# David Wood Plays for 5–12-Year-Olds:

## *The Gingerbread Man*; *The See-Saw Tree*; *The BFG*; *Save the Human*; *Mother Goose's Golden Christmas*

*The Gingerbread Man:* '. . . is told not only with the lightest and most stylish of touches, but is frequently very funny indeed.' *Observer* 'David Wood's strength has always been that he does not talk down to children: he gets down on his knees and looks at the world with their eyes instead.' *Times Educational Supplement*

*The See-Saw Tree:* 'David Wood – as the most successful children's playwright of this century – is trying through entertainment to teach the younger generation to preserve the world they live in and opt for conservation rather than commercial gain.' *The Stage*

*The BFG:* 'Joyous, exuberant and refreshingly un-pantomimic.' *Independent* 'Scrumdiddlyumptious! You'd be bogswinkled to miss it.' *Guardian*

*Save the Human:* '. . . raises crucial issues in a theatrical setting . . . a thought-provoking musical drama centred on an animal campaign to save the human . . . is a wonderfully astute conception.' *Northern Echo*

*Mother Goose's Golden Christmas:* 'The perfect family Christmas entertainment with all the traditions of panto. A really strong storyline which at the same time includes a host of fairytale characters . . . some marvellously inventive twists.' *Thurrock Gazette*

**David Wood OBE**, the 'national children's dramatist' (*The Times*), wrote the first of his seventy-five plays in 1967. Performed worldwide, they include *The Gingerbread Man*, *The See-Saw Tree* (recently produced by the China National Theatre for Children), *Save the Human*, *The Selfish Shellfish* and *The Ideal Gnome Expedition*. For twenty-five years he directed his plays for his Whirligig Theatre touring company. Among his adaptations are eight Roald Dahl stories, including *The BFG* and *The Witches* (three West End seasons each), *Goodnight Mister Tom* (Olivier Award 2013), *Tom's Midnight Garden* (two UK Theatre Awards), *Babe, the Sheep-Pig* and *The Tiger Who Came to Tea* (Olivier-nominated, now in its twelfth year touring the UK and internationally, including many West End seasons). He is President of Action for Children's Arts and received the J. M. Barrie Award 2017. The Story Museum, Oxford recently named its new theatre space after him – The Woodshed. www.davidwood.org.uk

**Paul Bateson** has been a drama teacher in primary and secondary schools in Yorkshire since 2008, and also works as a PGCE tutor for University of Huddersfield. He is a creative practitioner for Leeds Playhouse and Education Manager for Long Division Music Festival in Wakefield. Paul also works freelance as a writer, teacher trainer and workshop leader. www.paulbatesonis.co.uk

T0347836

# David Wood Plays for 5–12-Year-Olds

*The Gingerbread Man*

*The See-Saw Tree*

*The BFG*

*Save the Human*

*Mother Goose's Golden Christmas*

*With a foreword by the author and an introduction by*
PAUL BATESON

*methuen* | drama

LONDON • NEW YORK • OXFORD • NEW DELHI • SYDNEY

METHUEN DRAMA
Bloomsbury Publishing Plc
50 Bedford Square, London, WC1B 3DP, UK
1385 Broadway, New York, NY 10018, USA
29 Earlsfort Terrace, Dublin 2, Ireland

BLOOMSBURY, METHUEN DRAMA and the Methuen Drama logo are trademarks of
Bloomsbury Publishing Plc

This collection first published in Great Britain 2021
*David Wood Plays 1 and 2* first published in the United Kingdom in 1999 by Methuen Publishing Limited

*The Gingerbread Man* first published by Samuel French 1997
Copyright © David Wood 1997, 1999, 2021

*The See-Saw Tree* first published by Amber Lane Press 1987
Copyright © David Wood 1987, 1999, 2021

*The BFG* (stage version) first published by Samuel French 1991
Copyright © Trustees of the Estate of the late Roald Dahl and David Wood 1991, 1999, 2021

*Save the Human* first published by Samuel French 1990
Copyright © David Wood (book and lyrics) and Tony Husband (lyrics for Rock 'n' Roar), 1990, 1999, 2021

*Mother Goose's Golden Christmas* first published by Samuel French 1978
Copyright © David Wood 1978, 1999, 2021

Collection copyright © David Wood 1999, 2021
Foreword copyright © David Wood, 2021
Introduction to collection and plays copyright © Paul Bateson, 2021

David Wood and Paul Bateson have asserted their right under the Copyright, Designs and Patents Act,
1988, to be identified as authors of this work.

Cover design and illustration by Rebecca Heselton

A catalogue record for this book is available from the British Library.

A catalog record for this book is available from the Library of Congress.

ISBN:   PB:      978-1-3501-7492-4
        ePDF:    978-1-3501-7493-1
        eBook:   978-1-3501-7494-8

Series: Plays for Young People

Typeset by RefineCatch Limited, Bungay, Suffolk

To find out more about our authors and books visit www.bloomsbury.com
and sign up for our newsletters.

# Contents

# Foreword

What do you look back on with pleasure about your school days? Something you'll never forget. A sporting achievement? A special teacher? Your friends? Probably not the lessons or the tests. For many of us it's taking part in a school play. Being part of a team that creates a theatrical experience in which we tell a story to entertain our friends and families. Not just as actors, but as singers, musicians, puppeteers or stage managers. Or helping with building and painting the scenery, controlling the sound and lighting effects or learning to make props and costumes. Everyone contributes. Everyone tries to make sure they carry out their individual responsibilities well to help make the production go smoothly. And everyone shares in the excitement of the build-up, the rehearsals and the performance, basking in the end result with a glow of satisfaction and achievement. For the teachers and drama group leaders who produce the play, the rewards are just as exhilarating; by inspiring and galvanising the team, they have given the young people something perhaps more imaginative than they get in the classroom – a creative atmosphere of fun and discipline, teamwork and discovery, experiment and accomplishment.

Not every child will want to take part. It would be a boring world if we all had exactly the same interests. But putting on a play involves such a wide range of jobs that most children should find something to enthuse them. And teachers will be able to assess what aspect of the production might be most appropriate for them. I once directed a play in a primary school. Two classes were involved. Sixty children. Teachers helped me allocate roles and jobs. One girl was adamant she didn't want to take part. She clung to a radiator, refusing to even look up and show any interest. We certainly didn't want to force her to do anything, but let her observe and absorb the early stages of rehearsal for the actors and choir, as well as the scenery and prop preparations taking place in the art room. Eventually she became our prompter, and a very good one. Empowered to make sure the actors spoke the correct lines, she blossomed. Woe betide anyone who didn't pick up their cues!

Some people, including some teachers, argue that children's participation in the arts, including school plays, is a waste of time. It diverts them from their work routine and preparation for the dreaded tests. Some suggest it falsely gives children a desire to pursue a career in the arts. This is ridiculous. Most of them wouldn't give it a second thought. Furthermore, those of us who work in the theatre always advise young people to on no account think of entering the theatrical profession unless they are one hundred per cent certain that is truly where their ambitions lie and all they want to do. For most children participation in the play increases their self-confidence and sense of achievement. It also gives them much-needed fun. What's wrong with that? Article 31 of the UN Convention on the Rights of the Child says, 'Every child has the right to rest and leisure, to engage in play and recreational activities and to participate freely in cultural life and the arts.' Teachers and parents have a responsibility to facilitate this.

When I was growing up, things were different. It wasn't until I was fourteen that I was given the opportunity to be in a school play. But by then I had for some reason got the performing bug and had started doing puppet plays and giving magic shows at children's parties. I even sang songs with a local dance band. A residential drama course I attended just before acting in my first school play confirmed my passion. I still look back on that week as the best week of my life. Subsequently my headmaster encouraged me to follow my dream, but also persuaded me to go to university, where my love of theatre flourished further. I was very lucky. But the majority of those who shared my drama activities at school and university saw them as just a hobby and went on to have sensible jobs! And I'm sure their participation in theatre helped them become well-rounded, tolerant and empathetic team members in their lives and work.

The plays in this anthology will, I hope, be useful to teachers and drama group leaders. They were not originally written for children to perform. They were written for professional adult actors to perform for children and their families. But I believe, as do the publishers and editor of this book, that this is a virtue. Over the years many teachers have told me that the plays written specifically for children to perform are somewhat simplistic and patronising. They don't sufficiently challenge the audience or those taking part. It has been a pleasant surprise to find that schools and drama groups enjoy discovering ways to present my plays in spaces that don't possess the facilities of professional theatres. Their inventive solutions to the practical problems my plays pose never fail to delight me. As long as the story is told clearly, sophisticated settings and stage effects become less essential. Simplification and imaginative problem-solving can successfully substitute for professional gloss. And Paul Bateson has helpfully used his own experience as a drama teacher to suggest ideas to make these plays work without diluting their content.

And I believe the plays have a wider educational value too. Back in the 1990s I was asked to direct *The Gingerbread Man* for Unicorn Theatre. The play was already more than a decade old. Unicorn had, like many theatres around that time, acquired an education officer. Early in rehearsal she asked me if I had written the play with the National Curriculum in mind. I replied that the play had been written before the National Curriculum existed. Next day, having read the play, she came to see me. 'Are you *sure* that *The Gingerbread Man* wasn't written with the National Curriculum in mind?' I shook my head. She went on to say that the play incorporated so many of the core requirements of the Curriculum that she would have no problem creating a teachers' pack, detailing how the play could be used for follow-up work in the classroom. This made me think that perhaps any play of substance, relevance and integrity would most probably contain themes and ideas that would tick the necessary boxes. And it also reinforced my belief that it was pointless writing an 'educational play' for its own sake. An entertaining story should be the aim; educational spin-offs would automatically follow. I was once asked by a teacher if I could write a play about water. I asked why. 'Because water's on the Curriculum', came the reply. This was, I felt, a case of the tail wagging the dog. To begin creating a play with a purely educational objective was for me the wrong way round.

Nowadays I feel that theatre for children has a better balance. The entertainment and educational values can be integral and co-dependent, and theatre as a mere tool is no longer seen as a virtue. I hope I'm right and that these five plays fulfil both objectives. Please, teachers and drama group leaders, enjoy producing them, and may your children enjoy taking part in them.

David Wood
2021

# A Note on the Music

The music scores for my plays are all available from Concord Theatricals (see the info about performance rights), but, as Paul Bateson writes, it is not necessary to always use the music. Some songs might be spoken. Some might be omitted. But it may be of interest to know that some of the songs can be heard on my website, www.davidwood. org.uk. Go to the 'Sights and Sounds' section, then click on the names of the plays.

*The Gingerbread Man*: All the songs are sung by the original Old Vic cast.

*The See-Saw Tree*: The title song is sung by Simon Nicol (Fairport Convention) and a children's choir.

*Save the Human*: The title song and 'Rock 'n' Roar' are sung by the Whirligig Theatre cast.

*Mother Goose's Golden Christmas*: Click on link to 'The David Wood Songbook', where you will find the songs 'Getting Ready for Christmas' and 'When You're Feeling Worried', sung by the Allfarthing School Choir.

DW

# Introduction

'Doing' the school play as a teacher is a pleasure that only a handful of colleagues have ever experienced – I would like to change that.

As David Wood discussed in his Foreword, the joy of a school production is tangible for everyone involved, and far outweighs any worries that might creep in when considering it. The hard work, the camaraderie, the *fun* and the occasion of a great school show will stay with students, teachers and parents alike for a long, long time.

Rehearsing and performing drama with young people can create a rapport between staff and students that will spill positively into the classroom and it can be the first shoots of a love of creativity, culture and theatre arts for young people to explore further in their lives. However, as David says, it is not the easiest career path! All drama teachers are failed actors, they say . . . though I couldn't possibly comment.

I know my love of drama was fostered in primary school, performing *The Snow Must Go On*, a Mr Farrington self-penned Christmas classic, and another Roald Dahl work to go with *The BFG* here, his *Revolting Rhymes* which our teachers adapted for stage.

Drama can also happily support other areas of the curriculum such as literacy, geography, art and design, music, PSHEE and more.

To a busy teacher, though, introducing some drama into their usual classroom lessons, or going all out and staging a school show, can seem daunting and complicated – there never seems to be enough time. What play shall we choose? Will the children be able to pull it off?

Yes 'doing' the school play as a teacher is a labour of love, but this book will help with that.

David has written a quality selection of plays. This collection is not only a great leg up for any teacher wanting to stage a school production for the first time, ready-to-go plays with notes to help each step of the process. But it is also a brilliant go-to for professionally written scripts for the veteran play putter-on-erer, and a good resource for any teacher to try some drama in the classroom using the follow-up lesson activities. Different plays and activities here would be suitable for KS1, KS2 and KS3, along with drama groups or clubs.

David understands children's theatre need not mean dumbed down or lacking in quality, and he does that while making the plays *fun*.

Have a read, with your class, and get inspired – make this year the year that *you* do the school play using these beautifully written plays by David Wood.

I know I will be.

Paul Bateson – Teacher

# The Gingerbread Man – Teacher Notes

I love the *Toy Story* concept here; of the objects on the kitchen dresser coming to life while the 'Big Ones' are out of sight. The exaggerated characters are really fun to play and the acting exercises here focus on heightened characterisation to really bring them to life. Be mindful though that the performances do not become cartoon and too silly. There is potential for a real wow factor here in the set design and creating oversized kitchen utensils will be required – a giant teacup for capturing Sleek the Mouse is just one of the great production prospects here.

**Age range:** KS2/3
**Number of actors:** 6–10
This is a small-cast play and would be perhaps suited to a small committed drama club or a group of Y6/Y7 looking to perform to a younger audience.

**Running time:** Approx. 60 minutes (90 minutes with songs)

## Characters
The original production has six roles, and as only a small cast play, all six roles are substantial parts. Of course the Gingerbread Man is the title character and has a large number of lines. Originally the 'Voices of the Big Ones' were pre-recorded and played as audio, but for a school production there is potential here to cast these roles separately, and include these interactions as small scenes. Speaking into a microphone would help to create the booming human voices, contrasting with the characters on the dresser.

All of the characters can be played unisex with some basic adaptations of 'he/she', etc. and there is a good argument for a Gingerbread Woman as a playful approach.

Herr Von Cuckoo – for this character I might avoid stereotyped accents, which are unlikely to be done accurately by younger actors, and avoid the kissing if it brings about embarrassment! As always, clear, exaggerated movements, mannerisms and vocal expressions specific for each role will help characterisation (see activities).

## Costumes and props
A simple letter stitched or painted on a T-shirt would work, M = Sleek the Mouse, S = Salt, P = Pepper, T = Old Bag, etc.

Something more literal could be a pair of wings for Cuckoo, ears and a tail for Sleek, string vest for Old Bag, etc.

The costumes could be more human-like/natural, as the playwright suggests: lederhosen or at least a check shirt and braces for Herr Von Cuckoo, a blue and white stripy top for Salt, a velvet jacket for Pepper, a suit and sunglasses for Sleek the Mouse and a tatty cardigan for Old Bag. Sleek and Old Bag can indeed not look anything like a mouse or a tea bag, but instead be played and dressed as a 'smooth operator' and a crotchety old woman (or man) respectively.

Fun could be had making bigger costumes. A large cardboard box with neck, arm and leg holes and worn over the torso can be make decorated into a giant tea bag, or a salt/pepper mill; or baseball hats/bike helmets with cardboard beaks/mouse-snouts, whiskers or feathers can be worn for the others. Caution advised though: the characters need to be able to move and act freely, along with being heard clearly.

For the Gingerbread Man I am sure there are some orange-coloured 'onesies' out-there that can be adapted, or even costumes for hire; but again letters 'GB' on an orange T-shirt might suffice.

## Staging

The most exciting aspect to staging this play is the set. The action takes place in one location – the kitchen dresser – and it is integral to the concept of the play that we create a somewhat faithful representation. How can we do this in a school setting?

A simple projected backdrop could work well as a starting point and is a quick and easy method; though consideration must be given to shadows cast by actors from the position of a projector. Most schools have interactive screens now which mean the problem of shadows is solved.

The kitchen dresser is set on different heights, however, with the cuckoo clock centre at one level and the teapot further up on a 'high shelf'. It is important to get a sense of the fact that the Old Bag lives separately from the others. Wooden stage blocks can be painted white for sugar cubes and used as steps.

If you do not have staging platforms or blocks available, you could create raised areas by using tables, but there must be consideration for safety and ensuring actors are not in danger of stepping or falling off – a group of four tables cable-tied securely together works for the 'high shelf'.

Herr Von Cuckoo can stand on a block to announce the time.

A wooden or cardboard frame held by the actor with their head poked through can represent a character leaning out of their window/cuckoo clock door if desired.

Some of the bigger set pieces like the rolling pin, the envelope and the honey will certainly require some creative adaptation.

## Special props

The envelope can be made from a giant piece of card. The honey can be a yellow/orange cushion, or some orange balloons tied together in a clump.

The rolling pin can be a 2D cut-out shape mounted on the side of anything with trolley wheels, and the giant mug a one-man tent, perhaps painted.

The sequence where the characters use the rolling pin and string to pulley up the Gingerbread Man onto the high shelf and the finale of the play involving them trapping Sleek the Mouse under a giant mug will need a high hook and some rope.

## Music, sound effects and lighting

*The Gingerbread Man* is described as a 'musical play'; and there are some great song opportunities for singers and players, not to mention the wonderful choreographed movements to accompany the songs that are outlined in the stage directions.

In the absence of musical resource I would say the songs work well as spoken poems, and can be made visual by adding movements, actions and images to accompany the words (see 'Lesson plan').

The play works fine as a narrative without the songs at all, however.

**Other considerations**
There are a number of great set movement sections including a chase between the Gingerbread Man and Sleek when they first meet; and later when they capture Sleek, matador style. These sequences will depend on your set and staging, your actors and your choreography skills, but are really engaging sections and should be planned and rehearsed thoroughly. I would start small, perhaps using some simple mirroring movements, rather than allowing free-form running and chasing which often looks untidy. Simple slapstick tricks like a tap on the shoulder and a spin round, changing the chased to the chaser mid-action and bumping bums whilst walking back to back are a good place to begin.

**Lesson plan – Characterisation**
*Starter activity: Exaggeration circle*
Around a circle ask the students to repeat a given action and a sound one by one, exaggerating each time. 1 is normal, 10 is totally over the top.

Motifs could be: clenched fist and say 'Yes!', arms up with a 'Noooooo!', pointing and saying 'Oi!' As long as there is an action and a sound to copy and exaggerate.

*Engaging*
This can then be repeated as characters from the play, using a well-chosen line of dialogue and agreeing on an appropriate action. For example, Herr Von Cuckoo could say 'Guten Tag' and clutch at his sore throat, or Pepper enact a big sneeze.

*Developing: Movement, mannerisms and physicality*
Ask the students to move around the space. Call 'normal' walking speed 'level 5'. Call out different numbers that mean the actors walk faster and slower. Freeze the actors and question the audience: What kind of character might move fast? Slow? Why? Relate to the characters from the play.

Next, they move around the space they are being led around by certain body parts. The nose, knees, chest, etc. Freeze the actors and question the audience: What kind of character might move in this way? Why?

Discuss again how the characters from the play might move and let students experiment. Spotlight interesting versions. Finally, discuss the idea of mannerisms, small movements or actions that we associate with different characters. For example, Sleek the Mouse might run his hands through his hair, or Old Bag might stand with hands on hips. Again, experiment and share. Take extracts from the script and allow students to perform with exaggerated characterisation.

**Lesson plan – Songs as poems/poems with movements**
*Starter activity*
With the class sat in a circle, read through 'Sleek the Mouse' (song 7), with each student speaking a line each.

*Engaging – Sculptor and clay*
Using the previous character activities as inspiration, one pupil in a pair is the sculptor, the other is the clay. The sculptor's job is to mould the clay into a statue. This statue will

show Sleek the Mouse – perhaps being sneaky or looking cool. Remember facial expressions as well as gestures and body language!

*Developing*
Split the class into small groups and give each group a verse of the song. They should create an image to go with the words. For example, the first verse could be represented by four actors standing in a semi-circle with puzzled expressions and hands to ears like they have heard something strange, and another actor as Sleek in the middle striking his 'cool' pose.

*Main task*
Now the actors need to add the words from the song to the image as dialogue. They can distribute the lines however they wish. They can take a line each or speak in unison. They can use echo or repetition. Small movements and actions can be added. Perform and share in the order of the song as a quick way to bring poems or lyrics to life.

# The Gingerbread Man

**Book, music and lyrics by David Wood**

*The Gingerbread Man* was originally commissioned by the Towngate Theatre, Basildon, and produced there by the Theatre Royal, Norwich (Trust) Ltd, on 7 December 1976, with the following cast:

| | |
|---|---|
| **Herr Von Cuckoo** | Ronnie Stevens |
| **Salt** | Tim Barker |
| **Pepper** | Pearly Gates |
| **Gingerbread Man** | Jack Chissick |
| **Old Bag** | Veronica Clifford |
| **Sleek the Mouse** | Keith Varnier |

*Directed by* Jonathan Lynn
*Designed by* Susie Caulcutt
*Musical direction by* Peter Pontzen
*Lighting by* Martyn Wills

The play was subsequently presented at the Old Vic, London, by Cameron Mackintosh and David Wood, by arrangement with the Cambridge Theatre Company, for a Christmas season opening on 13 December 1977, with the following cast:

| | |
|---|---|
| **Herr Von Cuckoo** | Ronnie Stevens |
| **Salt** | Tim Barker |
| **Pepper** | Cheryl Branker |
| **Gingerbread Man** | Andrew Secombe |
| **Old Bag** | Vivienne Martin |
| **Sleek the Mouse** | Keith Varnier |

*Directed by* Jonathan Lynn
*Designed by* Susie Caulcutt
*Musical direction by* Peter Pontzen
*Lighting design by* Mick Hughes

**Characters**

**Herr Von Cuckoo**, *the Swiss-made cuckoo in the cuckoo clock. He wears lederhosen.*

**Salt**, *a salt cellar, based in design on the blue-and-white horizontal striped variety, thus making him look like a sailor, and indeed that's how he sees himself.*

**Pepper**, *a well-groomed, svelte, elegant female pepper-mill.*

**Gingerbread Man**, *who looks like what he is!*

**Old Bag**, *an elderly, short-tempered tea bag, who lives on the shelf, inside a cottage-style teapot.*

**Sleek the Mouse**, *an American gangster-style villain. Not as smooth as he'd like to appear.*

**Voices of the Big Ones**, *which can either be pre-recorded or doubled by other members of the cast. They are the voices of the family who own the house in whose kitchen and on whose dresser the action takes place.*

**Author's Note**

As this is a musical play, not a pantomime, it helps if all the cast play their lines and situations for truth and reality (even though their characters may seem to belong in the realm of fantasy!), rather than adopt a superficial, 'knowing' style of performance often associated, sadly, with panto. The original production of this play proved that audience participation and involvement works best when it is motivated by genuine concern for the characters and their problems; and this concern is created by the *cast's* genuine concern for them.

The action of the play takes place on a kitchen dresser.

Act One at night.
Act Two immediately following.

# Act One

*The action of the play takes place on a kitchen dresser. The characters are all but inches high; therefore the set is magnified. It is one structure, which remains throughout the play.*

*The stage surface is the 'top' of the dresser, in other words the working surface. The edge of the stage can therefore be the edge of the dresser. Positioned, say, 12 or 15 feet upstage is the back of the dresser, incorporating one practical shelf, and hopefully the beginnings of another (non-practical) shelf. Naturally at stage surface level there is a 'shelf-like area', under the practical shelf above. On the 'lower' shelf are two plates standing upright, one of which is practical in that it slides to one side to reveal a hole in the wooden back of the dresser, through which **Sleek the Mouse** enters; the other is practical in that it is used in the action to put things on. There is also a practical mug. There are several hooks along the edge of the shelf. There is also a length of string, which could be in a tin, or just the remains of an opened parcel; also a sugar bowl, with several practical lumps of sugar; and an egg cup. A gaily coloured pocket transistor radio can be either suspended from another hook, or horizontal on the top surface. On the 'upper' (practical) shelf is a cottage-style teapot. It has a practical front door. Next to it are various herb jars, which never move, but could have lids. There is a pot of honey. Other larger jars could be visible (probably painted, or simply the front façades). Beside or in the middle of the shelved part of the dresser is a cuckoo clock, with a practical door. **Herr Von Cuckoo** should be able to reach from his cuckooing position to the dresser working surface, perhaps by swinging on the short end of the pendulum or by having a pendulum with rungs, like a ladder. But as two characters have to make the return journey, i.e. from dresser to clock, it may be more feasible to make the 'podium' a sort of balcony, reachable by stepping up from the working surface. On the working surface itself sits a rolling pin. A tea cloth is somewhere handy. Other dresser clutter could be visible – non-practical fixed 'dresser dressing'. This could extend up to a non-practical top shelf, which could extend into the flies; or the very top of the dresser could be visible.*

*The set is backed by black tabs, and hopefully a floor cloth, with the dresser surface painted on; this should have black surrounds extending from the surface edges to the wings, thus truly defining the working area. If possible, a front cloth could be used instead of tabs. This would have the show's title and possibly a gingerbread man motif, plus a design of the dresser (on its own or as part of a kitchen scene). This could help the establishing of the large-scale set.*

*If an overture is required, it is suggested that a verse and chorus of 'Toad in the Throat' be played.*

*As the curtain rises we hear the ticking of the cuckoo clock, the hands of which point to twelve o'clock. The dresser is revealed in lighting which suggests moonlight, though it must obviously be bright enough to see everything clearly, as this will be the basic lighting for most of the play. **Salt** and **Pepper** stand, respectively back and front to the audience, under the practical shelf. An envelope stands between them, leaning against*

**Pepper**. **Salt** *and* **Pepper** *are in frozen positions. Suddenly the door of the cuckoo clock opens, and* **Herr Von Cuckoo** *enters. Rather ostentatiously he clears his throat.*

**Herr Von Cuckoo** (*warming up*)    Mi, mi, mi, mi. (*He looks up at the clock face to check the time, and launches into his rhythmic twelve-cuckoo call.*) Cuckoo! Cuckoo! Cuckoo! Cuckoo! (*The first four are confident and perky. Between each one he nods or turns his head in a clockwork manner. He keeps count on his fingers. Under his breath.*) Vier. Four. (*He carries on.*) Cuckoo! Cuckoo! Cuckoo! Cuckoo! (*During the second four, it becomes a bit of an effort, breathing-wise and counting-wise. Under his breath.*) Er – acht. Eight. (*He carries on.*) Cuckoo! Cuck-oo! (*Breath.*) Cuck-oo! Cu-ck-oooooh. (*The sound changes into one of disgust. During the last four he has developed a husky frog in the throat, and it is a real strain to get the sound out. He tries clearing his throat. A very husky note.*) Aaaah. What a noise horrible, nicht war? Hoppla! Ich ze toad in ze throat have. (*He tries a scale, but it cracks up nastily.*) Doh, ray, me, fah, so – (*Repeating.*) – fah – so – fah so . . . (*Speaking.*) So far so no good! (*Singing.*) La – (*Straining.*) – te . . . (*He tries 'doh', but nothing comes out; he has to go back down the octave to the lower 'doh'.*) DOH! (*He sighs.*) Oh . . .

SONG: **Toad in the Throat**

**Herr Von Cuckoo**
I was made in the mountains of Switzerland
(*Yodel.*)
From a fine piece of pine I was carved by hand
(*Yodel.*)
With all
My power
I call
The hour
On a clear and unwavering note
But I
Declare
To my
Despair
Today I've a toad in my throat.

(*Yodelling chorus.*)

'Cross the valleys of Switzerland you can hear
(*Yodel.*)
It's the sound of a yodelling mountaineer
(*Yodel.*)
He's all
Alone
Can't call
By 'phone
On a mountainside high and remote
When in

Distress
He's in
A mess
If he gets a toad in his throat.

(*Half chorus of yodelling.*)

Oh dear, oh dear
What can I do
I'm a cuckoo clock cuckoo who can't cuckoo.

So before people notice there's something wrong
(*Husky yodel.*)
I must try to recover my cuckoo song
(*Husky yodel.*)
A Swiss
You'll find
Is dis-
-inclined
To let a thing get on his goat
So I
Won't rest
I'll try
My best
To banish this toad from my throat.

*After the song,* **Herr Von Cuckoo** *shakes his head, checks to see that all is clear, then locks his door and, pocketing the key, makes his way on to the dresser. He arrives near* **Salt** *and* **Pepper**. **Salt** *is nearest him. Both are asleep.*

**Herr Von Cuckoo** (*in a husky whisper*)    Herr Salt. (*He tries to speak louder but cannot.*) Herr Salt. (*Giving up, he goes round to* **Pepper**. *He stands three paces from her.*) Fräulein Pepper. (*He moves in to her.*)

**Pepper** *wakes and starts to sneeze.*

**Pepper**    A – A – A . . .

**Herr Von Cuckoo**    Bitte . . .

**Pepper**    Tishoo!

**Pepper***'s sneeze sends him reeling back. He tries again.*

**Pepper**    A – A – A . . .

**Herr Von Cuckoo**    Entschuldigen Sie . . .

**Pepper**    Tishoo!

*Again* **Herr Von Cuckoo** *reels back. He tries again.*

**Pepper**    A– A– A . . .

**Herr Von Cuckoo**    Fräulein . . .

*Deftly he pulls out a handkerchief and puts it to her nose in the nick of time. This successfully stops the 'Tishoo'.* **Pepper** *holds in her breath.* **Herr Von Cuckoo** *waits a moment, checks to see he has stopped it, removes the handkerchief and meticulously starts to fold it and put it in his pocket.*

**Pepper** (*just when* **Herr Von Cuckoo** *least expects it*)    Tishoo!

**Herr Von Cuckoo** *jumps.* **Pepper** *wakes up.*

**Pepper**    What's going on? Oh, Herr Von Cuckoo, it's you.

**Herr Von Cuckoo** (*huskily*)    Ja. Guten Tag.

**Herr Von Cuckoo** *shakes her hand and kisses her on both cheeks.*

**Pepper**    Cuckoo, please! You'll knock me over. (*She becomes aware of the envelope leaning against her.*) Oh no, the Big Ones have done it again. (*Calling.*) Mr Salt. Mr Salt.

*The envelope is now leaning on* **Salt***. He wakes up.*

**Salt**    Shiver me timbers! Storm to starboard! Ready about! Man the lifeboats! We're running aground! SOS! (*He keeps the envelope from falling on him as he turns to face the audience.*)

**Pepper**    All right! It's all right, Mr Salt. Wake up. We're not running aground. You were having one of your nautical nightmares.

**Salt**    Sorry, Miss Pepper. I dreamed the windblown sails were enveloping us.

**Pepper**    No, Mr Salt, we are being enveloped by an envelope. Kindly remove it.

**Salt**    Ah. Aye, aye, ma'am. (*He salutes and starts to struggle with it.*)

**Pepper**    I refuse to be used as a letter rack.

**Herr Von Cuckoo** *helps with the envelope.*

**Salt**    We'll anchor it here. Thank you, shipmate. Couldn't have heave-hoed it on my own. Might have spliced my mainbrace. Ha, ha. Good morrow to you! (*He salutes.*)

**Herr Von Cuckoo** (*huskily*)    Guten Tag.

**Herr Von Cuckoo** *shakes* **Salt***'s hands and kisses him on both cheeks.*

**Salt**    Aye, aye. (*Rather embarrassed.*) Aye, aye! What can we do for you, shipmate?

*Sadly,* **Herr Von Cuckoo** *points to his mouth and opens and shuts it.*

**Salt**    Speak up. Don't be shy. (*To* **Pepper***.*) What's he doing? Looks fishy to me! (*He opens and shuts his mouth.*)

**Pepper**    Maybe he's hungry.

**Salt** (*to* **Herr Von Cuckoo**)    Are you hungry?

**Herr Von Cuckoo** (*whispering*)    Nein. Ich need your 'elp.

**Salt** (*whispering*)    What?

**Herr Von Cuckoo** (*whispering*)    Ich need your 'elp.

**Pepper** (*to* **Salt**)    What?

**Salt** (*to* **Pepper**, *whispering*)    Ich need your 'elp.

**Pepper** (*in normal voice*)    Why?

**Salt** (*whispering*)    I don't know.

**Pepper**    No. I mean ask *him* why.

**Salt** (*to* **Herr Von Cuckoo** *whispering*)    Why?

**Herr Von Cuckoo** (*whispering*)    Ich have ein difficulty.

**Salt** (*to* **Pepper**, *whispering*)    Ich have ein difficulty.

**Pepper**    What are you whispering for?

**Salt** (*to* **Herr Von Cuckoo**, *whispering*)    What are you whispering . . .

**Pepper**    No, no, I'm asking *you*. What are *you* whispering for?

**Salt**    I don't know.

**Pepper**    Then don't.

**Salt**    I won't.

**Pepper**    Now, what is your difficulty?

**Salt**    Well, I keep whispering.

**Pepper**    No, no. Ask *him*. 'What is your difficulty?' My, you're stupid.

**Salt** (*to* **Herr Von Cuckoo**)    What is your difficulty? My, you're stupid.

**Pepper**    No!

**Salt**    No!

**Pepper**    Out of the way.

**Salt**    I'm sorry, ma'am.

**Pepper** *and* **Salt** *swap places.*

**Pepper** (*to* **Herr Von Cuckoo**)    What is your difficulty?

**Herr Von Cuckoo** (*whispering*)    Ich have my voice lost.

**Salt** (*to* **Pepper**)    What?

**Pepper** (*to* **Salt**)    Ich have my voice lost.

**Salt** (*to* **Pepper**)    Well, that's very careless of you, Miss Pepper. When did you last see it?

**Pepper**   Not *me*. Him!

**Salt**   Ha, ha. I know. Only pulling your peppercorns! (*To* **Herr Von Cuckoo**.) Now then, shipmate, you have lost your voice, right?

**Herr Von Cuckoo**   Ja.

**Salt**   Why? I will hazard a guess you have lost it on account of all that 'cuckoo, cuckoo' palaver all day long. Take my advice, have a rest. Stop 'cuckoo, cuckooing' for a few days.

**Herr Von Cuckoo**   Impossible. Is my job.

**Salt**   What?

**Pepper**   Is his job. He means that a cuckoo clock that cannot 'cuckoo' is nothing short of useless. Correct?

**Herr Von Cuckoo**   Ja.

**Pepper**   I tend to agree. If you ask me, Mr Salt, Cuckoo could be a likely candidate for the Dustbin.

*Dramatic chord.*

**Herr Von Cuckoo**   Ach, nein. Nein. (*In panic, he flaps his wings.*)

**Salt**   Miss Pepper! What a cruel thing to say. Calm down, Cuckoo, calm.

**Pepper**   I'm only being realistic. What do the Big Ones do if they've finished with something or if something doesn't work? Throw it in the Dustbin.

**Herr Von Cuckoo** *trembles again.*

**Pepper**   Bang. The end. Never seen again.

*This is true. A gloomy pause.*

**Salt**   He must go on leave. (*He has an idea.*) To the seaside. Get some salty sea-air in your lungs and your voice'll come back loud as a fog-horn.

**Pepper**   How do you know? You've never seen the sea. The nearest the sea you've ever got was that willow-pattern sauce-boat on the top shelf. And what happened to that? One day the Big Ones found it was cracked and – bang –

**Salt**   – the Dustbin. All the more reason for Cuckoo to see the real sea. I've had salt in me all my life and I've never lost my voice. Go on, shipmate. Weigh anchor and fly away.

**Herr Von Cuckoo** *shakes his head.*

**Salt**   Why not?

**Herr Von Cuckoo**   You forget. Ich cannot fly. My wings are wooden. (*He begins to weep with despair.*)

**Salt**   You shouldn't have mentioned the Dustbin.

**Pepper** *thinks, then goes to comfort* **Herr Von Cuckoo.**

**Pepper**   Herr Von Cuckoo. I was very unkind. But standing on the shelf all day I get so bored and bad-tempered. When night-time comes I take it out on my friends. I'm sorry. Forgive me.

*After a pause,* **Herr Von Cuckoo** *accepts the apology, by kissing her on both cheeks.*

**Salt**   Now, come on. Show a leg. All hands on deck for a party. Eh? It's after twelve-hundred hours midnight, so we're safe. We can dance and sing.

**Herr Von Cuckoo** *points to his throat.*

**Salt**   Sorry, shipmate. You dance. We'll do the singing.

**Pepper**   Herr Von Cuckoo, may I have the pleasure of the next waltz?

**Herr Von Cuckoo** *cannot resist the invitation. He bows politely.*

SONG: **The Dresser Hop**

*This may be danced by all three, but it would be effective if* **Salt** *could play a squeeze-box to accompany the dancing of* **Pepper** *and* **Herr Von Cuckoo**. *If considered preferable the verses may be sung in unison.*

*Dramatic licence suggests that* **Herr Von Cuckoo** *could join in the chorus work!*

**Pepper**
     In approximately eighteen-fifty
     When the dresser was new
     Come midnight
     The dresser-folk
     Had nothing much to do

**Pepper** *and* **Herr Von Cuckoo**
     So one night they put their heads together
     Came up with the answer

**All**
     And ever since ev'rybody on
     The dresser's been a dancer.

     So kindly take your partners
     The dresser dance has begun
     Come skip and hop
     Round the working top
     With a one, two, three, one.

**Pepper**
     As we gaily trip the light fantastic
     All our cares we forget

**Herr Von Cuckoo**
> Avoiding
> The rolling pin
> We waltz and minuet

**Salt** *and* **Pepper**
> Palais glide or military two-step
> Quadrille or the Lancers

**All**
> We sing and sway till the break of day
> The dresser ballroom dancers.
>
> So kindly take your partners
> The dresser dance has begun
> Come skip and hop
> Round the working top
> With a one, two, three, one.

**Salt** *and* **Pepper**
> Herr Von Cuckoo
> Dashing as a white sergeant
> Jives to a gentle gavotte

**Pepper**
> No one can fault
> Mister Salt
> As he saunters

**Salt**
> And at the foxtrot
> Miss Pepper is hot.

**All**
> So kindly take your partners
> The dresser dance has begun
> Come skip and hop
> Round the working top
> With a one, two, three, one
> Come skip and hop
> Round the working top
> With a one, two, three,
> One, two, three,
> One, two, three,
> One.

**Salt**    Bravo!

**Herr Von Cuckoo** (*with a bow*)    Danke schön.

**Pepper**    Thank you.

**Herr Von Cuckoo** *starts towards his clock.* **Pepper** *sighs.*

**Salt**   Well, that was fun.

**Pepper**   Old-fashioned.

**Salt**   I enjoyed it.

**Pepper**   Only did it to cheer up Cuckoo. Oh, if only something exciting, out of the ordinary, would happen.

*Suddenly* **Herr Von Cuckoo,** *who has just passed the rolling pin, flaps his wings excitedly.*

**Herr Von Cuckoo** (*croaking*)   Herr Salt, Fräulein Pepper. Schnell, schnell!

**Salt**   Smell, what smell? What's he croaking about?

**Pepper**   Schnell. Quick.

**Salt** *and* **Pepper** *go to the rolling pin. All look behind it.*

**Herr Von Cuckoo**   Was ist das? What is zat?

**Salt**   Let's heave-ho it over here and have a good look.

**Salt** *and* **Herr Von Cuckoo** *pick 'it' up and carry 'it' over the rolling pin, standing 'it' up, facing away from the audience.*

**Salt**   Funny, it's warm. (*To the audience.*) Anyone seen one of these before? What is it?

*The audience should shout out 'a Gingerbread Man'.*

A what?

*The audience shout again.*

**Pepper**   Of course! A Gingerbread Man. The Big Ones must have baked him.

**Herr Von Cuckoo**   Guten Tag.

*He goes to shake hands, but at this point the* **Gingerbread Man** *bends at the stomach.*

**Salt**   They didn't bake him very well. He's all rubbery. Hey up.

*They lift the* **Gingerbread Man,** *but he collapses again. Business repeated a couple of times. His arms flail wildly. Eventually, he is still.*

**Salt**   Phew! I hope you're finished! You're heavy!

**Pepper**   That's it! He's not!

**Salt**   He *is*! He's very heavy.

**Pepper**   No. Finished. He's not finished. Look. No eyes, no mouth, no nose . . .

**Salt**   No nose?

**Pepper**   No, no nose.

**Salt**   No no nose?

**Pepper**   Yes!

**Herr Von Cuckoo** (*an idea*)    Ich knows.

**Salt**   *Your* nose?

**Herr Von Cuckoo**   Nein. Ich *knows*. Ich idea have. Let us him finish.

**Pepper**   How?

**Herr Von Cuckoo**   Give him eyes und mouth und nose . . .

**Pepper**   Good idea, Cuckoo; now what could we use? (*To the audience.*) What could we use for the Gingerbread Man's eyes?

**Audience**   Currants.

**Pepper**   Yes! Currants. And we'll use another currant for his nose as well.

**Cuckoo**   Yes, but what can we use for the Gingerbread Man's mouth? Something red.

**Audience**   A cherry.

**Cuckoo**   A cherry. Danke! Danke! Good idea. A cherry.

**Salt**   So we want currants and a cherry. Let's find some. And while we're looking (*To the audience.*) would you look after the Gingerbread Man for us please?

**Audience**   Yes.

**Salt**   You would?

**Audience**   Yes.

**Salt**   Thankee.

*They all rush to the back, in search. Slowly, the* **Gingerbread Man** *begins to topple sideways. The audience may call out. In any case,* **Salt** *suddenly sees and rushes back to catch him in time.*

**Salt**   Hey! Hup!

**Salt** *rebalances the* **Gingerbread Man** *and returns to work.*

(*To the audience.*)    Thankee.

*After a moment, the* **Gingerbread Man** *topples the other way.* **Herr Von Cuckoo** *has to rush in and stop him falling.*

**Herr Von Cuckoo**   Ach! Ach! Ach! Hup! (*He rebalances him. To the audience.*) Danke!

*Meanwhile currants and a cherry have been collected behind the rolling pin. The* **Gingerbread Man** *begins to topple once more – towards* **Salt***'s side.*

**Salt** (*rushing back*)   Hey! (*He catches the* **Gingerbread Man**.)

**Pepper** (*holding up the currants and cherry*)   Got some!

**Salt**   Well done, Miss Pepper. (*To* **Herr von Cuckoo**) Let's heave-ho him on to the rolling pin.

*He and* **Herr Von Cuckoo** *lift him and sit him, back to the audience, on the rolling pin. Tension music is heard as they 'finish' the* **Gingerbread Man**'s *face. This can be mimed or cheated as he is sitting back to the audience.*

**Herr Von Cuckoo**   One eye.

**Salt**   Aye.

**Herr Von Cuckoo**   Two eyes.

**Salt**   Aye, aye.

**Herr Von Cuckoo**   Three eyes.

**Salt** *and* **Pepper**   No!

**Herr Von Cuckoo**   One nose, one mouth.

**Salt**   Right. Reception party – assemble. I'll pipe him aboard.

**Pepper** *and* **Herr Von Cuckoo** *stand formally.* **Salt** *blows his whistle.*

**Salt** (*to the* **Gingerbread Man**)   Welcome aboard this dresser, shipmate.

*They stand back.* **Salt** *salutes. Tension music builds – but nothing happens.*

**Herr Von Cuckoo**   Is he all right?

**Salt**   No, he's all wrong. Why won't he wake up? He's got all his tackle.

**Pepper**   I know. Make him sneeze.

**Salt**   How, Miss Pepper?

**Pepper**   Me. Herr Von Cuckoo, kindly twist my grinder a touch.

**Herr Von Cuckoo** *obeys. Percussion accompaniment.*

**Pepper**   Thank you.

*She bends and picks up the pepper (this can be imaginary), then gingerly holds it under the* **Gingerbread Man**'s *nose. Tension music. The* **Gingerbread Man** *builds to an enormous sneeze, which blows everyone back a little.*

**Gingerbread Man**   A – a – a – tishoo!

*The* **Gingerbread Man** *slowly starts to move, one limb at a time, until he is standing. A sudden jump turns him to face the audience for the first time. He looks excitedly about – he can see for the first time. The others come forward to watch. Suddenly he sees them and does not know how to react.* **Salt** *comes forward to shake hands.*

**Salt**    Welcome aboard, shipmate. I'm Salt.

**Pepper**    How do you do? I'm Pepper.

**Herr Von Cuckoo**    Hallo! Herr Von Cuckoo at your service. (*He bows politely.*)

*With an effort, the* **Gingerbread Man** *opens his mouth and tries to speak.*

**Gingerbread Man**    H – ha – hall – o. Ha – llo. (*He laughs with pleasure at being able to speak.*) Hallo! Salt, Pepper, Herr Von Cuckoo, hallo! (*Leaping and shouting with excitement, he jumps about, nearly knocking people over.*) Hallo! Hallo! Hallo! Hallo!

**Pepper**    Maybe I made his mouth a little large.

**Salt**    No, no. Only the excitement of his first voyage.

*The* **Gingerbread Man** *comes bounding back. He talks very loudly.*

**Gingerbread Man**    I say, where am I?

**Salt**    In the kitchen.

**Pepper**    On the dresser.

**Herr Von Cuckoo**    You are baked freshly.

**Gingerbread Man**    Baked freshly?

**Salt**    By the Big Ones.

**Gingerbread Man**    The Big Ones?

**Pepper**    The human people who live here.

**Salt**    Talking of whom, I wonder, shipmate – could you turn down the volume a little? If they should wake up . . .

**Gingerbread Man** (*just as loudly*)    Certainly, Salty! Ha, ha. (*He slaps* **Salt** *on the back heartily.*) Say no more.

**Herr Von Cuckoo** *attempts to 'Shhhh' the* **Gingerbread Man** *but in vain. He leaps off to explore, moving behind a plate.*

**Gingerbread Man**    Hallo! Hallo!

**Herr Von Cuckoo**    Shhhh!

**Salt** (*trying to be broadminded*)    Just high spirits . . .

**Salt** *turns to see the* **Gingerbread Man** *peering behind the plate.*

**Salt**    Hey, mind that plate! Oh my.

**Herr Von Cuckoo**    What have we done?

**Pepper** *starts laughing.*

**Pepper**    I think it's splendid.

**Salt**    It won't be if he disturbs the Big Ones on the upper deck.

**Pepper**    Why not? A spicy whiff of excitement. Danger. Exactly what we need. Just what I wanted.

*The* **Gingerbread Man** *finds the transistor radio.*

**Gingerbread Man** (*loudly*)    I say! Salty, what's this?

**Salt**    Shhh! What?

**Herr Von Cuckoo** (*concerned*)    Aah! Ze radio.

**Salt** (*to* **Herr Von Cuckoo**)    Oh no. (*To the* **Gingerbread Man***, trying to be calm.*) That, shipmate? Nothing special. I wouldn't touch it if I . . .

*Too late. The* **Gingerbread Man** *finds the switch and turns it on. Rock music blares out.*

**Salt**    Oh no!

*The* **Gingerbread Man** *starts gyrating to the rhythm.*

**Salt** (*loudly*)    Miss Pepper, what are we to do?

**Pepper** *smiles at* **Salt** *gleefully and goes over to the* **Gingerbread Man***, and starts happily gyrating with him.*

**Salt**    Mutiny! That's all we need!

**Gingerbread Man** (*loudly*)    Hey, Pepper!

**Pepper** (*loudly*)    Yes?

**Gingerbread Man**    One thing nobody told me.

**Pepper**    What?

**Gingerbread Man**    Who *I* am?

**Pepper**    You? You're the Gingerbread Man!

*During the song,* **Salt** *and* **Herr Von Cuckoo** *eventually relent and join in.*

SONG: **The Gingerbread Man**

**Gingerbread Man**
　　Newly baked this morning
　　Take a look at my tan
　　Hey hey
　　I'm the Gingerbread Man
　　Like a magic spell I
　　Just appeared with a bang

Hey hey
I'm the ginger, ginger
Ginger, ginger, ginger
Ginger, ginger
Gingerbread Man.

**All**

Ginger, ginger
Ginger, ginger, ginger
Ginger, ginger
Gingerbread Man.

**Gingerbread Man**

Suddenly you found me
Like a flash in the pan
Hey hey
I'm the Gingerbread Man
Bold and brown and bouncy
As an orang-utan
Hey hey
I'm the ginger, ginger
Ginger, ginger, ginger
Ginger, ginger
Gingerbread Man.

**All**

Ginger, ginger
Ginger, ginger, ginger
Ginger, ginger
Gingerbread Man.

**Gingerbread Man**

From the tips of my toes
To the top of my head
I'm guaranteed genuine
Gingerbread

**All**

Gingerbread, gingerbread.

**Salt, Pepper** *and* **Herr Von Cuckoo**

Soon as you arrived the
Dresser party began
Hey hey
You're the Gingerbread Man

**Pepper**

Ginger you're the greatest
I'm your number one fan

**All**

> Hey hey
> You're the ginger, ginger
> Ginger, ginger, ginger
> Ginger, ginger,
> Gingerbread Man.
>
> Ginger, ginger
> Ginger, ginger, ginger
> Ginger, ginger,
> Gingerbread Man.

**Gingerbread Man**

> One more time

**All**

> Ginger, ginger
> Ginger, ginger, ginger
> Ginger, ginger,
> Gingerbread Man.

*At the end of the song they all applaud happily.*

**Pepper**    That's more like it!

**Herr Von Cuckoo**    Encore! Encore!

**Salt**    I must say that was invigorating.

**Gingerbread Man** (*turning up the volume*)    Go on then!

**Salt**    What?

**Gingerbread Man**    Say it!

**Salt**    That was invigorating!

*All laugh as the music starts again. They all start dancing once more.*

*Suddenly, we hear, loudly, the noise of a door opening. Then a violent lighting change – all up to a blinding full – tells us someone has come into the kitchen.*

*All react with horror to this.* **Herr Von Cuckoo** *scurries back to his clock, and goes inside.* **Pepper** *dashes to her original position, maybe even trying to replace the envelope.* **Salt** *has finished up near the radio, which is still blaring out. He starts to dash back to join* **Pepper**, *but suddenly remembers to turn the radio off. Then he freezes, but can see the* **Gingerbread Man**, *who has never experienced the blinding light before. He is standing transfixed.*

**Salt** (*whispering through clenched teeth*)    Hey, Gingerbread Man. Down! Lie down!

*In the nick of time, the* **Gingerbread Man** *lies down, virtually in the position he had been left. Now, as the voices of the* **Big Ones** *are heard, perhaps we see their shadows looming threateningly over the set.*

**Mrs Big One**    There you are, dear, nothing.

**Mr Big One**    Extraordinary, darling. I could have sworn I heard the radio blaring out.

**Mrs Big One**    Well, you were wrong, dear, weren't you?

**Mr Big One**    Must have been, I suppose.

**Mrs Big One**    Anyway, it couldn't have just switched itself on, could it?

**Mr Big One**    Ah, but – it might have been left on.

**Mrs Big One**    What do you mean?

**Mr Big One**    Well, darling, you er – might – not have switched it off.

**Mrs Big One**    Of course I never switched it off –

**Mr Big One**    Aaaah!

**Mrs Big One**    – because *I* never switched it on in the first place. *You* did. For the football results. If anyone left it on, you did.

**Mr Big One**    I didn't.

**Mrs Big One**    What?

**Mr Big One**    Leave it on.

**Mrs Big One**    Then what are we arguing for?

**Mr Big One**    I'm not arguing. I thought I heard music, that's all.

**Mrs Big One**    Well, it must have come from next door. Come on, dear, I'm getting cold.

**Mr Big One**    All right, darling. But I could have sworn I heard music.

*During the last speech, the clock door opens and* **Herr Von Cuckoo** *emerges and clears his throat (with difficulty).*

**Herr Von Cuckoo** (*huskily*)    Mi, mi, mi, mi. (*He looks up to check the time – one o'clock. Very huskily.*) Cuckoo! (*He shrugs his shoulders, shakes his head and goes back inside, curled up with embarrassment.*)

**Mrs Big One**    What a weedy little noise.

**Mr Big One**    Needs a bit of oil, maybe.

**Mrs Big One**    Past it, more like. Have to get rid of it if it can't do better than that.

*The lights return to 'normal' and we hear the door slam. The shadows have gone. Pause. First to emerge is* **Herr Von Cuckoo**. *He comes out of his door, and locks it, in a terrible state.*

**Herr Von Cuckoo**    Ach! Ach! Ach! Ach! 'Have to get rid of it', she said. Herr Salt!

*He goes towards* **Salt** *and* **Pepper** *and meets the* **Gingerbread Man**, *who is nervously shaking.*

**Gingerbread Man**   Hey! What was all that about?

**Herr Von Cuckoo** (*avoiding the* **Gingerbread Man**)   Bitte, Herr Salt.

**Salt** *and* **Pepper** *move.* **Salt** *ignores* **Herr Von Cuckoo**.

**Pepper** (*recovering*)   A-a-tishoo!

**Salt** (*angrily*)   Gingerbread Man!

**Gingerbread Man**   What happened?

**Salt**   You woke up the Big Ones, that's what happened. Now listen. You're very young, the youngest member of the crew; you were only baked today. But this ship will sink if you behave . . .

**Pepper** (*intervening*)   Please, Mr Salt. Let me. Gingerbread Man. You're very welcome here; you've given us more excitement tonight than we've had for years, *but* we dresser folk, for our own good, should never cross with the Big Ones.

**Herr Von Cuckoo** *reacts to this remark.*

**Gingerbread Man**   I'm sorry.

**Pepper**   They can be very cruel.

**Herr Von Cuckoo** *starts sobbing.*

**Salt**   Cheer up, Cuckoo.

**Herr Von Cuckoo**   Did not you hear? Zey will throw me in the Dustbin.

**Gingerbread Man**   What's the Dustbin?

**Pepper**   Anything they don't want, the Big Ones throw in the Dustbin and it's never seen again.

**Herr Von Cuckoo** *sobs even more.*

**Pepper**   Sorry, Cuckoo, but he must be told.

**Gingerbread Man**   Why should they want to throw Cuckoo away?

**Herr Von Cuckoo** *sobs even more.*

**Herr Von Cuckoo**   Because ich have a toad in ze throat.

**Salt**   I think you mean 'frog', shipmate.

**Herr Von Cuckoo**   Frog, toad, what is ze difference?

**Salt**   Well, a toad is larger with fatter cheeks . . .

**Herr Von Cuckoo** *sobs again.*

**Salt**   I'm sorry, shipmate. Most unfeeling.

**Pepper**   The point is, he can't sing his cuckoos; he's a cuckoo-less cuckoo clock cuckoo.

**Herr Von Cuckoo** *sobs harder.*

**Gingerbread Man**    Listen. Let me help. To make up for waking the Big Ones.

**Herr Von Cuckoo**    What could you do?

**Gingerbread Man**    Find something to make you better.

**Pepper**    Something to soothe a sore throat.

**Salt**    What have we got on board that's soothing? Silky smooth, full of goodness?

*Hopefully the audience will help by shouting out 'honey'. This will work if the pot (on the shelf) is marked clearly enough to have been established.*

**Pepper**    Of course, honey!

**Gingerbread Man**    Honey. Right, where is it?

**Salt**    It means a voyage of exploration to the High Shelf.

*Dramatic chord. All look up at the honey.*

**Gingerbread Man**    Simple! Back in a jiffy.

*The* **Gingerbread Man** *walks towards the back. The others look at each other.*

**Salt**    Wait!

*The* **Gingerbread Man** *turns.*

**Salt**    Before you set sail . . .

**Pepper**    Beware.

**Gingerbread Man**    Beware?

**Herr Von Cuckoo**    Of ze Old Bag.

**Gingerbread Man**    Of what?

**All Three**    The Old Bag.

**Pepper**    The most horrible, dangerous, ruthless – tea bag.

**Salt**    The terror of the High Shelf.

SONG: **Beware of the Old Bag**

*If considered preferable the verses may be sung in unison.*

**Pepper**
　　She lives in the teapot up there

**Salt**
　　But to visit her – don't you dare.

**Herr Von Cuckoo**
　　She keeps herself
　　To her shelf

**Salt**
> And her shelf
> To herself

**All**
> And trespassers had better . . .
>
> Beware
> Of the Old Bag
> She's not fond of company
> Take care
> She's an old hag
> She's nobody's cup of tea.

**Pepper**
> She's the terror of the teapot
> And her temper's quick to brew

**Salt**
> From the gloom she will loom
> Like a ghost to frighten you

**Salt**
> So look out,

**Pepper**
> Look out,

**Herr Von Cuckoo**
> Look out,

**All**
> She's lying in wait
> Ev'ry perforation oozing hate.
>
> Beware
> Of the Old Bag
> She's not fond of company
> Take care
> She's an old hag
> She's nobody's cup of tea.

**Salt**
> And she hides behind the herb jars
> Looking out for passing spies

**Pepper**
> If you peep, out she'll creep

**Herr Von Cuckoo**
> And you'll get a big surprise

**All**

So look out, look out, look out
For Gingerbread Man
She will surely catch you if she can.

Beware
Of the Old Bag
She's not fond of company
Take care
She's an old hag
She's nobody's cup of tea.

**Herr Von Cuckoo**

So look out,

**Pepper**

Look out,

**Salt**

Look out,

**All**

Take care
Beware.

*Towards the end of the song, the* **Gingerbread Man** *has been 'frightened' by the others to hide behind the rolling pin. Now, at the end of the song, as the others freeze in their final positions, arms outstretched for the big finish, we hear a ghostly noise.*

**Gingerbread Man** (*behind the rolling pin*)    Woooooh, woooooooooh!

*Dramatic rumble. The others face front and react frightened, as a ghostly figure looms from behind the rolling pin. It is the* **Gingerbread Man** *with a tea cloth over his head.*

**Salt, Pepper** and **Von Herr Cuckoo** (*in a frightened whisper*)    It's the Old Bag!

*The* **Gingerbread Man** *creeps to one side, making his ghostly noise. The others tremble with fear. All together they turn their eyes to the noise, see the apparition, react, turn, bump into each other, and then, all together, run screaming to the side edge of the dresser. The* **Gingerbread Man** *pursues. They, having apparently nearly fallen off the dresser, run in their group to the other side. He pursues them to the edge. They nearly 'fall off', then in their huddle escape to the centre. The* **Gingerbread Man** *throws the tea cloth over them. They punch around inside it, and then emerge from it. The* **Gingerbread Man** *is laughing.*

**Pepper**    It was him all the time. (*She sneezes to recover.*)

**Gingerbread Man** (*laughing*)    Sorry, Pepper. Just a little joke.

**Salt**    Just a little joke? We nearly fell overboard, didn't we Cuckoo?

**Herr Von Cuckoo** *opens his mouth to reply, but nothing comes out.*

**Salt**    Eh?

**Herr Von Cuckoo** *tries again. Now all take notice. Not a sound comes out. He shakes his head.*

**Salt** (*to the others*)   Listen.

**Gingerbread Man**   I can't hear anything.

**Salt**   Exactly. There's nothing to hear. Cuckoo's got no voice at all. Come on, shipmate, I'll take you home.

*Music, as the sad* **Herr Von Cuckoo** *is led by* **Salt** *to his door. As they go in,* **Pepper** *and the* **Gingerbread Man***, who have watched in a sort of worried reverie, snap out of it.*

**Pepper**   The honey. Please. You'll have to hurry. It's an emergency now.

**Gingerbread Man**   Certainly, certainly, quick as I can. You can rely on the Gingerbread Man!

*Music as the* **Gingerbread Man** *flexes himself in preparation.* **Pepper** *watches as he advances to the shelf. He jumps to reach it, but cannot (or reaches it but cannot pull himself up). He tries this a couple of times, unsuccessfully, then looks at* **Pepper** *in consternation. She looks around.*

**Pepper**   Sugar lumps! Use them as steps!

*She runs to the sugar bowl. She and the* **Gingerbread Man** *take out three or four lumps and make a pile, leaving a 'step' on each one. Gingerly the* **Gingerbread Man** *climbs the pile, but at the last minute he topples over and the pile collapses. He lands on the 'floor'. At this moment,* **Salt** *emerges from the cuckoo clock.*

**Salt**   Ahoy there! What's up?

**Gingerbread Man**   I'm down! (*Setting up the sugar lumps again.*) Just on my way.

**Salt**   You'll never get up there like that.

**Pepper**   Think of a better way.

**Salt**   Well . . . Well . . . Well . . .

*As* **Salt** *thinks, the* **Gingerbread Man** *again climbs the sugar lumps, topples and falls again. He makes an angry frustrated noise.*

**Pepper**   Well?

**Salt**   Well . . .

**Pepper**   Come on. Here's a chance to show off your nautical know-how.

**Salt**   I'm thinking, I'm thinking. What would a real old salt of the sea do? Got it! A capstan.

**Gingerbread Man**   Of course! A capstan! (*Pause.*) What's a capstan?

**Salt**   I'll show you, shipmate. Miss Pepper, be good enough to heave-ho that piece of string that came on the Big Ones' parcel yesterday.

**Pepper**   String. (*She goes to find it, stops and turns, and smiles.*) Aye, aye, Captain! (*She salutes and carries on. She is thoroughly enjoying the excitement.*)

**Salt**   Gingerbread Man. Give us a hand rolling the rolling pin.

**Gingerbread Man**   Aye, aye, Captain.

**Salt** *and the* **Gingerbread Man** *push the rolling pin to beneath the shelf, under a vacant cup hook on the shelf edge above their heads.*

**Pepper** (*returning*)   String, Captain.

**Salt**   Splendid. Thank you, Miss Pepper. Now, everybody, I'll show you the Captain's capstan!

*Music – shanty-style, the intro to the next song, as* **Salt***, helped by the other two, prepares the capstan. First he throws the string over the cup hook, above. Then he gives one end to the* **Gingerbread Man***, showing him how to tie it round his waist as a kind of sling-hoist. (The slip-knot could already be there.) The other end of the string is tied round the thick part of the rolling pin, which should be upstage. The string should be taut. Then* **Salt** *and* **Pepper** *roll the rolling pin forwards (downstage), having the effect of lifting the* **Gingerbread Man** *off the ground. He will probably have to help himself, by using the side of the dresser, and finally helping himself climb on to the shelf.*

SONG: **Heave-Ho, A-Rolling Go**

**Salt**
   Haul on the halyard, hard as we can

**All**
   Heave-ho, a-rolling go

**Salt**
   Hup, mates, and hoist the Gingerbread Man

**All**
   Way hay and yo ho ho.

**Salt**
   Lifting our load and taking the strain

**All**
   Heave-ho, a-rolling go

**Salt**
   Turning the capstan, cranking the crane

**All**
   Way hay and yo ho ho.

**Salt**

Higher and higher, t'ward the crow's nest

**All**

Heave-ho, a-rolling go

**Salt**

Fair wind and fortune follow the quest

**All**

Way hay and yo ho ho.

*The music continues as the* **Gingerbread Man** *removes the loop of string and hangs it from the hook, and waves down to* **Salt** *and* **Pepper***, who then sit and wait on the rolling pin. Lighting changes to the shelf area only. Tension music as the* **Gingerbread Man** *sets off towards the honey, treading on tiptoe.*

*Suddenly the door of the cottage teapot creaks menacingly open, and the* **Old Bag** *peeps out, then seeing the invader of 'her' territory, surreptitiously creeps out and starts stalking the* **Gingerbread Man***.*

*The audience will pretty certainly react, by shouting a warning to the* **Gingerbread Man***, who by this time has reached the honey and is starting to remove the lid. The* **Old Bag***, looming like a ghost, advances and the* **Gingerbread Man** *senses danger; he mimes to the audience 'Is there someone behind me?'; 'Yes', comes back the reply. He works himself up to a sudden quick turn; but the* **Old Bag** *has been too quick for him, and hidden behind other jars and bottles. The* **Gingerbread Man** *assumes the audience is leading him up the garden path, and returns to the honey jar. The business is repeated as the* **Old Bag** *creeps out and advances again. This time, encouraged by the audience, he turns suddenly, and sees the* **Old Bag** *– surprising her at the same time. Both scream and run to hide in opposite directions. They re-emerge and go into a panto-style stalking – the* **Gingerbread Man** *never seeing the* **Old Bag** *and vice versa – back to back, until they bump into each other, jump violently and confront one another.*

**Old Bag** (*sharply*)   Who are you?

**Gingerbread Man**   The G-G-G-Gingerbread Man.

**Old Bag**   Never heard of you.

**Gingerbread Man**   I was only b-b-baked today. By the Big Ones.

**Old Bag**   You're trespassing.

**Gingerbread Man**   But . . .

**Old Bag**   This is *my* shelf.

**Gingerbread Man**   But this is an emergency. Herr Von Cuckoo . . .

**Old Bag**   What about him?

**Gingerbread Man**   He's lost his voice.

**Old Bag**    You mean he can't 'cuckoo'?

**Gingerbread Man**    Yes. I mean no.

**Old Bag** (*with a sudden cackle*)    Ha, ha, ha.

**Gingerbread Man**    So I thought . . .

**Old Bag** (*with a sudden change back to sharpness*)    What did you think?

**Gingerbread Man**    I thought I'd get him some honey. It might help him.

**Old Bag**    You thought wrong.

**Gingerbread Man**    You mean honey won't help him?

**Old Bag**    I mean you're not getting him any. I'm glad, delighted he's lost his voice. I've always hated that stupid noise every hour of the day and night. 'Cuckoo, Cuckoo, Cuckoo.' Now perhaps I can get a bit of peace and quiet.

**Gingerbread Man**    But the Big Ones may throw him in the Dustbin.

**Old Bag**    Good riddance. And good riddance to you, too. Clear off. (*To the audience.*) And *you* can clear off too. All of you.

**Gingerbread Man**    What have *they* done?

**Old Bag**    They don't like me.

**Gingerbread Man**    How do you know?

**Old Bag**    Nobody likes me. I'm all alone. All the other tea bags in my packet were used up ages ago. The Big Ones missed me and I hid in the teapot. No one ever visits me.

**Gingerbread Man**    Well, it's not easy getting here.

**Old Bag**    It's not easy *living* here.

**Gingerbread Man**    Are you lonely?

**Old Bag**    I never said that.

**Gingerbread Man**    I'll be your friend, if you like.

**Old Bag**    Huh. Bribery. Get round me. Let's be friends. Then I give you the honey. Whoosh, down. Never see you again.

**Gingerbread Man**    I don't think you want a friend.

**Old Bag**    I never said that. I'm quite enjoying a bit of company.

**Gingerbread Man**    Good (*Indicating the honey.*) Then will you let me take some . . .

**Old Bag** (*interrupting*)    I'll tell your fortune for you, if you like.

**Gingerbread Man**    Will you? How?

**Old Bag**    Tea leaves have always had special magic fortune-telling properties. They send messages through my perforations. Show me your hand.

**Gingerbread Man**    Well . . .

*He tentatively stretches out his hand.*

**Old Bag**    Come along. Don't be shy.

SONG: **The Power of the Leaf**

**Old Bag**
    If you want to know the future
    You don't need a horoscope
    You don't need to study stars
    Through a telescope
    You don't need a pack of tarot cards
    You don't need a crystal ball
    For the power of the tea leaf
    Is more potent than them all.

    So
    Put your belief
    In the power of the leaf
    It can tell you things you never knew before
    Put your belief
    In the power of the leaf
    If you want to know what lies in store.

    No, there isn't any secret,
    There's no club you have to join
    And you needn't cross my palm
    With a silver coin
    You don't need to say a magic word
    You don't need a medium
    Through the power of the tea leaf
    See the shape of things to come.

    So
    Put your belief

**Gingerbread Man**
    (*spoken echo*) Put your belief

**Old Bag**
    In the power of the leaf

**Gingerbread Man**
    (*spoken echo*) In the power of the leaf

**Old Bag**
    It can tell you things you never knew before

**Both**
Put your belief
In the power of the leaf
If you want to know what lies in store.

*The music continues.*

**Old Bag**    I can see! I can see!

**Gingerbread Man** (*speaking*)    What can you see?

**Old Bag**    A message.

**Gingerbread Man**    For me?

**Old Bag**    Yes. Listen and learn.
'When trouble comes, if you can cope,
Three lives will shortly find new hope.'

**Gingerbread Man**
'When trouble comes, if I can cope,
Three lives will shortly find new hope.'

What does it mean?

**Old Bag**    You'll find out – soon.

**Gingerbread Man**    Thank you, Old Bag.

**Old Bag**    Don't thank me, thank the power of the leaf.

**Old Bag** and **Gingerbread Man** (*singing*)
So
Put your belief
In the power of the leaf
It can tell you things you never knew before
Put your belief
In the power of the leaf
If you want to know what lies in store.

Put your belief
In the power of the leaf
It can tell you things you never knew before
Yes! Put your belief
In the power of the leaf
If you want to know what lies in store.

**Old Bag**    Don't forget.

**Gingerbread Man**    Thank you, Old Bag. Well, it's time for me to go down again.

**Old Bag** (*sharply*)    Why? Don't you enjoy my company?

**Gingerbread Man**    Yes, but the others are . . .

**Old Bag** (*charmingly*)   Let me show you round my shelf. (*She grabs him by an arm, and leads him across.*) See my herb garden? Bay, cinnamon, mint, rosemary.

**Gingerbread Man**   What are they for?

**Old Bag**   They contain remarkable medicinal powers. I have studied them hard and long. They can cure diseases, make sick folk better.

**Gingerbread Man**   Nobody told me you could do that.

**Old Bag**   Nobody else knows.

**Gingerbread Man**   But think of the good you could do for the dresser folk. The help you could be.

**Old Bag**   Nobody's ever asked for my help.

**Gingerbread Man**   I'm asking you now. To help Cuckoo.

**Old Bag**   That noisy bird?

**Gingerbread Man**   Just a small lump of honey . . .

**Old Bag**   No, no, no! I must be getting senile. Soft. I was beginning to like you. But you weren't being friendly at all.

**Gingerbread Man**   I was!

**Old Bag**   All you want is your rotten honey. And if I give you some I'll never see you again.

**Gingerbread Man**   You will.

**Old Bag**   Clear off.

**Gingerbread Man**   I'll come back.

**Old Bag** (*shouting*)   Get off my shelf.

*Furious, the* **Old Bag** *stomps back to the teapot and goes inside.*

*Music, as the* **Gingerbread Man** *considers what to do. He looks at the honey, then at the place of descent, perhaps checking for confirmation with the audience.*

**Gingerbread Man** (*whispers to audience*)   Shall I?

*He makes his mind up, and, having checked that the teapot door is still closed, he tiptoes to the honey jar and steals a chunk. He checks once more that the coast is clear, then creeps to where he left his string harness. He looks over the edge.*

**Gingerbread Man** (*whispering*)   Salty. Pepper. Psssst. Salty.

**Salt** *and* **Pepper** *are dozing on the rolling pin.* **Salt** *stirs and wakes up. The lighting changes to reveal below.*

**Gingerbread Man**   Pssst.

**Pepper** (*waking*)   A-a-a-tishoo!

**Salt**    What? What?

**Gingerbread Man** (*whispering*)    Up here!

**Salt** (*looking up; loudly*)    It's Gingerbread Man!

**Gingerbread Man**    Shhhhh!

*Music. The* **Gingerbread Man** *shows* **Salt** *the honey, and mimes throwing it down.* **Salt** *understands, wakes up* **Pepper***, hushing her and pointing up to the* **Gingerbread Man***.*

*They whisper briefly, then go to the back and bring forward a plate. Meanwhile, the* **Gingerbread Man** *looks anxiously back at the teapot door.* **Salt** *and* **Pepper** *hold the plate underneath, and the* **Gingerbread Man** *prepares to throw down the honey. At this point the teapot door creaks open. The audience will probably shout a warning, as a result of which the* **Gingerbread Man** *throws the honey down on to the plate, and desperately puts on the string harness. Meanwhile, below,* **Salt** *and* **Pepper** *place the plate down, out of the way, and return to the 'capstan' rolling pin. With a cry of 'anchors away', they lower him to their level.*

*During this, the* **Old Bag** *emerges, shouting abuse. She reaches the edge of the shelf and very nearly catches the* **Gingerbread Man***.*

**Old Bag**    You double-crossing little thief! I saw you! Let me get my hands on you! I'll make you squirm! Stealing deserves punishment and punished you will be! You evil little trickster. Come back.

*By this time the* **Gingerbread Man** *has reached the floor and* **Salt** *and* **Pepper** *help him off with the string harness. During the next speech the* **Gingerbread Man** *becomes subdued. Music to heighten the situation.*

**Old Bag** (*with a deliberately nasty change of tack*)    You won't get away with it, you know. Gingerbread Man. Can you hear me? You'll soon suffer. You won't be around much longer. The Big Ones bake Gingerbread Men – to eat them. While they're fresh and crisp and tasty. Eat them. Goodbye, Gingerbread Man. Goodbye for ever.

*Laughing, the* **Old Bag** *backs away and returns inside the teapot.*

*The* **Gingerbread Man***, stunned by her words, is led to the rolling pin by* **Salt** *and* **Pepper***; they sit him down.*

**Gingerbread Man**    Is it true?

**Salt**    Well, shipmate, we can't say for certain . . .

**Pepper**    But – well, normally, if the Big Ones bake anything . . .

**Gingerbread Man**    I see.

**Salt**    Sorry, shipmate.

**Pepper**    We didn't say anything because – well, you seemed so happy. And you cheered all of us up.

**Salt**    *And* you were brave enough to answer Cuckoo's SOS.

**Gingerbread Man**    Cuckoo! (*He jumps up.*) I must tell him we've got his honey. (*He sets off, then stops and looks back.*) And don't worry about me! (*He smiles.*) I'm not beaten – till I'm eaten! And I won't be eaten – till I'm beaten!

*Music as the* **Gingerbread Man** *leaves* **Salt** *and* **Pepper** *to relax on the rolling pin, and crosses to the cuckoo clock, on the way possibly placing the plate in a central position. He reaches the clock and knocks on the door.*

**Gingerbread Man**    Herr Von Cuckoo!

*The door opens. The sickly* **Herr Von Cuckoo** *emerges. He starts to speak.*

**Gingerbread Man**    Don't speak! Save your voice! Look what I've got for you. (*Pulling the plate towards* **Herr Von Cuckoo**.) Honey. For your throat.

**Herr Von Cuckoo** *takes in the news, then grabs the startled* **Gingerbread Man** *and kisses him on both cheeks, making husky noises meaning 'Danke, danke!'*

**Gingerbread Man**    My pleasure, Cuckoo.

**Herr Von Cuckoo** *turns.*

**Gingerbread Man**    Don't go! Aren't you going to eat some?

**Herr Von Cuckoo** *shakes his head and points to the clock face, which says ten to two. Then he mimes 'cuckoo, cuckoo'.*

**Gingerbread Man**    You've got to do some 'cuckooing' first?

**Herr Von Cuckoo** *nods.*

**Gingerbread Man**    Can't you give it a miss this once? You're not well.

**Herr Von Cuckoo** *shakes his head effusively. He must do his duty.*

**Gingerbread Man**    All right. But you'll try the honey afterwards?

**Herr Von Cuckoo** *nods and grunts, 'Ja, danke.'*

**Gingerbread Man**    Fine. Your throat is sore, you're feeling sick –

A dose of honey will do the trick!

**Herr Von Cuckoo** *goes back into the clock. Music as the* **Gingerbread Man** *leaves, and returns to* **Salt** *and* **Pepper**, *on the rolling pin. He yawns, and sits on the floor, against the rolling pin, as if to go to sleep.* **Salt** *and* **Pepper** *smile at him.*

**Pepper**    Goodnight. (*She yawns and nods off.*)

**Salt**    Goodnight. (*He yawns and nods off.*)

**Gingerbread Man**    Goodnight. (*He yawns and nods off.*)

*Pause. Suddenly there is a loud noise, scratching and scuffling. The* **Gingerbread Man** *jumps awake and listens. The noise stops. He settles again. The noise starts* *again. He listens again. He decides to investigate. Meanwhile* **Salt** *and* **Pepper** *have gone to sleep.*

*The* **Gingerbread Man** *halts in his tracks. The noise stops. He takes a couple of steps. The noise starts again. He listens. It stops. Two steps. It starts again. The* **Gingerbread Man** *tracks down the noise to behind a plate, which stands vertical in the corner of the back of the dresser. Inquisitively, he tentatively slides the plate to one side. A hole is revealed in the back of the dresser.*

**Sleek the Mouse** *enters, sniffing hungrily, at the same time looking around to make sure the coast is clear.*

*The* **Gingerbread Man** *watches, half hidden behind the plate.*

**Sleek** (*to nobody in particular*)    O guys you K – I mean, OK, you guys. This is a raid. One move and you'll feel my false teeth – no, I mean, one false move and you'll feel my teeth.

SONG: **Sleek the Mouse**

*NB: To prick the balloon of* **Sleek***'s cool exterior, the song should be staged in such a way that little things suddenly frighten him or go wrong – then he has to work hard to cover his embarrassment and preserve his image.*

**Sleek**
>    You hear scratching
>    In the skirting
>    In the kitchen
>    Of your house –
>    Then it's odds on
>    That you're list'ning
>    To yours truly –
>    Sleek the Mouse.
>
>    I mean business
>    No one bugs me
>    I'm not playing
>    Hide and squeak
>    Double-cross me
>    At your peril
>    I'm the boss mouse –
>    Call me Sleek.
>
>    I went raiding
>    In the pantry
>    In the middle
>    Of the night
>    When the Big Ones
>    Caught me nibbling

Pink blancmange
They got a fright.

Tried to catch me
In a mouse trap
But I fooled them
With such ease
And next morning
Trap was empty
No one told them –
I hate cheese!

Any showdown
I can handle
With a human,
Mouse or cat
And my whiskers
Start to tremble
If you call me –
(A) dirty rat!

I'm a hungry
Desperado
So I'm forced to
Use my nouse
That comes easy
To the ruthless
One and only
Mafia mouse.

Super-mouse
Call me Sleek
Sleek the Mouse
Pretty chic

Sleek!

*He goes to lean nonchalantly in a final position, against the mug – but misses it and falls to the ground.*

*He gets up and sniffs hungrily again.*

Somewhere I snack a sniff – sniff a snack. A lip-smackin', paw-lickin', whisker-itchin', nose-twitchin' supersnack. And I'm gonna track it down. For days my belly's been empty and I've had a bellyful! (*He sniffs.*)

*The* **Gingerbread Man** *emerges. Not suspecting danger, he approaches and stands by* **Sleek** *during the following.*

**Sleek**    I'm gonna nose my follow and nothing's gonna stand in my way . . . (*He turns and bumps into the* **Gingerbread Man**.) Aaaaaah!

**Gingerbread Man**    Hallo.

**Sleek**    You're standing in my way, stranger.

**Gingerbread Man**    I'm the Gingerbread Man.

*He shakes hands with* **Sleek***.*

**Sleek**    Hi, Ginger. I'm Sleek the Mouse. And I'm telling you this dresser ain't big enough for both of us.

**Gingerbread Man**    I don't know what you mean.

**Sleek** *sniffs, realises the scent is near, sniffs his hand which was shaken by the* **Gingerbread Man***'s – and realises.*

**Sleek**    Hey. It's you! You're my little snackeroo!

**Gingerbread Man**    What?

**Sleek**    You smell good enough to eat, Ginger.

**Gingerbread Man** (*realising the threat*)    I am, (*Suddenly.*) but not by you! Look! (*Points up, distracting* **Sleek***, then dashes off.*)

*Music, as a chase starts.*

*The* **Gingerbread Man** *escapes through* **Sleek***'s legs, possibly making him fall over. The* **Gingerbread Man** *runs back to the plate and hides behind it.* **Sleek** *follows, and goes behind the plate. As he does so, the* **Gingerbread Man** *emerges from the other side of the plate and runs round it.* **Sleek** *follows. The chase round is repeated.*

*The* **Gingerbread Man** *emerges, and stops, then gingerly backs towards the other side of the plate. Suddenly* **Sleek** *comes out from that other side, having tricked the* **Gingerbread Man** *by not going the full circuit. He pounces. The* **Gingerbread Man** *manages to struggle free, but is forced to back away to the edge of the dresser.* **Sleek** *pounces again, but the* **Gingerbread Man** *slips sideways out of the way, leaving* **Sleek** *perilously near falling off. He teeters and totters alarmingly. Meanwhile, the* **Gingerbread Man** *dashes back to the rolling pin and wakes up* **Salt** *and* **Pepper***, who react animatedly to the situation. They quickly decide that the* **Gingerbread Man** *should go aloft to the shelf. So* **Salt** *helps him up, winding the capstan.*

*Meanwhile,* **Sleek** *recovers his balance and turns to be faced by* **Pepper***. They size each other up, then* **Pepper** *twists her grinder, picks up some pepper and throws it towards* **Sleek***, who sneezes violently, but half-heartedly carries on the chase, which continues in the rolling pin area, involving* **Salt** *too. Up on the shelf, the* **Gingerbread Man***, supposedly out of harm's way, watches and shouts encouragement.*

*Suddenly the teapot door opens, and a furious* **Old Bag** *pops out, screaming vengeance.*

*The* **Gingerbread Man** *senses her approach and a mini-chase starts. Everyone is in motion on both levels when we hear, as before, the loud noise of the door opening. Then the violent lighting change up to a blinding full. All except* **Sleek** *pause frozen for a second, realise what has happened and dash to their normal positions. The* **Old Bag** *returns in the teapot,* **Salt** *and* **Pepper** *to their spot, and the* **Gingerbread Man**, *not being able to climb down in time, lies flat on the shelf.* **Sleek**, *unaware of what has happened, stands transfixed and wide-eyed. Then we hear the voices of the* **Big Ones**.

**Mrs Big One**    There was no need for you to come down, dear.

**Mr Big One**    But you said you heard noises, darling.

**Mrs Big One**    I did, dear, funny scuffling noi . . . Aaaaaaah! Look.

**Mr Big One**    Heavens. A mouse!

**Mrs Big One** (*screaming*)    Aaaaaah!

**Mr Big One**    Shoo, shoo, you verminous little rodent. Shoo, shoo.

*The 'Aaaaaaahs' and the 'Shoo shoos' continue ad-lib, until* **Sleek** *comes to his senses and scurries to shelter – towards his hole behind the plate.*

**Mr Big One**    He's gone, darling.

**Mrs Big One**    He hasn't, he's hiding! Ughhh!

**Mr Big One**    All right, all right. I'll put some poison down.

*We hear noises of, say, a cupboard door and a tin opening.*

Here you are. Here's some poison. This'll teach you. One gulp and you're a gonna.

*Music, as from above the stage some poison (glitter?) floats down on to the plate on which the honey waits for* **Herr Von Cuckoo**.

**Mrs Big One**    Thank you, dear.

**Mr Big One**    Come on, darling, (*Yawn.*) let's go back to bed.

*At this moment* **Herr Von Cuckoo** *slowly and painfully comes out of his clock. It is two o'clock. He sadly croaks.*

**Herr Von Cuckoo**    Cuckoo, cuckoo. (*Hardly any noise comes out. He shakes his head.*)

**Mr Big One**    Huh. That cuckoo's no better. Hopeless.

**Mrs Big One**    I'll deal with it in the morning, dear.

*The door slams shut, and the bright light goes out. Everybody except* **Herr Von Cuckoo** *remains frozen after all the panic.* **Herr Von Cuckoo**, *reacting to the last words of the* **Big Ones**, *looks over to the plate, and smiles.*

**Herr Von Cuckoo** (*huskily*)    Herr Von Cuckoo will show you. In ze morning, thanks to ze Gingerbread Man's honey, ich will quite better be!

*Happily, he leaves the clock, arrives on the dresser and starts walking towards the poisoned plate of honey. He was in his clock when the* **Big Ones** *put down the poison, and therefore has no idea there is any danger.*

*The audience, hopefully, scream a warning, and as he reaches the plate and prepares to eat –*

*Curtain.*

# Act Two

*Act Two begins where Act One ended. It is suggested, to avoid the possibility of the audience missing the vital first minutes of this act (because of late return to seats, taking time to settle, etc.) that an entr'acte be played,* after *the house lights go down and* before *the curtain rises.*

*The curtain rises. A smiling* **Herr Von Cuckoo** *rubs his hands in anticipation, bends down – and eats some of the poisoned honey. The audience may shout out another warning. The* **Gingerbread Man**, *still flat out following the* **Big Ones'** *visit, opens his eyes and sees* **Herr Von Cuckoo** *eat just too late. He shouts down to him.*

**Gingerbread Man**   Cuckoo!

**Herr Von Cuckoo**   Mein friend. How can ich danke you? Ich better already feel!

*He goes to take more. The* **Gingerbread Man** *stops him, shouting.*

**Gingerbread Man**   No!

**Salt** *and* **Pepper** *bustle across and pull away the plate. Then* **Salt** *helps the* **Gingerbread Man** *down, using the string.*

**Salt**   Did he eat any?

**Gingerbread Man**   One mouthful.

**Herr Von Cuckoo**   Was is ze matter? You honey fetchen me, zen away taken.

**Pepper**   It was poisoned, Cuckoo. Poisoned by the Big Ones.

**Herr Von Cuckoo** (*disbelieving*)   Nein. (*He laughs.*) You make ze bit of a joke with me, hah? Listen. (*He happily shows how improved his voice is.*) Cuckoo! Cuckoo! Cuckoo! (*But after a couple of smiling 'Cuckoos', he clutches his stomach and sways. He goes on cuckooing, but it becomes more and more painful, until finally he faints backwards into the arms of* **Salt** *and the* **Gingerbread Man**.)

**Pepper**   Quick, lie him down.

**Salt**   Aye, aye, ma'am.

**Pepper**   Where's the tea cloth?

**Salt**   Behind the rolling pin.

**Pepper** *fetches the tea cloth and covers* **Herr Von Cuckoo** *to keep him warm.*

**Gingerbread Man**   What are we going to do?

**Salt** *listens to* **Herr Von Cuckoo**'s *heart.*

**Pepper**   Nothing much we *can* do. Just wait and hope he didn't eat too much.

**Salt**   He's still breathing. Just. If only we had a ship's doctor.

*Pause.*

**Gingerbread Man**    But we have!

**Salt**    What?

**Gingerbread Man**    Well, not a doctor exactly, but she could help.

**Pepper**    Who?

**Gingerbread Man**    The Old Bag. With her herbs. 'They can cure diseases, make sick folk better', she said.

**Salt**    She won't help. Never has before. Remember that jelly mould, Miss Pepper?

**Pepper**    Yes. Top shelf she was. In the shape of a rabbit.

**Salt**    She was made of metal – one day she started getting rusty.

**Pepper**    Next day. Bang. The Dustbin.

**Salt**    The Old Bag never lifted a leaf to help.

**Gingerbread Man**    Did anyone ask her to help?

**Pepper**    Huh. No one dared to go near her.

**Salt**    Waste of time, anyway.

**Gingerbread Man**    If you didn't ask her, you could hardly expect her to help. (*He turns and looks up to the shelf, and the teapot.*) Hey! Old Bag. Can you hear me? (*Pause.*) Old Bag! We need your help. Please.

*No response.*

**Salt**    It's no use, shipmate.

**Herr Von Cuckoo** *groans with pain. The* **Gingerbread Man** *hears; it makes up his mind for him. He goes to the string hoist and starts putting it on.*

**Salt**    What are you doing?

**Gingerbread Man**    Come on. Hoist me up again. The Old Bag is Cuckoo's only chance.

**Salt**    But . . .

**Pepper**    He's right, Mr Salt. Let him try.

**Gingerbread Man**    Quick.

**Salt** (*after a pause*)    Aye, aye, sir!

**Salt** *and* **Pepper** *man the rolling pin capstan.*

SONG: **Heave-Ho, A-Rolling Go** (*reprise*)

**Salt**
Haul on the halyard, hard as we can

**All**
Heave-ho, a-rolling go

**Salt**
Hup, mates, and hoist the Gingerbread Man

**All**
Way hay and yo ho ho.

**Gingerbread Man**
SOS – urgent! I'll do my best,

**All**
Heave-ho, a-rolling go

**Salt**
Fair wind and fortune follow your quest

**All**
Way hay and yo ho ho.

*The* **Gingerbread Man** *arrives on the shelf. Below,* **Salt** *and* **Pepper** *sit on the rolling pin, looking at the prostrate* **Herr Von Cuckoo**. *The lighting intensifies on the shelf as the* **Gingerbread Man** *takes off his string hoist and leaves it on the cup hook. Music continues as he approaches the teapot. He is determined, though not over-confident. He knocks on the door, turning away from it as he waits for a reply. Nothing. He knocks again, and again turns away. No response at first, but then silently the door opens. The* **Gingerbread Man** *is unaware of this.*

*The* **Old Bag** *slowly emerges.*

*The* **Gingerbread Man** *goes to knock on the door again, but in fact knocks the* **Old Bag** *on the nose.*

**Old Bag**   Ow!

*The* **Gingerbread Man** *jumps with surprise.*

**Gingerbread Man**   Ooh!

**Old Bag** (*furious*)   First you pinch my honey, now you knock me on the nose.

**Gingerbread Man**   I'm sorry. I didn't hear you.

**Old Bag**   Clear off!

**Gingerbread Man**   No, please.

**Old Bag**   Clear off! And if you ever come on my shelf again, I'll . . .

**Gingerbread Man** (*shouting*)   I need your help.

*Pause.*

**Old Bag**   What?

**Gingerbread Man** (*sincerely*)   I need your help.

**Old Bag** (*softening*)    What for?

**Gingerbread Man**    It's Cuckoo.

**Old Bag**    That noisy bird again? I helped him when you helped yourself to my honey.

**Gingerbread Man**    He's been poisoned –

**Old Bag** (*losing her temper*)    How dare you? My honey is pure and healthy-giving . . .

**Gingerbread Man**    – by the Big Ones.

**Old Bag**    The Big Ones? Why?

**Gingerbread Man**    They put poison on his honey –

*The* **Old Bag** *looks indignant for a second.*

**Gingerbread Man** – I mean *your* honey. Look.

*He leads the* **Old Bag** *to the edge of the shelf and shows her the sight of the prostrate* **Herr Von Cuckoo** *below.*

**Old Bag**    But why?

**Gingerbread Man**    They wanted to get rid of Sleek the Mouse.

*At the mention of* **Sleek the Mouse**, *the* **Old Bag** *becomes nervous.*

**Old Bag**    Mouse? What mouse?

**Gingerbread Man**    Sleek. The mouse that's trying to eat me.

**Old Bag**    Eat you? Where? Has he followed you? (*She looks around, wild-eyed.*)

**Gingerbread Man**    No. Probably went home when he saw the poison pouring down.

**Old Bag**    I hate mice. Vicious creatures. They try to chew my perforations.

*Suddenly, from a hole behind the herb jars, if necessary pushing between them, comes* **Sleek the Mouse**.

**Sleek**    OK, Ginger, don't move.

*The* **Old Bag** *screams.*

**Sleek**    Show for a timedown – time for a showdown.

**Old Bag**    Aaaaah. A mouse! Help! Help! (*She gathers in her perforations in terror.*)

**Gingerbread Man**    Shhh! Go away, Sleek. I'm not frightened of you. (*He does not sound convincing.*)

*Meanwhile,* **Salt** *and* **Pepper** *have heard the* **Old Bag**'s *screams and stand below, looking at the scene above.*

**Sleek**   No? Reckoned you were safe up here, huh? Reckoned I couldn't climb dressers too? Think again, Ginger. I used the back entrance.

**Old Bag** (*wailing*)    Get rid of him! (*Pushes the* **Gingerbread Man** *towards* **Sleek**.)

**Sleek** *cannot see the* **Old Bag** *behind the* **Gingerbread Man**.

**Sleek**   You've had your fun, Ginger. Now it's my turn. I'm starving.

**Gingerbread Man**   You may be hungry, but try as you can, you'll never eat the Gingerbread Man.

*Music.* **Sleek** *and the* **Gingerbread Man** *move towards each other 'High Noon' style. Left on her own, the* **Old Bag** *trembles at the edge of the shelf.* **Sleek** *and the* **Gingerbread Man** *circle each other. Then, say, three times* **Sleek** *lunges at the* **Gingerbread Man***, who steps aside to avoid him. Then they clasp hands in a trial of strength. Slowly but surely* **Sleek** *gains supremacy till the* **Gingerbread Man** *is down. Then* **Sleek** *sniffs hungrily at the* **Gingerbread Man***'s arm, and prepares to bite it. He has his back to the* **Old Bag***. Very bravely, seeing the situation, the* **Old Bag***, who has started to creep home to her teapot, decides she should help the* **Gingerbread Man***. She looms up on* **Sleek***, and pulls his tail.*

**Sleek**   Aah!

*In this second or two of panic, the* **Gingerbread Man** *rolls away from* **Sleek***'s grasp and dashes to the hole behind the herb jars. He disappears.*

**Sleek** (*realising what has happened*)    You miserable Old Bag. You'll pay for that.

*Music continues as they stalk each other. Finally, the* **Old Bag** *is backed towards the edge of the shelf. The* **Gingerbread Man** *arrives below (through the mouse hole behind the plate). He rushes to* **Salt** *and* **Pepper***, who have been watching. They consult in a huddle, then grab the tea cloth off the prostrate* **Herr Von Cuckoo***, and hold it under the shelf (firemen's blanket-style). Alternatively the others position the upturned mug for her to step down on. The tension builds as* **Sleek** *advances and finally the* **Old Bag** *jumps or falls from the shelf into the tea cloth. She is taken care of, as the lights focus on the furious* **Sleek** *above. During his next speech, the* **Gingerbread Man***, taking the tea cloth with him, goes back through the hole behind the plate.*

**Sleek**   I've been boozlebammed! Bamboozled! You dirty, stinking rats! (*Petulantly whining.*) There were two of you against one of me. (*He suddenly cries with frustration and injustice, the aim being to get the audience to laugh at him.*) It's not fair! Boo hoo hoo hoo! (*He hears the audience laughing at him and looks up, furious.*) Hey! It's not funny. Nobody laughs at me, OK? I'm the baddie. The tough guy. A savage brute. And I'm telling you – (*He crumples again.*) – it wasn't fair! Boo hoo hoo!

*Hopefully the audience are laughing again.*

Shut up! I'm warning you. I'm a mouseless ruth – ruthless mouse – (*He has an idea.*) – and I'm so hungry that one more squeak from you and I'll be down there – raiding your sweets. All those toffees, and sherbet lemons and chocolate eclairs . . . (*He laughs and sniffs greedily. His sniffs suddenly change as he realises he can detect something tasty nearby.)*

*Through the hole, carrying the tea cloth, the* **Gingerbread Man** *appears.*

**Gingerbread Man**    Coo – ee!

*Music, as* **Sleek** *sees the* **Gingerbread Man** *and prepares to attack. He charges a few times, warded off by the* **Gingerbread Man**, *who uses the tea cloth like a bullfighter's cape – with appropriate music. Finally the* **Gingerbread Man** *manoeuvres himself to the teapot, the door of which is still open. With a final flourish he makes* **Sleek** *charge him and steps aside, forcing* **Sleek** *to run into the teapot. Swiftly, the* **Gingerbread Man** *slams the door shut, and either locks it or places something against it to stop it opening. (In the original production, a matchbox was used.) The others below have been watching, and now applaud. The* **Gingerbread Man** *bows graciously and throws down the tea cloth to be put back on* **Herr Von Cuckoo.** **Pepper** *returns to tend* **Herr Von Cuckoo.**

**Gingerbread Man**    Thank you, thank you. (*Looking over the edge.*) All right, Old Bag?

**Old Bag**    No. You've shut him in my teapot. (*Wailing.*) There's a mouse in my house!

**Gingerbread Man**    Oh, sorry. I'll let him out, shall I?

**Old Bag**    What?

**Gingerbread Man**    Let him come down and nibble your perforations.

**Old Bag**    No, no. Leave him.

**Gingerbread Man**    Some folk are never satisfied. (*He sits on the edge.*)

**Old Bag**    I am. I am. Thank you. Thank you *all* for saving me.

**Salt** (*uncomfortably*)    Our duty, ma'am. Anyone in danger on the high shelf . . .

**Old Bag**    But you'd rather it hadn't been me, eh?

**Salt**    No, but . . .

**Old Bag**    You don't like me, do you?

**Salt**    I . . .

**Old Bag**    You think I'm a miserable Old Bag who doesn't deserve saving! Eh?

*An embarrassed pause.*

Well, you're right. All this time I've kept myself to myself and then complained that I was lonely. Stupid. I can see that now.

**Salt**    Well, ma'am. Crisis brings folk together, so they say!

*He offers his hand.*

**Old Bag**    Thank you.

**Salt** *and the* **Old Bag** *shake hands. A sickly groan comes from* **Herr Von Cuckoo**.

**Pepper**   I hate to interrupt your touching little scene, but Cuckoo is getting worse.

**Salt**   I'm sorry, Miss Pepper. Excuse me, ma'am.

*He hastens to help, leaving the* **Old Bag** *on her own, thinking.*

**Old Bag** (*after a pause, whispering to the shelf above*)   Psst. Gingerbread Man.

**Gingerbread Man**   Yes?

**Old Bag**   You said that bird was poisoned?

**Gingerbread Man**   By the Big Ones. And they'll chuck him in the Dustbin if he's not better when they come down. But, as you said, his cuckoos are very noisy. Good riddance.

*Pause.* **Salt** *and* **Pepper**, *who have heard this exchange, look on in anticipation.*

**Old Bag** (*to everybody*)   May I examine Herr Von Cuckoo? I may be able to help.

*Music starts as the* **Old Bag** *goes and looks at* **Herr Von Cuckoo**. *Then after a quick examination . . .*

SONG: **Herbal Remedy**

**Old Bag**
>I can cure this malady
>With a pure herbal remedy
>I will effect it
>With expedience
>When you've collected
>The ingredients.

>Dill
>Helps you sleep when you're ill
>Horseradish
>Eradicates the pain
>Sage
>Helps you live to old age
>Rosemary
>Strengthens the brain.

>Chives
>Are the savers of lives
>Sweet Basil
>A pow'rful antidote
>Bay
>Makes the aches go away
>Bilberry
>Soothes a sore throat.

Thyme
Puts you back in your prime
Witch hazel
The antiseptic brew
Mint
Gives the eyes a fresh glint
Cinnamon
Fends off the 'flu.

**All**

Dill, Horseradish, Sage, Rosemary,
Chives, Sweet Basil, Bay, Bilberry,
Thyme, Witch hazel, Mint, Cinnamon

**Old Bag**

Tarragon, and lastly
Parsley.

*The music continues.* **Herr Von Cuckoo** *groans and writhes in pain.*

**Old Bag** (*rushing to him*)    It's all right, Herr Von Cuckoo. It's only me!

**Herr Von Cuckoo** *raises his head and sees who it is. He groans even louder – in horror and fright; he knows how unpleasant the* **Old Bag** *can be.*

**Old Bag** (*calming him*)    Don't flap. I'll get your voice back for you – (*Turning from him; in a cross sotto voce.*) – even if it *does* upset my nerves.

**Herr Von Cuckoo** *half sits up, having heard this remark. He looks with inquisitive worry.*

**Old Bag** (*Correcting herself*) I said – I'll just get my herbs . . .

**Herr Von Cuckoo** *is satisfied by this and lies flat again. The song continues. During the next section, the* **Gingerbread Man** *throws down the ingredients; the others place them in the egg cup which they drag forward for the purpose. (NB: In the first production,* **Salt**, **Pepper** *and the* **Gingerbread Man** *all went to the top shelf (using the back entrance) and sang the names of the herbs as solo lines while finding the herbs and throwing them in the egg cup below. The* **Old Bag** *therefore sang the lines describing the herbs' properties. This may or may not be practical in other productions.)*

**Gingerbread Man**    Dill

**All**    Helps you sleep when you're ill

**Gingerbread Man**    Horseradish

**All**    Eradicates the pain

**Gingerbread Man**    Sage

**All**    Helps you live to old age

**Gingerbread Man**    Rosemary

**All**    Strengthens the brain.

**Gingerbread Man**    Chives

**All**    Are the saver of lives

**Gingerbread Man**    Sweet Basil

**All**    A pow'rful antidote

**Gingerbread Man**    Bay

**All**    Makes the aches go away

**Gingerbread Man**    Bilberry

**All**    Soothes a sore throat.

**Gingerbread Man**    Thyme

**All**    Puts you back in your prime

**Gingerbread Man**    Witch hazel

**All**    The antiseptic brew

**Gingerbread Man**    Mint

**All**    Gives the eyes a fresh glint

**Gingerbread Man**    Cinnamon

**All**    Fends off the 'flu.

**Old Bag**    A final touch of tarragon,
    Soon you'll be the paragon
    Of health, once again, fighting fit.

    Lastly
    Pass me
    The parsley . . .

*The* **Gingerbread Man** *throws it. The* **Old Bag** *adds it to the other ingredients. (NB: In the original production* **Pepper** *and* **Salt** *arrived back down below in time for* **Pepper** *to pop it in the egg cup.)*

**Gingerbread Man**    That's it.

**Old Bag**    It is ready. Herr Von Cuckoo must now drink.

*Tension music as* **Salt** *and* **Pepper** *help* **Herr Von Cuckoo** *up and lead him to the egg cup. The* **Gingerbread Man** *watches from the shelf above.*

**Salt**    Come on, shipmate.

**Herr Von Cuckoo** *groans.*

**Pepper**    Drink this, Cuckoo.

**Herr Von Cuckoo** (*recoiling from the smell of the brew*)   Ugh!

**Old Bag**   The nastier it smells, the more good it does you. Drink. It will make you sleepy.

**Herr Von Cuckoo** *drinks, helped by the others. He makes faces at the taste.*

**Old Bag**   Do you feel sleepy?

**Herr Von Cuckoo** *shakes his head and shrugs his shoulders. Then suddenly he relaxes into sleep as if by magic.*

**Old Bag**   That's good. Mr Salt, please help me lead him home.

**Salt**   Aye, aye, ma'am.

*They set off for the clock.*

**Pepper**   Will he get better?

**Old Bag**   I think so. But not for a few hours. I'll stay with him.

**Salt**   As long as he's shipshape by eight o'clock. The Big Ones will be down by then. They'll expect to hear him cuckoo.

**Old Bag**   I'll do my best.

**Salt**   Thank you, Old Bag.

**Old Bag**   Thank me when he's better.

*The* **Old Bag** *takes* **Herr Von Cuckoo** *inside. The door shuts.* **Salt** *returns to* **Pepper***.*

**Salt**   Well, Miss Pepper, something exciting, out of the ordinary; that's what you wanted.

**Pepper**   And that's what I've had. Those shivers of terror. That awful uncertainty. The dreadful frights. My, it's been a wonderful night. (*She grins.*) I do hope it hasn't finished yet!

**Gingerbread Man** (*from the shelf above*)   It's hardly started.

**Salt** *and* **Pepper** *jump.*

**Pepper**   I'd forgotten you were up there.

**Gingerbread Man**   You've forgotten something else as well.

**Pepper**   What's that?

**Gingerbread Man**   Sleek the Mouse is up here too! (*He indicates the teapot.*) In there.

**Salt**   Can't we leave him there?

**Gingerbread Man**   In the Old Bag's teapot?

**Pepper**   Give him the poison.

**Gingerbread Man**   He wouldn't fall for that. He saw it being put down.

**Pepper**    You'll just have to let him out and order him home.

**Gingerbread Man**    I can't do that. He's starving. He won't stop to listen. He'll just start nibbling. Me.

**Salt**    Where does he live, anyway?

**Gingerbread Man**    Behind the dresser. (*He has an idea.*) Wait a minute. He's only here because I was curious and let him in. If we could get him back through this hole (*Indicating the hole on the shelf.*), block it up, *and* push the plate back down below, he'd be shut out.

**Salt**    He'd never fall for that! You just said, he's starving. He won't disembark from this dresser till he's had his nibble.

**Gingerbread Man**    Well, he's not nibbling *me*.

**Pepper**    No. We won't let him. We'll have to catch him and *then* force him back through the hole.

**Salt**    But how?

*All think and look around.*

**Gingerbread Man** (*suddenly*)    Your mug!

**Salt** (*thinking he means 'face'*)    What?

**Gingerbread Man**    Your mug!

**Salt**    What about it?

**Gingerbread Man**    It's big enough.

**Salt**    Are you being cheeky?

**Gingerbread Man**    No. You've got a big mug.

**Salt**    How dare you?

**Gingerbread Man**    Over there. (*He points.*) We could use it.

**Salt**    Oh. *That* mug.

**Gingerbread Man**    Yes. When he comes down, drop it over him.

**Pepper**    Yes, that could work. (*She goes to fetch the mug.*) Then push him to the hole, let him go through and block it up again. How thrilling!

**Gingerbread Man**    Exactly.

**Pepper**    But how do we drop the mug over him? He'll see it coming.

*Pause.*

**Salt**    Got it. Watch, shipmates!

*Music, as* **Salt** *takes the string from the rolling pin and attaches it to the handle of the upturned mug. He then mimes to the* **Gingerbread Man** *to throw down the sling hoist* *end, keeping the rope passing over the hook (or another hook if this is more convenient). By hauling on the string, the mug will rise – at least, the* handle *side will, leaving the opposite side still on the deck.*

**Salt** (*excitedly*)    Demonstration.

**Gingerbread Man**    Roll up, roll up. See Mr Salt's Patent Mug Mouse Trap.

*Music, as* **Salt** *pulls the string, and makes the mug rise.*

**Salt**    Now, Miss Pepper, could you hang on to the halyard please?

**Pepper**    Certainly. What do I do?

**Salt**    Nothing, ma'am, till I give the order. Then let down the mug.

**Pepper**    I hope I don't get too excited.

**Salt**    Now. I'm Sleek.

*Tension music, as* **Salt** *goes to his starting position and does a* **Sleek** *impersonation, sniffing towards the mug.*

**Salt**    OK, you guys, I'm the boss around here. Go, Miss Pepper!

**Salt** *stands under the inverted mug.* **Pepper** *lets the string up, which brings the mug down over* **Salt**.

**Gingerbread Man**    Bravo, bravo. (*He applauds from the shelf above.*)

**Pepper**    Congratulations, Mr Salt. (*She comes forward, leaving the string, and joins the applause.*)

**Salt**    Hey! Let me out!

**Pepper**    Oh! (*Loudly.*) Sorry.

*She returns to the string and pulls. The mug rises and* **Salt** *comes out.*

**Salt**    Right. Let him out, Gingerbread Man, and I'll stand by on the Mug Trap.

**Gingerbread Man**    Hang on.

**Salt**    Exactly. Hang on the halyard.

**Gingerbread Man**    No. Hang on. Problem.

**Salt**    Problem?

**Gingerbread Man**    How do we make sure Sleek gets in the right position for the trap to work?

**Pepper**    He's right. We can't just expect Sleek to happen to arrive there.

**Gingerbread Man**    No. What would make Sleek want to go under the mug?

**Salt**    Food! Cheese?

**Gingerbread Man**    He hates cheese.

**Pepper**    Something sweet. (*Idea.*) A sweet? (*Excited.*) A sweet!

**Gingerbread Man**    Of course! A sweet! Under the mug. Any sweets on the dresser, Salty?

**Salt**    Sorry, shipmate.

**Gingerbread Man**    Has *anyone* got a sweet we could use? Hands up. Don't throw them. Miss Pepper, perhaps you could select one!

**Pepper**    Certainly. Now, let's see. (*She looks at the audience, and selects a donor.*) You. Could we use your sweet? . . . Thank you. Can you throw it to me? (*She receives it.*) Oh yes, this should work. It looks very tempting. Smells it too. (*She describes the sweet.*)

**Salt**    Right, Miss Pepper. Under the mug. Heave-ho!

*He raises the mug, and* **Pepper** *carefully positions the sweet.*

**Pepper**    Ready.

**Salt**    Gingerbread Man, let him out!

**Gingerbread Man**    Hang on.

**Salt**    Again?

**Gingerbread Man**    Yes. We need something else to make the plan foolproof.

**Salt**    Go on then.

**Gingerbread Man**    Something to make sure that Sleek doesn't fool us by grabbing the sweet very quickly – before the mug has time to catch him.

**Salt**    Yes. Something to make him freeze, still as a statue, perhaps.

**Pepper**    Of course! He did that when the Big Ones came in.

**Salt**    What?

**Pepper**    Stood transfixed. They were shouting at him.

**Gingerbread Man**    What were they shouting?

**Pepper**    They were going 'Aaaah!' and 'Shoo, shoo, shoo!'

**Gingerbread Man**    That's it, then. We'll go 'Aaaah!' and 'Shoo, shoo shoo!'

**Salt**    I doubt if we can do it as loud as the Big Ones . . .

**Gingerbread Man**    Perhaps – (*To the audience.*) – would *you* help us again? You will? Thank you.

**Pepper**    Splendid. Now, if some of you could scream very loudly, the moment Sleek arrives under the mug . . .

**Salt**    I could use my whistle as a signal!

**Pepper**    Yes.

**Salt**   So, when I blow my whistle, some of you scream and some of you go 'Shoo, shoo, shoo'. Let's try it. All together. After the whistle.

**Pepper**   I'll pretend to be Sleek.

*She acts as* **Sleek** *approaching the mug.* **Salt** *blows his whistle. The audience practise their noises and* **Salt** *encourages.* **Pepper** *acts transfixed.*

**Pepper** (*when satisfied*)   Thank you. Excellent.

**Salt** (*manning the string*)   Ahoy there, Gingerbread Man. Let him out!

*He hauls up the mug. Tension.*

**Gingerbread Man** (*breaking the tension*)   Hang on!

**Salt**   Not again!

**Gingerbread Man**   Last time.

**Pepper**   Go on, then.

**Gingerbread Man**   Well, if – (*Indicating the audience.*) – everybody is going to be kind enough to help us, we ought to make sure they're protected.

**Salt**   How do you mean?

**Gingerbread Man**   Suppose Sleek decides to leave the dresser and invade *them*?

*Pause.*

**Pepper**   Got it! When he goes to the mug, they – (*Indicating the audience.*) – make him freeze; if he goes to the edge – *I* make him *sneeze*! Mr Salt! Twist my grinder!

**Salt**   Oh, Miss Pepper. You're hot stuff!

SONG: **Hot Stuff**

*During the song,* **Salt** *and* **Pepper** *place pepper all around the edge of the dresser, and* **Salt** *acts out the effects of pepper mentioned in the lyrics.*

**Pepper**
  I can make him sneeze
  Like a tickle with a feather
  I can make him sneeze
  Like a change of weather
  I can make him sneeze
  Just a sniff's enough
  Ev'ryone agrees
  I'm
  Hot stuff.

  I can make him sneeze
  Like a duster that is dusty

Splutter like a breeze
When it blows up gusty
I can make him sneeze
With a huff and puff
Ev'ryone agrees
I'm
Hot stuff.

First his nose will itch
On his brow a puzzled frown
Then his nose will twitch
Atishoo atishoo
And all fall down.

I can make him sneeze
Like the pollen in the summer
Ev'ryone agrees
I'm a red hot Momma
I can make him sneeze
Like a pinch of snuff
Ev'ryone agrees
I can make him sneeze
Make him cough and make him wheeze
Ev'ryone agrees
I'm
Hot stuff.

Atishoo!

**Salt**    Gingerbread Man, can we set sail now?

**Gingerbread Man**    Aye, aye, sir! You two keep out of sight as much as you can. (*To the audience.*) And don't forget, everybody . . .

**Salt**    Wait till Sleek is under the mug, then . . . (*He blows his whistle; the audience screams and shoos.*)

**Gingerbread Man** (*calming the audience*)    But wait till you hear the whistle. Good luck.

*Tension music, as the* **Gingerbread Man** *creeps to the teapot, removes whatever he has blocked the door with and gingerly opens the door an inch; then he runs to hide. Below, all is set:* **Salt** *has hauled on the string, the mug is in the up position and the sweet is in position. Pause.*

*Suddenly,* **Sleek the Mouse** *enters.*

**Sleek**    OK, Ginger, I've had enough of your tricks. Prepare to beat your maker – I mean prepare to meet your baker . . . (*He sees the audience.*) And as for you – you're the creepiest, crawliest critters I've ever sniffed. Did you stop laughing at me when I asked? Not on your life! When Ginger shut me up, did you warn me? Not on your life! And do you think I'm gonna forgive and forget? Not on your life! You've asked for a sweetie raid and a sweetie raid you're gonna get. I'm coming down! Yes I am!

**Audience**   No you're not!

**Sleek**   Oh yes I am!

**Audience**   Oh no you're not!

**Sleek**   On yes I am!

**Audience**   Oh no you're not!

**Sleek**   You just watch this!

*He jumps, or slides down, from the shelf to the stage level. The* **Gingerbread Man** *quickly blocks the mousehole with a herb jar or the honey pot, then hides again, occasionally peeping out to survey the scene.*

**Sleek**   Sweetie raid! (*He advances towards the audience, sniffing all the while.*) You just rustle 'em up ready or I'll nibble *you* instead. Mmmm. Caramel whirls, fruit gums, gob stoppers . . . (*He reaches the edge of the dresser, sniffs and . . .*) A . . . a . . . a . . . tishoo! (*He backs away a little, then comes forward, at a different angle.*) Chewy bullseyes, liquorice sticks, peppermints . . . (*The sniffing of pepper is repeated.*) A . . . a . . . a . . . tishoo! (*He backs away again, then chooses another angle to go. As he starts, he suddenly reacts to a new scent, and stands, excitedly sniffing and trying to place the smell.*) Oh! That sure is a swell smell! Kind of juicy and crunchy and – (*Etc., improvising to describe the type of sweet under the mug – which will vary from performance to performance.*) – my favourite sweetie! Where is it, where is it?

*The audience should lead* **Sleek** *to the mug. He can veer the wrong way a couple of times, but eventually he reaches the mug, and spots the sweet.*

Mmmmm! There it is! (*He starts to creep under the mug, then stops.*) This isn't a trick, is it?

**Audience** (*encouraged by the* **Gingerbread Man** *above*)   No.

**Sleek**   It's not a trap?

**Audience**   No.

**Sleek**   'Cos if it *is* – you've had it!

*The tension music builds as* **Sleek** *goes under the mug and reaches for the sweet. At the appropriate moment,* **Salt** *blows his whistle.*

**Audience** (*encouraged by the* **Gingerbread Man** *above*)   Aaaaaah! Shoo! shoo! Aaaaaah! Shoo, Shoo!

**Sleek**, *as expected, reacts by staring transfixed. After enough time to establish this,* **Salt** *lowers the mug, enveloping* **Sleek**. **Salt**, **Pepper** *and the* **Gingerbread Man** *cheer. The* **Gingerbread Man** *triumphantly jumps down from the shelf on to the mug.*

**Gingerbread Man**    Well done, everyone! Thank you.

*Suddenly he nearly falls as* **Sleek** *causes the mug to move like a bucking bronco. The* **Gingerbread Man** *jumps off. The mug darts about on the worktop.* **Salt**, **Pepper** *and the* **Gingerbread Man** *chase it and eventually push it to the corner, where the hole is, and carefully line it up in the correct position.*

**Salt**    One more time! (*He blows his whistle.*)

**Audience**    Aaaaaah! Shoo, shoo! Aaaaaah! Shoo, shoo!

**Salt**, **Pepper** *and the* **Gingerbread Man** *tip up the mug, allowing* **Sleek** *to scuttle out. He reacts terrified to the audience's noises and runs to and then through the mousehole.*

*The* **Gingerbread Man** *slides the plate to its original position. All is safe. All cheer. Victory! They shake hands and thank the audience for their help.*

*The door of the cuckoo clock opens, and the* **Old Bag** *comes out.*

**Old Bag**    Shhh! Quiet! Herr Von Cuckoo is asleep.

**Gingerbread Man**    Sleek's gone home!

**Old Bag**    My home!

**Gingerbread Man**    No, behind the dresser.

**Old Bag**    Good riddance.

**Salt**    How is Cuckoo?

**Old Bag**    Much better. But he must have hush. If he can sleep till just before eight o'clock he should be fine again.

**Pepper**    And his cuckoos?

**Old Bag**    Back to their irritating, noisy selves!

**Gingerbread Man**    Hooray!

**Salt, Pepper** *and* **Old Bag**    Shhh!

(*Optional line to help calm the audience for the song.*)

**Old Bag**    We must have quiet! For Cuckoo.

SONG: **Come the Light**

**Salt, Pepper, Gingerbread Man** *and* **Old Bag**
    Come the light
    The light of day
    The problems of the night
    May fade away
    Faint ray of hope
    May you shine bright

Making ev'rything come right
Come the light.

Hear the tick tick tock
Of the cuckoo clock
Ticka taking us towards the dawn
Hear the time tick by
Hear the seconds fly
Ticka telling us tomorrow's born.

And
Come the light
The light of day
The problems of the night
May fade away
Faint ray of hope
May you shine bright
Making ev'rything come right
Come the light.

Hear the tick tick tock
Of the cuckoo clock
Ticka tocka never going wrong
Hear the time tick by
Hear the seconds fly
Ticka telling us it won't be long.

And
Come the light
The light of day
The problems of the night
May fade away
Faint ray of hope
May you shine bright
Making ev'rything come right
Come the light.

Come the light
Come the light,
May ev'rything come right
Come the light.

*At the end of the song, they all fall fast asleep.*

*Tick-tocking music is heard, to suggest a time lapse. If possible, the lighting narrows
to the face of the cuckoo clock, where the hands turn round till they reach about ten
minutes to eight. (During the next scene they creep up to eight o'clock.) The lighting
changes to suggest the early morning.* **Salt**, **Pepper**, *the* **Gingerbread Man** *and the*
**Old Bag** *are still asleep.*

*The music continues as the door of the cuckoo clock opens, and* **Herr Von Cuckoo** *emerges, yawning and tentative at first, as though testing himself to make sure he is better. He checks the time on the clock face. He clears his throat . . .*

**Herr Von Cuckoo**    Mi, mi, mi, mi. (*He is pleased. He yodels – without difficulty.*) La, la, la, la, la, te, teeeee. (*He smiles, delighted. Then, as a final test, he sings.*) Cuck – oo! Cu – ckoo! (*They sound back to normal.*) Ze toad has flown! My voice is found!

SONG: **Toad in the Throat** (*reprise*)

**Herr Von Cuckoo**
I was made in the mountains of Switzerland
(*Yodel.*)
From a fine piece of pine I was carved by hand
(*Yodel.*)
With all
My power
I call
The hour
On a clear and unwavering note
It's my
Belief
To my
Relief –
I haven't a toad in my throat.
(*Yodelling chorus.*)

*During the chorus, the others wake up, and, pleased and relieved to see* **Herr Von Cuckoo** *is better, gather round the clock. The music continues as they applaud him. He sees them.*

**Herr Von Cuckoo**    My friends. Ich danke you much for better me making. (*He bows politely.*)

**Gingerbread Man** (*indicating the audience*)    Everybody helped.

**Herr Von Cuckoo** (*to the audience*)    My friends. Ich danke too you. (*He bows to the audience.*)\* Ich would like to danke you all, as is ze custom in Switzerland, by inviting you all to join me in my yodel! You all will do zat, ja?

**All including audience**    Ja/Yes!

**Herr Von Cuckoo**    Danke. After drei – three. Eins, zwei, drei . . .

*All sing the yodelling chorus – those on stage should find it difficult. The audience will probably not be very good either! . . .*

(*After a while.*) Nein, nein, nein. Das ist *horrible*! Listen, I teach you.

---

\*Optional cut between asterisks; the yodelling 'songsheet', originally included as an enjoyable Christmas pantomime-style bit of fun, may seem unnecessary at other times of the year.

**Herr Von Cuckoo** *teaches everyone line by line. If it is thought desirable, he could pull down a roller-blind-style song sheet from above his door, with the 'words' on it.*

> Yodel oddle oddle
> Yodel oddle oddle
>     Yo ho ho
> Yodel oddle oddle
> Yodel oddle oddle
>     Yo tee hee
> Yodel oddle oddle
> Yodel oddle oddle
>     Yo yoo hoo
> Yodel oddle oddle
> Yodel oddle oddle
>     Dee.

*Depending on audience response,* **Herr Von Cuckoo** *leads everyone in the whole chorus, once or twice. He then sings a verse to lead into a chorus sung by everyone. The audience are encouraged to cough and 'Mi, mi, mi' before they sing.*

**Herr Von Cuckoo**
> I was made in the mountains of Switzerland
> (*Yodel.*)
> From a fine piece of pine I was carved by hand
> (*Yodel.*)
> With all
> My power
> I call
> The hour
> On a clear and unwavering note
> It's my
> Belief
> To my
> Relief –
> I haven't a toad in my throat.

**Herr Von Cuckoo** *sings the chorus with the audience.*

Bravo, bravo.*

*All on stage clap the audience. Suddenly a loud door noise stops everyone in their tracks, and a bright light snapped on tells us that the* **Big Ones** *have arrived. Tension music. All scuttle to their number one positions –* **Herr Von Cuckoo** *in his clock, and* **Salt** *and* **Pepper** *below the shelf, if possible with the letter between them. The* **Gingerbread Man** *and the* **Old Bag** *both go behind the rolling pin – the* **Gingerbread Man** *flat out as he was at the beginning.*

*We hear the voices of the* **Big Ones**. *The clock points to eight o'clock. The shadows of the* **Big Ones** *are seen against the dresser.*

**Mrs Big One**　Hurry up, dear. We'll be late.

**Mr Big One**　Sorry, darling. I must have overslept.

**Mrs Big One**　Well, I've got to be at work by nine.

**Mr Big One**　No time for breakfast then.

**Mrs Big One**　Any sign of that mouse?

**Mr Big One**　No. I should think he's gone for good.

*Indignantly, the* **Gingerbread Man** *pops up for a second, as if to say 'You sent him packing? We did!' Realising what he is doing, he stops and drops down again.*

**Mrs Big One**　Thank heavens.

**Herr Von Cuckoo** *enters from his door, and with great confidence proclaims the time.*

**Herr Von Cuckoo**　Cuckoo! Cuckoo! Cuckoo! Cuckoo!

　Cuckoo! Cuckoo! Cuckoo! Cuckoo!

*He stands there, listening.*

**Mr Big One**　Did you hear that, darling? Eight perfect working-order cuckoos.

**Mrs Big One**　He's not past it after all! No Dustbin for him!

**Herr Von Cuckoo** *smiles radiantly. He has forgotten to go back inside.*

**Mr Big One**　Probably a bit of fluff in his works.

**Herr Von Cuckoo** *looks indignant.*

**Mr Big One**　Come on, darling.

**Mrs Big One**　Do you want the Gingerbread Man to nibble in the car?

**Mr Big One**　Yes, that's an idea.

*The* **Gingerbread Man**'s *head emerges nervously from behind the rolling pin.*

**Mrs Big One**　Otherwise you'll be hungry with no breakfast.

**Mr Big One**　Hang on. No. He's probably all germy –

*The* **Gingerbread Man** *looks indignant.*

**Mr Big One**　– that mouse's dirty paws must have run all over him.

**Mrs Big One**　Ugh, you're right. Don't eat him. Might make yourself ill.

*The* **Gingerbread Man** *looks relieved. The* **Old Bag** *pops her head up to congratulate him.*

**Mr Big One**　No. I'll throw him in the Dustbin.

*Their reactions change to fright.*

**Mrs Big One**    Oh no, don't do that. He's nice. He's got a cheeky face. Let's keep him – as a sort of decoration. He can stand on the shelf next to the teapot. Come on, dear, we'll be late.

*The bright light is switched off, and a door slam tells us the **Big Ones** have gone. Pause. Then all five emerge cheering, and converge centre, shaking hands with each other, and **Herr Von Cuckoo** kissing cheeks.*

**Salt**    Congratulations, Cuckoo. You've never sung better.

**Herr Von Cuckoo**    Danke. Danke you all.

**Pepper**    Gingerbread Man . . .

**Gingerbread Man** (*fiercely*)    Don't come near me!

**Pepper**    Why not?

**Gingerbread Man** (*laughing*)    I'm all germy and nasty and horrible – (*He jokingly advances on her like a monster.*)

*All laugh.*

– but I'm not to be beaten, and not to be eaten!

**Salt**    A happy end to the voyage.

**Old Bag** (*angrily*)    Happy? First that bird is better, and second, I have to share my shelf with *him*! (*She indicates the **Gingerbread Man**.*) You think I'm *happy*? (*Awkward pause. Then she breaks into a huge smile.*) I'm delighted, thrilled . . .

*The **Gingerbread Man** runs to the **Old Bag**.*

**Old Bag**    And if you don't visit me at least twice every day, there'll be trouble!

**Gingerbread Man**    Trouble! I can cope with trouble. Your fortune telling was right.

**Old Bag**    Of course!

**Gingerbread Man**
  'When trouble comes, if you can cope
  Three lives will shortly find new hope.'

**Herr Von Cuckoo**    One is me. I escaped the Dustbin.

**Gingerbread Man**    Two is me. I escaped being eaten!

**Salt**    And three?

**Old Bag**    Three is – me!

**Pepper**    What did you escape?

**Old Bag**    I escaped – from myself. And found you – my friends.

*All cheer.*

**Herr Von Cuckoo**    And who do we owe it all to?

**All**    The Gingerbread Man!

SONG: **The Gingerbread Man** (*reprise*)

**Pepper**
Ginger

**Salt**
Ginger

**Old Bag**
Ginger

**Herr Von Cuckoo**
Ginger

**Gingerbread Man**
Ginger?

**All**
Ginger, ginger,
Gingerbread Man.

Soon as you arrived the
Dresser party began
Hey hey
You're the Gingerbread Man
Ginger you're the greatest
I'm your number one fan
Hey hey
You're the ginger, ginger
Ginger, ginger, ginger
Ginger, ginger,
Gingerbread Man.

Ginger, ginger
Ginger, ginger, ginger
Ginger, ginger,
Gingerbread Man.

**Gingerbread Man**
Newly baked this morning
Take a look at my tan
Hey hey
I'm the Gingerbread Man
Like a magic spell I
Just appeared with a bang
Hey, hey
I'm the ginger

**All**
Ginger

**Gingerbread Man**
Ginger

**All**
Ginger

**Gingerbread Man**
Ginger

**All**
Ginger

**Gingerbread Man**
Ginger, ginger,
Gingerbread Man.

**All**
Ginger, ginger
Ginger, ginger, ginger
Ginger, ginger,
Gingerbread Man.

**Gingerbread Man**
One more time

**All**
Ginger, ginger
Ginger, ginger, ginger
Ginger, ginger,
Gingerbread Man.

*Curtain.*

# The See-Saw Tree – Teacher Notes

I really love the premise of *The See-Saw Tree*, putting the audience in role and confronting them with a big decision . . . and the subject matter here could not be more pertinent for a modern-day audience. There is much fun to be had using sound and lighting to create a dramatic climax, and building a giant tree for a set!

**Age range:** KS2
**Number of actors:** 8–16
**Running time:** Approx. 60 minutes

## Characters

The original production has eight actors playing dual roles, one human character and one animal character; this can be easily increased to sixteen by casting them all individually. Opportunities for extra parts could be: using several actors to bring to life Mr Bunn's first description of the See-Saw Tree as a flashback, or, originally the 'Big Ones' are heard as voices off-stage but there is potential here to cast a number of builders in hi-vis jackets and hard hats, and include these interactions as small scenes. The animals on stage should freeze still when the builders arrive, and ideally be dimmed into darkness. There is scope to play the builders' scenes in the audience, or back of the hall, depending on your space.

All of the characters can be played unisex with some basic adaptations.

The animal characters are the most substantial roles, with most lines to learn, though the human characters must be able to carry off some audience interaction confidently.

## Costumes and props

If you are casting actors in dual roles then costumes should be small and simple, as there will not be much time to change from their human roles to their animal roles; but either way they need not be realistic in any way. Again, dressing all actors in one uniform, of black or green, and then using one-chosen piece of costume to represent each character may be more suited to a school production. For example, a simple pair of glasses signifies Mrs Wise, and with a leather jacket an actor becomes Mr Batty. For the animal costumes a spotty jumper will work for Mistlethrush, or a snazzy jacket and suitcase for Jay. Some other basic identification factors could be ears, a tail, wings or baseball cap adapted with a beak.

Overall, clear characterisation is the most important factor and movement, body language and voice should portray character.

**Staging** The action takes place in three locations, the village hall, the bottom of an oak tree and further up the oak tree, all of which can be represented rather than perfectly re-created.

The village hall needs nothing more than a table and chairs. A circle drawn or taped on the floor can represent a tree trunk and upturned buckets painted brown are stumps for sitting. There are a number of stage directions in the play which require movement between the tree levels; a small set of stepladders with plastic ivy entwined creates some height, for a Mistlethrush nest or a Bat balcony. I would think carefully about hanging actors upside down though – sat on a table swinging legs might suffice. A children's play tunnel is a good rabbit hole, and a leafy version of a curtain can create a closed-off area for Owl's home and Squirrel's drey.

## Special props

There are a number of special props that would be purpose made in a professional production and really bring the characters to life and so will help the actors.

Jay's suitcase and special coat filled with all his wares is important to the character and should be made from an adapted jacket.

The acorns and eggs can be made as a part of a creative project in class using pâpier-maché or bean bags; I would avoid balloons or balls or anything that bounces, pops or rolls away.

You will need a builders' 'electric cable' which should *absolutely not be electric*. A washing line works and can be strung across by the builder characters we mentioned earlier. Caution should also be taken as to how you demonstrate branches crashing down when cut; this can be done in slow motion, or using branches that are made from cardboard tubes/art straws will ensure a soft landing.

## Music, sound effects and lighting

There are some great songs here and the sing-a-long with the audience at the end can be really joyous. Some adaptations could be: the Mistlethrush's song is meant to be out of tune and can be funny in this sense; the Bat's song is half sung and hummed as he is listening through ear phones; and the Tree Folk protest song can be chanted or at least sections of it.

Lots of the smaller sound effects like birdsong, whistles, trees creaking, etc. can be created by the actors just using their voices (see 'Soundscapes' lesson plan). There are, however, lots of sound effects resources online that might help create more tension, especially when re-creating machinery and chainsaws, etc.

If lighting can be used in the production it will be beneficial, not only to differentiate between the village hall (all house lights up) and the tree (some stage lighting, green wash), but especially the moments the builders are around, where the stage can grow darker, builders perhaps even using torches. Red light works well as an ominous light, and the climactic sequence where the tree is felled and Rabbit bites the cable can look great using a strobe light and/or bright white light. Some productions even use pyrotechnics to really ramp up the impact.

## Other considerations

Both the opening and ending of the play require some interaction with the audience and this should be rehearsed with a willing test audience in advance. There is potential for some playful immersive work, by having the actors in role as the audience come in, welcoming them to the parish meeting in character and showing them to their seats. Similarly at the end they can shake hands and celebrate in the audience at the closing song.

You should give some thought as to any unexpected reactions from the audience and how the actors should deal with it. Perhaps at the start a modern-day eco-friendly audience might vote against the playground as they see that losing the tree is an issue; in which case an actor might have to overrule them: 'Well, the council has the final say, and we want it gone!' The playwright has provided alternative endings for different outcomes of the final vote, but again these should be rehearsed. The forum theatre exercise might help actors become comfortable with small improvisations (see lesson plan).

**Lesson plan – Soundscapes**

*Starter activity*

Tape a large circle on the floor and gather the students around it. Tell them: 'This is a large oak tree in the middle of Turner's Field; it is called the See-Saw Tree – why might it be called that?

*Engaging*

Next: 'There are lots of plants and animals that live around here. What kinds of things might there be?' Ask the students to write an idea on a post-it note and then stick it somewhere on or around the 'tree'. Suggestions might be things like flowers, a badger, a dry-stone wall, etc. You can extend this activity depending on your desired literacy focus, for example asking students to use more detailed descriptions, alliteration, rhyme, or adjective/noun/verb sentences like 'A sneaky orange fox creeping along'. Students can create individual mimes or images for their idea.

*Developing*

Group the students into pairs, and ask them to go and stand next to one of their post-it notes and consider what sounds might be heard there. For instance, if there is 'a wise old Owl hooting' the students can re-create that sound. Begin to hear each pair's sounds and then layer them up to create a soundscape of all the noises together. Some can be repeated or made louder/quieter, there can be echoes, we can hear all, some or just one sound – the teacher acts as conductor.

*Main task*

Split the story of the See-Saw Tree into five or six main events:

> The See-Saw Tree is big and strong and the children love playing on it
> The animals are happy and live in peace
> There is meeting to discuss chopping the tree down
> There is a protest
> The builders begin to chop the trees down anyway
> One of the animals is hurt and the town must decide to keep the tree or not

In small groups students should create an image for each sentence, speak the sentence in some way and create a soundscape to illustrate each section of the story. Pause for four seconds between each one.

**Other activities**

*Paired role play*

Taking inspiration from the characters in the parish meeting, one pupil takes the role of someone in favour of the supermarket, and the other adopts the role of a someone who wishes to dissuade them. Ask pupils to improvise their discussion. Then swap over so that both get an opportunity to try both roles.

**Forum theatre**

The whole premise of the play puts the audience in role to affect the outcome of the story. Forum theatre plays with this idea of alternative endings, and also helps actors practise improvisation if it ends up being needed!

As a whole group stage the parish meeting in the village hall, with some actors around the meeting table and the rest in the audience watching. Give the actors a basic overview and allow them to improvise around the idea that one character proposes the chopping down of the tree and the building of a playground, with one character in favour and one against. The scene should not reach a resolution as such. After a while, when the scene is running out of steam call out 'stop'; and the actors should freeze. Explain that with forum theatre we can stop the action, and re-play in many different ways, for different outcomes. For example the business man could be played as very stern, or very charming in his proposal; the other members of the meeting could be angry, or more worried in their responses. Replay the scene in several ways taking suggestions of how it can differ from the audience. You can also freeze the action and swap the actors over to try out an idea, or even introduce a new character. For a more detailed look into this technique, research Augusto Boal's theatre practice.

*Persuasive writing*

After reading or watching the play, or even running through the brief synopsis above, ask the students to write a letter to the council persuading them to keep or remove the tree. They must use the key features of persuasive writing and write in an appropriate tone. This could be adapted to be a speech instead and a new conference staged, or extended into looking at protest posters/songs.

*Leaf making*

A quick and easy way to make some scenery for *The See Saw Tree* is to ask students to cut and design leaf shapes to be scattered around the stage or attached to the set. You can even write on dried leaves themselves.

# The See-Saw Tree

**Book, music and lyrics by David Wood**

*The See-Saw Tree* was originally commissioned by the Redgrave Theatre, Farnham. The first performance was given by the Farnham Repertory Company, sponsored by Arundell House Securities, on 18 March 1986, with the following cast:

| | |
|---|---|
| **Mrs Wise/Owl** | Patricia Samuels |
| **Mrs Dunnock/Dunnock** | Alex Kingston |
| **Mr Storer/Squirrel** | Christopher Reeks |
| **Mr Jay/Jay** | Kit Thacker |
| **Mrs Thrush/Mistlethrush** | Brenda Longman |
| **Mrs Cook/Cuckoo** | Sharon Courtney |
| **Mr Bunn/Rabbit** | Andrew Sargent |
| **Mr Batty/Bat** | Paul Benzing |

*Directed by* Stephen Barry and Kit Thacker
*Designed by* Juliet Shillingford
*Musical direction by* Peter Pontzen
*Lighting by* Vincent Herbert

The play was subsequently presented at Sadler's Wells Theatre, London, and on tour by Whirligig Theatre in the autumn of 1987, with the following cast:

| | |
|---|---|
| **Mrs Wise/Owl** | Susannah Bray |
| **Mrs Dunnock/Dunnock** | Mary Ann Coburn |
| **Mr Storer/Squirrel** | Mike Elles |
| **Mr Jay/Jay** | Richard Hague |
| **Mrs Thrush/Mistlethrush** | Caroline High |
| **Mrs Cook/Cuckoo** | Shelaagh Ferrell |
| **Mr Bunn/Rabbit** | David Bale |
| **Mr Batty/Bat** | Michael Seraphim |

*Directed by* David Wood
*Designed by* Susie Caulcutt
*Musical supervision by* Peter Pontzen
*Musical direction by* Michael Haslam
*Lighting by* Roger Frith

**For Common Ground, the conservation group who sowed the seed**

TREES, WOODS & THE GREEN MAN · COMMON GROUND
IMAGE BY BEN NICHOLSON

I wish to acknowledge with gratitude the helpful advice given me by Jim Flegg, whose excellent book *Oakwatch* (published by Pelham Books) confirmed my belief that here was subject matter for a play, and encouraged me to proceed. The subsequent use of Jim Flegg as a sounding-board for ideas and as an oracle of the oak has been not only extremely useful but also most enjoyable. Thank you, Jim!

D.W.

# Characters

Each actor plays two parts, the human role linked with the animal role.

ACTOR 1: **Mrs Wise**, *the Chairperson of the Parish Council. Solid, fair and authoritative.*
**Owl**, *the leader of the oak community.*

ACTOR 2: **Mrs Dunnock**, *Secretary of the Parish Council. Keeps a low profile. Efficient, helpful, knowledgeable, but unshowy.*
**Dunnock**, *a rather drab, hardworking bird, willing to perform menial tree tasks, cleaning, taking messages, etc.*

ACTOR 3: **Mr Storer**, *businesslike, financially orientated Treasurer of the Parish Council.*
**Squirrel**, *home-loving, conservative, occasionally excitable member of the tree community.*

ACTOR 4: **Mr Jay**, *rather flashy supermarket owner, smarmy businessman, ingratiating.*
**Jay**, *a flash itinerant member of the tree community, popping in and out almost as a travelling salesman, on the lookout for a good opportunity.*

ACTOR 5: **Mrs Thrush**, *a fairly outspoken woman, who takes public service seriously and loudly espouses a cause.*
**Mistlethrush**, *a strident member of the tree community, builder of untidy nests, not afraid to be outspoken.*

ACTOR 6: **Mrs Cook**, *not a local person, but not afraid to put her views. Might be regarded as somewhat common by the residents.*
**Cuckoo**, *an itinerant visitor to the tree, a colourful character from Africa, whose sole motive for visiting is to dump her egg in some unsuspecting bird's nest.*

ACTOR 7: **Mr Bunn**, *a concerned conservationist. Outspoken.*
**Rabbit**, *a member of the animals' underground movement. Resistance leader. Practical.*

ACTOR 8: **Mr Batty**, *entrepreneur, whizz-kid smooth operator.*
**Bat**, *hi-tech way-out member of the tree community. His radar comes in useful. He has big headphones connected to a 'Walkman'-style radio.*

The play takes place in three locations:

1) A village hall
2) The bottom of an oak tree
3) Further up the oak tree

## Act One

*As the audience arrives, the stage resembles a public platform with table and chairs.*

**Mrs Dunnock**, *a few minutes before 'curtain up', sweeps the platform.*

**Mrs Wise**, *the Chairperson, arrives and bids 'Good day' to* **Mrs Dunnock**, *then settles herself in the chair.*

**Mr Jay** *and* **Mr Storer** *also arrive, greet each other and* **Mrs Wise**, *then sit down.* **Mr Jay** *prepares some maps and pictures.*

*In the auditorium,* **Mr Batty**, **Mrs Thrush**, **Mrs Cook** *and* **Mr Bunn** *sit amongst the audience, near the front.*

*When the play is due to start,* **Mrs Dunnock** *rings a small bell, and takes her seat at the table, as Secretary, taking notes. The house lights stay up.*

**Mrs Wise**    Welcome, everybody, to this public meeting. Thank you for taking the trouble to come along to discuss the future of Turner's Field, the patch of waste land next to Jay's Supermarket. As Chairperson of the Parish Council, I invite you to make your views known. Mrs Dunnock, our Secretary, will make notes on the proceedings.

**Mrs Dunnock** (*shyly*)    Thank you, Mrs Wise. (*Correcting herself.*) Madam Chairman.

**Mrs Wise**    First, the Treasurer, Mr Storer, will outline our proposals.

**Mr Storer**    Thank you, Madam Chairman. As you may know, Turner's Field was left in his will to the Council by Farmer Turner, who died last year. For a long time it has been unused – except as an unofficial unsightly rubbish tip, and we feel the time has come to decide its future. We are pleased that Mr Jay, here –

**Mr Jay** (*smiling broadly, almost smarmily*)    Good afternoon.

**Mr Storer**    – the owner of the supermarket, has offered a substantial sum for the land, and, let's face it, the Council desperately needs the cash to help improve local services . . .

**Mrs Thrush** (*from the floor, standing*)    Hear, hear. They could do with it. Our road's in a shocking state. Like driving on cobblestones . . .

**Mr Storer**    Yes, indeed. So, Mr Jay, please reveal your plans.

**Mr Jay** (*rising*)    Certainly, Mr Storer. As you know, Jay's Supermarket aims to provide a service. High quality, low prices, that's our motto. For some time, in our quest to make shopping a happy, *family* experience, we have improved our facilities – more tills for speedier checkouts, easy-push trolleys, music to soothe the harassed housewife. And now, in our usual caring way, we propose to create, (*Showing a map.*) on Turner's Field . . . guess what?

**Mrs Cook** (*from the floor, standing*)    More car parking space. That's what's needed. I'm not a local, but I come here to shop and it's always a dreadful problem finding a space, then humping the shopping to the car . . .

**Mr Jay**    Maybe, Mrs er –

**Mrs Cook**    Cook.

**Mr Jay**    Cook. Maybe. But, may I be so bold – do you have children?

**Mrs Cook**    Yes, but I never bring *them* here. They get bored. I leave them with a friend.

**Mr Jay**    Exactly. They get bored. That's why we propose to create a children's playground, where our customers' children can safely play till the shopping is successfully accomplished.

**Mrs Thrush**    I support that. There's so little for the kids to do in this place. Not even a cinema any more.

**Mrs Wise**    Yes, well, Mrs er –

**Mrs Thrush**    Thrush.

**Mrs Wise**    Mrs Thrush. Thank you. Let's have a vote. Please raise your hands if you like Mr Jay's idea of a children's playground. (*She encourages the audience to raise their hands.*) Fine. Thank you.

*Whatever the outcome . . .*

**Mr Bunn** (*from the floor, standing*)    Madam Chairman, before I vote, could I know more of what this playground will be like? Will it be an adventure playground? Swings, slides, that type of thing?

**Mrs Wise**    Mr Jay.

**Mr Jay**    Ah, yes, well to answer that, may I, Madam Chairman, invite Mr Batty to speak? I will be giving Mr Batty the concession to create the playground and operate it.

**Mr Bunn**    Concession? You mean this is a business deal?

**Mr Jay**    Well, life's a business, Mr er –

**Mr Bunn**    Bunn.

**Mr Jay**    Mr Bunn. Mr Batty, please . . .

**Mr Batty** *joins the others on the platform. He displays a diagram.*

**Mr Batty**    Yes, well, like I'm going to clear the land and have an open play area with swings and slides, all free for the use of, plus a special building for the machines.

**Mr Bunn**    Machines?

**Mr Batty**    Yes. The space invaders, the pin tables, the fruit machines . . .

**Mrs Wise**    And, Mr Batty, will these be er . . . free for the use of?

**Mr Batty**    Ah. Well. No. Like I've got to make a living, Madam Chairman.

**Mr Jay**    Seems fair enough to me. Only providing what the kids of today really want.

**Mr Bunn**    So, Mr Batty, you are going to clear the land, are you?

**Mr Batty**    Yes.

**Mr Bunn**    On that land are several trees. Healthy trees.

**Mr Batty**    Can't help that. They'll have to come down.

**Mr Bunn**    But one of those trees is an oak. It's been there for nearly three hundred years.

**Mr Batty**    So what?

**Mr Bunn**    So what? (*He goes on to the platform.*) That tree has a history. In the old days people called it the See-Saw Tree.

**Mr Batty**    The See-Saw Tree?

**Mr Bunn**    The See-Saw Tree.

*Lighting changes.* **Mr Bunn** *remains in a pin-spot, while the rest of the stage grows dark. The actors clear the stage as* **Mr Bunn** *speaks.*

One of its branches grew straight out, near to the ground. Children used to balance a plank over the branch and use it as a see-saw. The villagers loved that oak. And the tree was itself like a village. A living community of animals, birds and insects, going about their daily business. It still is.

*During the following speech, an actor hands* **Mr Bunn** *his 'Rabbit' costume and, if necessary, helps him on with it.*

Just imagine what that community will feel like should it be threatened. Just imagine what might happen if Mr Jay's plan went ahead and Mr Batty was allowed to cut down that oak tree, that special oak tree. Just imagine. (*Echo effect.*) Just imagine, just imagine . . .

*The lighting changes as the curtains part to reveal the base of the oak tree. The trunk is wide, bearing in mind that the characters are small. Various knob-like shapes and root formations sprout from the bottom, which might be used as 'seats'. The entrance to* **Rabbit**'s *burrow is incorporated. Ivy climbing the tree could afford masking for scaffolding or ladder-like rungs, down which and up which the characters can climb. Foliage is visible above. A few acorns lie on the ground. Grass grows around the roots. A large white cross has been painted or chalked on the trunk.*

**Mr Bunn** *becomes* **Rabbit**.

*It is dawn. A chorus of birdsong is heard.*

**Rabbit** *chooses a likely blade of grass and begins eating it. He makes for his burrow, but suddenly sees the white cross. Mystified, he approaches it and stretches up to feel it. It is still wet. He examines the paint on his paw, then looks at the cross again.*

*Suddenly* **Dunnock**'s *head peers through the foliage above.*

**Dunnock**   Morning, Rabbit.

**Rabbit** *jumps and turns.*

**Rabbit**   Oh it's you, Dunnock. Morning. You're up early.

**Dunnock**   Lots to do, Rabbit. A Dunnock's work is never done. Owl's hollow to clean, Squirrel's drey to muck out . . .

**Rabbit** (*idea*)   Squirrel?

**Dunnock**   Yes, he's doing his annual acorn tally. Stock-taking. Takes it so seriously . . .

**Rabbit**   Dunnock, give him a message, will you? It's urgent.

**Dunnock**   S'pose so. If he's in.

**Rabbit**   Please. There's a mystery to solve.

**Dunnock**   How exciting. The only mystery I've got to solve is how I'm going to get all my jobs done. You've no idea how –

**Rabbit**   Go. Now. Tell Squirrel to meet me here. As soon as possible.

**Dunnock**   All right, all right. Keep your fur on. (*Disappearing.*) Dear oh dear oh dear.

**Dunnock** *exits.*

**Rabbit** (*to himself*)   Silly little bird.

*Sudden noises from a distance make* **Rabbit** *turn and listen eagerly. Heavy vehicles approaching. Headlamps swing across the stage momentarily dazzling* **Rabbit**. *The vehicles stop. Doors bang. Distant voices are heard.*

**Voice One**   Right, lads. Cup of tea. Then unload.

**Voice Two**   OK. Brew up, Charlie.

**Voice Three**   Righto.

**Voice Four** (*singing*)   Charlie put the kettle on . . .

*Laughter.* **Rabbit** *listens transfixed.*

**Rabbit** (*to himself*)   Big Ones.

*He scuttles to his burrow and disappears.*

*The noises of the* **Big Ones** *recede.*

**Squirrel** *descends the tree.*

**Squirrel**   Make it snappy, Rabbit. I can't afford to dilly dally, shilly shally, mystery or no mystery. (*He notices* **Rabbit** *is not there.*) Rabbit? Rabbit. (*He goes to the burrow entrance. Calling.*) Rabbit? (*Louder.*) Rabbit? (*He gives up and calls up the tree.*) Dunnock?

*Pause.*

Dunnock!

**Dunnock** *appears through the foliage.*

**Dunnock**    Dear oh dear oh dear. What is it, Squirrel?

**Squirrel**    Play a little game with me, would you?

**Dunnock**    I beg your pardon?

**Squirrel**    Play a little game with me, would you?

**Dunnock**    Sorry, Squirrel, too busy. Didn't know you liked games. Ask Rabbit to play with you.

**Squirrel**    No!

**Dunnock**    He likes games.

**Squirrel**    No, you bird of little brain. I mean, is this your idea of a joke?

**Dunnock**    Joke?

**Squirrel**    Leading me on a wild rabbit chase.

**Dunnock**    Sorry, you've lost me.

**Squirrel**    I've lost Rabbit.

**Dunnock**    Him too? Dear oh dear. Where is he?

**Squirrel**    If I knew that, I wouldn't be saying I'd lost him. He's not here. You really are very thick, Dunnock.

**Dunnock**    There's no call for rudeness. Rabbit wanted to see you about some mystery.

**Squirrel**    The mystery is, where's Rabbit?

**Dunnock**    Search me, Squirrel.

*She disappears.*

**Squirrel** *tries the burrow again.*

**Squirrel** (*calling*)    Rabbit!

*No reply.* **Squirrel** *goes to leave. He spies an acorn.*

Ah!

(*Picking it up.*) At least it's not a totally wasted journey. (*He goes to climb the tree, and suddenly sees the white cross. He reacts mystified, then, like* **Rabbit** *earlier, stretches up to feel it. He, too, gets paint on his paw. Bemused, he climbs back up the tree, carrying his acorn. As he climbs.*) Out of my way, Dunnock.

**Squirrel** *disappears.*

**Dunnock** (*off*)    Charming. (*Calling after him.*) It's not my fault he's not there.

**Dunnock** *reappears through the foliage and climbs down the trunk.*

(*To herself.*) Hope he's all right. It's not like him to be unreliable. He did seem in a bit of a state, though. (*She goes to the burrow and calls down it.*) Rabbit? Rabbit! Are you there? I took your message. Rabbit!

**Rabbit** *enters from off-stage – from the direction in which the* **Big Ones***' voices came from. He is breathless and agitated.*

**Dunnock** (*still looking down the burrow*)    Rabbit!

**Rabbit**    What are you doing?

**Dunnock** (*turning*)    Looking for Rabbit. (*Turning back and calling down the burrow.*) Rabbit!

**Rabbit**    Yes?

**Dunnock**    What? Oh it's you! Silly me. Where did you spring from?

**Rabbit**    My back door. Over there. Where's Squirrel?

**Dunnock**    He's been and gone.

**Rabbit**    Been and gone?

**Dunnock**    Arrived and departed.

**Rabbit**    But I haven't spoken to him yet.

**Dunnock**    That's on account of the fact that you weren't here when he arrived. He arrived after you departed. *You* arrived after *he* departed. A matter of bad timing, if you ask me.

**Rabbit**    I'm not asking you, Dunnock, I'm telling you, to get Squirrel down here. Now.

**Dunnock**    Again?

**Rabbit**    Quickly, please. It's serious.

**Dunnock**    It *is*. I'll never get my jobs done at this rate.

**Rabbit**    Go!

**Dunnock**    Oh, all right.

**Rabbit**    Hurry!

**Dunnock** (*climbing the tree*)    Dear oh dear oh dear oh dear.

**Dunnock** *disappears.*

*As* **Rabbit** *watches her depart, the noises of the* **Big Ones** *return.*

**Rabbit** *freezes.*

**Voice One**    Right, lads, the party's over. We got a job to do.

**Voice Two**    OK. Unload the gear.

**Voice One**    Shift yourself, Charlie!

*Laughter.*

**Rabbit** *reacts frightened and scampers down his burrow.*

*As he does so, the lights fade. The noise of heavy mechanical gear being unloaded and an engine being turned on fills the air and increases in intensity as the scene change takes place. The base of the tree disappears (flown or revolved) and the main set, halfway up the tree, is revealed.*

*It incorporates several levels, dominated by, at stage level, the 'hollow' – the home of* **Owl**. *This should include a closed-off section, which could be like a hut, complete with door; however, it might be more appropriate, and less fantasy-orientated, to have a section partitioned off by a leafy equivalent of a bead curtain.* **Owl**'s *hollow becomes the dominant acting area, in which meetings of the tree community take place. Other important locations are a hole in the trunk, in which* **Squirrel** *has his drey, an upper level, partly covered with foliage, where* **Mistlethrush** *has her nest, and a branch the other side from which* **Bat** *can 'hang'. The actor playing* **Bat** *should appear to be upside down, with his head on his arms. Branches should provide walkways between these locations, perhaps using scaffolding and steps disguised with leaves and ivy.*

*As the noises of the* **Big Ones**'*working recede, lighting reveals* **Dunnock** *climbing towards* **Squirrel**'s *drey. She carries cleaning implements – brush (made of twigs) and dusters (made from leaves). The brush could be strapped on her back. She whistles as she climbs.*

*As* **Dunnock** *reaches* **Squirrel**'s *drey, we hear his voice from inside.*

**Squirrel** (*inside*)    Twenty-three, twenty-four, twenty-five . . .

**Dunnock**    Excuse me. Squirrel.

**Squirrel** (*inside*)    Twenty-five, twenty-six . . .

**Dunnock** (*louder*)    Squirrel!

**Squirrel**    What is it? I'm busy. Twenty . . .

**Dunnock**    It's Rabbit.

**Squirrel** (*popping out, carrying acorns, or perhaps an improvised abacus*)    Rabbit? Where?

**Dunnock**    Down there.

**Squirrel**    Down where?

**Dunnock**    Down there. Waiting.

**Squirrel**   Oh not again. Where was I? Twenty-five? Twenty-six? I've lost count now. I'll have to start all over again.

**Dunnock**   Sorry, Squirrel.

**Squirrel**   *You're* sorry? My annual acorn tally's important, Dunnock. I don't do it for fun. Winter has a nasty habit of creeping up on us. I must be prepared. It's serious.

**Dunnock**   I know, Squirrel. But Rabbit's serious too. I've never seen him so serious.

**Squirrel**   Oh, very well. But this is the last time. Up, down, up, down.

**Dunnock**   Life's full of them, they say.

**Squirrel**   What?

**Dunnock**   Ups and downs. Shall I clean out your drey while you're gone?

**Squirrel**   Yes, please, Dunnock. But don't interfere with my acorns, please. They're all sorted.

**Dunnock**   Right. Mind how you go.

**Squirrel** *climbs down, round the trunk and out of sight.*

**Squirrel** (*as he goes*)   Dilly dally, shilly shally . . .

**Squirrel** *disappears.*

**Dunnock** *starts sweeping the entrance to the drey. Suddenly, from above her, comes a strident, shrill, out-of-tune singing, the sort of singing that human beings might practise in the bath. It is* **Mistlethrush**.

**Mistlethrush**
   La la la la laaaah!
   La la la la laaaah!

*A bundle of nesting material falls from above on or near* **Dunnock**. *She reacts irritated, and sweeps it up.*

**Mistlethrush**
   Spring, spring
   Makes me sing
   My happy tuneful song.

*More nesting material descends on* **Dunnock**.

**Dunnock**   What's going on up there? (*She clears up the nesting material.*)

**Mistlethrush**
   La la la la laaaah!
   La la la la laaah!

*More nesting material falls.*

**Dunnock** (*calling*)   Hey! Up there, whoever you are.

*Foliage parts, revealing* **Mistlethrush** *in the throes of making her nest. She untidily builds it around her in a slap-dash manner. She leans out.*

**Mistlethrush**    'Allo, dearie.

**Dunnock**    Oh it's you, Mistlethrush. Morning.

**Mistlethrush**    Nice one! (*She sets to work on her nest again, slapping on grass and twigs and odd shreds of Polythene bag material. She sings even more stridently.*)

Spring, spring
Makes me sing
'Cos summer won't be long!

*More nesting material gets flung out on to and around* **Dunnock**, *who gamely tries to collect it.*

**Dunnock**    Mistlethrush, must you be so messy?

**Mistlethrush**    Sorry, dearie, I'm building my nest.

**Dunnock**    I can see that. (*Holding up the fallen nesting material she has collected.*) I thought you were building it down here for a moment.

**Mistlethrush**    Sorry, dearie. Just getting sorted out. Be a love and bring me those bits back.

**Dunnock** (*resigned*)    On my way. (*She climbs up to* **Mistlethrush***'s nest.*)

**Mistlethrush**    Got some lovely bits of plasticy stuff this year. Big Ones leave it behind after their picnics. Very good stuff for insulting, that, my fella says.

**Dunnock**    Insulting?

**Mistlethrush**    Yeah, insulting, infiltrating, something like that.

**Dunnock**    Insulating.

**Mistlethrush**    Exactly! Keeps the eggs warm. And the babies when they hatch. (*Receiving the nesting material from* **Dunnock**.) Ta, dearie. You're a treasure. (*She starts building again, making a terrible mess.*) Now, this bit here, that bit there. Whoops! Lost that bit.

**Dunnock**    Do you want a bit of help?

**Mistlethrush**    Oh, would you? I'm not much good at it, am I? Funny, I'm not what you'd call domesticised . . .

**Dunnock**    Domesticated.

**Mistlethrush**    Exactly. But come springtime I get this feeling, all warm and cosy and material . . .

**Dunnock**    Maternal.

**Mistlethrush**    Exactly. And I fling myself into a flavour of activity getting ready for the big day. Oo, I can't wait. What about you, dearie? Are you laying this year?

**Dunnock**    In a few weeks, I expect.

*She works away.* **Mistlethrush** *does very little.*

**Mistlethrush**   Lovely. Listen, I've written this pretty little lullaby for my babies. I'll teach it to you. Might come in useful. (*She sings, loudly and off-key.*)

Hush your beak
Close your eyes
Go to sleep
And rest all the rest of you
Mum is tired
Don't squawk or squeak
Hush your beak.

**Dunnock** *has listened with a pained, patient expression.*

**Mistlethrush**   Good, innit? That'll nod 'em off in no time.

**Dunnock**   I think it might keep them awake!

**Mistlethrush**   Eh?

**Dunnock**   It's excruciating.

**Mistlethrush**   Exactly. Knew you'd like it. (*Looking at her nest.*) Oo, you are getting on a treat. A palace! Ta, dearie, everso. (*She starts to sing again – a dreadful din.*)

Spring, spring –

**Dunnock** (*interrupting*)   I'd, er, better be off. Squirrel's drey to muck out. (*She starts to leave.*)

**Mistlethrush**   Bye, dearie. (*Singing.*)
Spring, spring
Makes me sing
My happy tuneful song

*She works away on her nest again as* **Dunnock** *descends and enters* **Squirrel***'s drey. More nesting material falls down.*

**Mistlethrush**
Spring, spring
Makes me sing
'Cos summer won't be loooooooong!

*Suddenly* **Jay** *arrives – on the branch below, near* **Squirrel***'s drey. He is brashly confident, and carries a kind of 'suitcase' for his wares.*

**Jay**   What music fills my ears?

**Mistlethrush** (*looking down*)   Who's that?

**Jay**   Such tone. Such pitch. Such artistry.

**Mistlethrush**   Ooh! You flashy flatterer.

**Jay**   Jay's the name, madam. Travelling salesbird supreme.

**Mistlethrush**   I know you! Long time no see.

**Jay**   I have been on a flight of exploration, madam, spreading my wings far and wide in search of marketable merchandise. Scouring the countryside for new and exciting lines to offer my lucky customers at bargain prices. What do you fancy?

**Mistlethrush**   Nothing, dearie. I'm too busy building my nest.

**Jay**   Aha! See my selection, perfect for the use of. (*He opens his coat. Inside his wares are neatly displayed.*) Dried grasses, bracken, quality mosses, badger hair, sheep's wool for extra warmth, polythene and paper. Pick your own, mix 'n' match, yours for the modest sum of two acorns. Can't say fairer than that.

**Mistlethrush**   Not today, thank you, Jay.

**Jay**   Do me a favour.

**Mistlethrush**   I've got all I need, dearie. I'm almost ready to lay.

**Jay**   Aha! Think ahead, madam. Think of when your eggs hatch. Think of all those hungry little beaks to feed. No problem. (*He opens the other side of his coat, revealing more merchandise.*) I've got crab apples, juicy slugs, calorie-stuffed caterpillars, mouthwatering worms, specially selected spiders, meaty maggots and crunchy moths. Take your pick.

**Mistlethrush**   Sorry, dearie, come back next week.

**Jay**   Your loss, dear lady, not mine. Happy laying.

**Mistlethrush**   Tata, Jay.

*She disappears into her nest, dropping more nesting material by* **Jay**. *He eagerly picks it up, then drops it.*

**Jay**   Ugh. Most inferior. (*He thinks again.*) Might sell it second-hand. (*He approaches* **Squirrel**'*s drey.*) Wakey, wakey! Anyone at home?

**Dunnock** *appears, carrying rubbish from the drey.*

**Dunnock**   Not today, thank you, Jay.

**Jay**   Give a bird a chance, Dunnock! Where's Squirrel?

**Dunnock**   Out. I'm doing his cleaning.

**Jay**   Aha! Glad you said that. Ideal for the use of. (*He opens his suitcase, displaying more wares.*) Look at this little lot. Bark scourer, lichen loosener, fungus flusher, mildew stripper, leafmould remover. Tried and tested. Satisfaction guaranteed.

**Dunnock**   No thanks.

**Jay**   I'm only asking one acorn per item.

**Dunnock**   I've got no acorns. Squirrel's your best bet for acorns. He's got stacks of them in there.

**Jay**   Really?

**Dunnock**   Nightmare it is trying to clean round them, believe you me.

**Jay** (*apparently sympathetic*)   I'm sure, I'm sure.

**Dunnock**   Now, if you'll excuse me, I must get rid of Squirrel's rubbish. (*She sees* **Mistlethrush***'s nesting material.*) Oh, no. (*To herself.*) Mistlethrush, I've just cleaned this branch. Dear oh dear oh dear.

*She passes* **Jay** *and starts clearing up. She doesn't notice* **Jay** *take the opportunity to enter* **Squirrel***'s drey. He checks no one is looking, then darts inside, returning almost immediately carrying two acorns.* **Dunnock** *finishes clearing and turns round.* **Jay** *hastily hides the acorns.*

**Dunnock**   You still here?

**Jay**   Er . . . thought I'd wait for Squirrel. Any idea when he'll be back?

**Dunnock**   Anybody's guess. I must get on, anyway. Owl's hollow to muck out yet. See you.

**Jay**   Good day, dear lady.

**Dunnock** *sets off for* **Owl***'s hollow. When she arrives, she disappears inside the inner sanctum.*

**Jay** *stows away the two acorns in his suitcase or in his pockets. He checks the coast is clear and pops back inside* **Squirrel***'s drey.*

*Suddenly* **Squirrel** *appears, scrambling up from behind the tree. He is breathless and agitated.*

**Squirrel** (*calling*)   Owl! Owl!

*He goes towards* **Owl***'s hollow, as* **Jay** *emerges from the drey with two more acorns.* **Squirrel** *doesn't see* **Jay,** *who nervously pops back in the drey.*

**Squirrel**   Owl!

**Dunnock** *appears from* **Owl***'s inner sanctum.*

**Squirrel** (*shouting*)   Where's Owl?

**Dunnock**   Owl's out.

**Squirrel**   She would be.

**Dunnock**   See Rabbit?

**Squirrel**   Yes, yes. Where is she?

**Dunnock**   Still hunting, I dare say.

**Squirrel**   Never around when she's needed.

**Dunnock**   Don't blame me, Squirrel. I only work here.

**Squirrel**   I know, Dunnock. I'm sorry, but it's urgent.

**Jay** *sees his chance. He hurries out with two acorns, grabs his things and hides behind the trunk, unseen by* **Squirrel***.*

**Dunnock**   It's always urgent.

**Squirrel** (*shouting*)   It's *very* urgent.

**Mistlethrush** (*leaning out of her nest*)   Excuse me. Could I ask you to lower your voices?

**Squirrel**   Don't you start, Mistlethrush.

**Mistlethrush**   That's just it, dearie. I *have* started. My eggs are coming and I have to conserve.

**Dunnock**   Concentrate.

**Mistlethrush**   Exactly. So, please. A bit of hush for Mistlethrush. (*She disappears.*)

**Squirrel** (*in a loud whisper*)   Dunnock! Please. Let me know the moment Owl gets back.

**Dunnock**   Right. (*She goes back into* **Owl**'s *inner sanctum.*)

**Squirrel** (*muttering as he returns to his drey*)   What a day! (*He enters his drey.*) What a – (*With a shriek.*) What on earth? (*He darts out again. Calling.*) Dunnock! Dunnock!

**Mistlethrush** *leans out of her nest.*

**Mistlethrush**   Hush, please!

**Squirrel**   Sorry, Mistlethrush.

**Mistlethrush** *flounces out of sight.*

**Squirrel** (*calling*)   Dunnock!

**Dunnock** *emerges from* **Owl**'s *inner sanctum as* **Squirrel** *arrives.*

**Dunnock**   Not again. I told you. Owl's out.

**Squirrel**   I know, I know, you silly little bird. Listen, I thought I asked you not to interfere with my acorns.

**Dunnock**   You did and I didn't. Devil of a job I had cleaning round them.

**Squirrel**   They're not all there.

**Dunnock**   *You're* not all there, if you ask me. Been funny all morning.

**Jay** *creeps back from behind the tree, and enters* **Squirrel**'s *drey again.*

**Squirrel**   Come with me. I'll show you. (*He drags* **Dunnock** *towards his drey.*) Come on.

**Dunnock**   Oh dear, oh dear. Calm down, Squirrel.

**Squirrel**   I'm perfectly calm. I –

*He is cut short by the sight of* **Jay** *emerging from the drey, carrying another two acorns.*

**Squirrel**    Thief! Thief!

**Jay**    Ah! No! I can explain.

**Squirrel**    Caught in the act!

**Jay**    No, no. Listen, Squirrel. I er . . . I lost my way.

**Squirrel**    Lost your way? I've lost my acorns. You've stolen them!

**Jay**    No, no, no. These are *my* acorns.

**Squirrel**    Your acorns?

**Jay**    Yes. I was hoping to sell them to you. You're one of my best customers.

**Squirrel**    Liar!

**Jay**    Squirrel, please! My reputation!

**Squirrel**    Clear off!

**Jay**    You're making a big mistake!

**Squirrel**    Clear off!

**Dunnock** *looks on philosophically as* **Mistlethrush** *looks down from her nest.*

**Mistlethrush** (*shrill*)    Will you shut up!

*The others freeze in surprise.*

Have a little consternation.

**Dunnock**    Consideration.

**Mistlethrush**    Exactly.

**Squirrel**    Sorry, Mistlethrush. Serious business down here.

**Mistlethrush**    It's not exactly a barrel of laughs up here! Laying eggs is a very painful progress.

**Dunnock**    Process.

**Mistlethrush**    Exactly. And you can shut up too, clever dick Dunnock. Ooh! (*A cry of pain as her labour pains force her back into the nest.*)

**Dunnock**    I'd better go up and help her.

**Dunnock** *climbs up to* **Mistlethrush**. *Both remain hidden behind the foliage.*

**Squirrel** (*to* **Jay**)    You see the havoc you cause?

**Jay**    Havoc? Have a heart, Squirrel. Just a bit of honest trading.

**Squirrel**    Honest? You stand there holding my acorns and call it honest?

**Jay**    Yes. Well. Perhaps I overstepped the mark. Call it quits, eh? (*He hands the acorns back to* **Squirrel**.)

**Squirrel**    Call it what you like. Just flap your wings and fly away. (*He throws an acorn at* **Jay**.)

**Jay**    All right. All right. Keep calm.

**Squirrel**    I'm perfectly calm! (*He throws another acorn.*)

**Jay**    Ow! You've made your point!

**Squirrel** *quickly gets more ammunition from inside the drey, and throws it.*

**Squirrel**    Scarper!

**Jay**    Ow!

**Squirrel**    Now!

(*NB: In the original production, to really throw the acorns proved impractical:* **Squirrel** *mimed throwing in threatening fashion, and* **Jay** *reacted.*)

*He has forced* **Jay** *back towards* **Owl***'s hollow.*

*Suddenly they are both frozen by the appearance of* **Owl** *from her inner sanctum.*

**Owl**    Enough!

*Both* **Squirrel** *and* **Jay** *react nervously.*

**Squirrel**    Sorry, Owl.

**Jay**    No harm meant.

**Owl**    I will not suffer brawling. This is a civilised tree.

**Squirrel**    Yes, Owl.

**Owl**    We are a civilised society.

**Jay**    Yes, Owl.

*Pause.*

**Squirrel**    Good hunting, Owl?

**Owl**    Disastrous. (*Threateningly.*) I'm starving.

**Squirrel**    Oh dear.

**Jay**    May I be of service, Owl? (*He opens his coat.*) Caterpillar? Slug? Very tasty.

**Owl**    Insubstantial. Junk food. Do you have a mouse?

**Jay**    Er, no. But I could do you a vole.

**Owl** *advances, as* **Jay** *starts to delve in his suitcase.* **Owl** *simply takes the suitcase, calmly turns and heads back to her hollow.*

**Owl**    Thank you, Jay.

**Jay**    That's four acorns, please.

**Owl** (*turning threateningly*)    I beg your pardon?

**Jay** (*nervously*)    Four acorns?

**Owl**    No, thank you.

**Jay**    I meant . . .

**Owl** (*charmingly threatening*)    But I'm sure Squirrel would appreciate four acorns.

**Jay**    But Owl!

**Owl**    Now.

**Jay** (*defeated*)    Yes. Yes. My pleasure. Here you are, Squirrel. (*He hands over the acorns he stole earlier.*) One, two, three, four.

**Squirrel**    Thank you, Jay. How generous. Good day.

**Owl**    Good day, Jay.

**Jay** *mumbles and disappears behind the tree.*

**Squirrel**    Thanks, Owl.

**Owl**    I think justice prevailed.

**Squirrel**    Yes, indeed. Er . . . Owl, could I have an urgent word? You see . . .

**Owl**    Not now, Squirrel. Hunting makes me tired. Unsuccessful hunting makes me exhausted.

**Squirrel**    Yes, but –

*A sudden scream of pain from* **Mistlethrush***'s nest above.*

**Mistlethrush**    Aaaaagh!

**Owl** (*with a jump*)    What on earth's that?

**Squirrel**    Mistlethrush laying. It's a painful process.

**Owl**    I know the feeling.

**Dunnock** *leans from above, by the nest.*

**Dunnock** (*excited*)    One egg laid. Number two coming! (*She sees* **Owl**.) Morning, Owl, I've cleaned your hollow.

**Owl**    Thank you, Dunnock.

*Another shriek from* **Mistlethrush**.

**Mistlethrush**    Aaaaaah!

**Dunnock**    Excuse me. (*She disappears to help* **Mistlethrush**.)

**Owl** (*yawning*)    See you later, Squirrel. (*She turns to go.*)

**Squirrel**    But please, Owl, it's important. Let me –

**Owl**    Later, Squirrel, later.

**Squirrel**    But *please*, you see, Rabbit –

*Another interruption. Loud singing:*

**Bat** (*from behind the tree*)
    You gotta keep
    Hanging on
    Baby
    Gotta keep
    Hanging on . . .

**Owl**    Oh no, Bat's back!

**Bat** *enters, heavily 'into' the rock song playing (unheard by us) through his large headphones. A 'Walkman'-style battery pack is attached to his belt.*

**Bat**
    You gotta keep
    Hanging on
    Baby
    Gotta keep
    Hanging on . . .

*As though in a trance, he jigs up and down, making loud percussion-type noises in accompaniment to the music.*

    Shubba dubba boom boom
    Shubba dubba wow!

**Owl**    He's in one of his trances again. Wake him up.

**Squirrel** *goes to* **Bat** *and waves frantically at him.* **Dunnock** *peers down to see what all the noise is about.*

**Squirrel**    Bat! Bat!

**Bat**
    Be-dum dum dum dum
    Pow!

*He nearly knocks* **Squirrel** *over.*

**Bat**
    You gotta keep
    Hanging on –

*In desperation* **Squirrel** *pulls the plug out of the battery pack.* **Bat** *immediately stops dancing.*

**Bat**    Hey, Squirrel, baby, you turned me off! I was all turned on and in the groove. In the groove and on the move. Pow! Pow! Pow! My, what a night! (*He sees* **Owl**.) Hi, Owl, baby!

**Owl**    Don't baby me, Bat. Where have you been? You stink.

**Bat**    I've been raving, Owl baby. Down the Battery Disco Tree. Where all the best bats hang out. The joint was jumping and I was flying.

**Owl**    He's high as a kite. Go to your perch and sleep it off. Help him, Squirrel.

**Bat**    I'd far sooner swing in your cosy little hollow, Owl baby.

*He tries to reach it, but* **Squirrel** *leads him away to his perch.*

**Owl**    You come near my cosy little hollow and I'll swallow you for breakfast.

**Bat**    OK, Owl baby. Don't get uptight, right? (*He tries to perch upside down.*) Let it all hang out, like little old me.

*He keeps losing his balance.* **Squirrel** *tries to help him. He sings jerkily.*

**Bat**
> You gotta keep . . .
> Hanging on . . .
> Baby . . .
> Gotta keep . . .
> Hanging . . . on . . .

*He finally balances and starts snoring.* **Squirrel** *returns to* **Owl**.

**Owl**    Did I say this was a civilised tree? A civilised society? Sometimes I wonder.

**Squirrel**    *I* wonder, Owl, if you could please listen . . .

**Owl**    I've told you, Squirrel.

**Squirrel**    But it's vital that you listen. Rabbit has news. *The Big Ones* . . . ⎫
**Owl**    I want some rest. Now go away and leave me alone – ⎭ (*together*)

**Owl**    The Big Ones? (*She pays attention immediately.*)

**Squirrel**    Yes.

**Owl**    What? Where?

**Squirrel**    I don't know, but Rabbit says please come.

**Owl**    Why didn't you tell me before?

**Squirrel**    I tried, Owl, I did try.

**Owl** (*preparing to leave*)    I'll meet you down there. I don't like flying so low in broad daylight, but it's a risk I'll have to take.

*She disappears round the trunk, preparing to fly down.*

**Squirrel**    Thank you, Owl.

**Squirrel** *hastens to climb down the tree. He disappears.*

**Jay** *emerges from hiding. He checks the coast is clear, laughs softly, retrieves his suitcase from* **Owl**'s *hollow, then enters* **Squirrel**'s *drey.*

**Bat** *wakes and looks at* **Owl**'s *hollow.*

**Bat** (*delighted*)    Owl's out! Groovy! (*He goes down to it and settles upside down, enjoying the comfort.*)

*Suddenly a shriek from above –* **Mistlethrush**.

**Mistlethrush**    Aaaaaah!

**Bat** *loses his balance and topples.* **Jay** *pops his head out of the drey in alarm.* **Dunnock** *leans out over* **Mistlethrush**'s *nest.*

**Dunnock**    Two!

*Blackout.*

*As the scene changes back to the base of the tree, we hear the grating mechanical sound of a digger. The sounds continue as the lights come up on the base of the tree.*

**Squirrel** *is descending. He goes to* **Rabbit**'s *burrow.*

**Squirrel** (*calling*)    Rabbit! Owl's coming! Rabbit!

**Owl** *arrives, as though she has just landed.*

**Owl** (*tense*)    Where is he?

**Squirrel**    He'll be here. Look, Owl. The mystery. (*He shows* **Owl** *the white cross.*) What does it mean?

**Owl**    I wish I knew, Squirrel. (*Suddenly.*) What's that noise?

*The digger noise increases.* **Owl** *and* **Squirrel** *listen intently. Then, distant voices.*

**Voice One**    Another one over here, Tom.

**Voice Two**    OK. (*Calling.*) Charlie. More earth. Get a move on.

**Voice Three**    Coming.

**Owl**    Rabbit was right. Big Ones.

*Suddenly* **Rabbit** *emerges from his burrow, caked with earth and terrified.*

**Rabbit** (*breathless and almost hysterical*)    No! No! Please! No!

**Squirrel**    Rabbit, Owl's here.

**Rabbit**    Owl, Owl. Tell me I'm dreaming. Tell me it's not true. It can't be true! Help me! Help me!

**Owl**    Pull yourself together, Rabbit. What's happened?

**Rabbit**    I tried. I did try. There was nothing I could do. Murderers! Murderers!

**Owl**    Rabbit! Tell us. Calmly.

**Rabbit**    Big Ones. Filling in the burrow. Earth pouring down. Friends and relatives struggling, suffocating. Buried alive. (*He breaks down, sobbing, and collapses into* **Squirrel**'s *arms.*)

**Squirrel**   He's fainted. Oh, Owl, what are we going to do?

**Owl**   Back up the tree, quick.

**Squirrel**   What about Rabbit?

**Owl**   Him too.

**Squirrel**   Up there? But how, Owl, how?

**Owl**   Like before.

**Squirrel**   Before?

**Owl** (*taking hold of* **Rabbit**)   Before you were born, Squirrel. One winter it rained for days. The waters rose and flooded out Rabbit's burrow. I lifted Rabbit and his friends and relatives to safety in the tree till it was over. Emergency rescue. Like this one.

*The noise of the digger and earth pouring into the burrow interrupt.* **Owl** *and* **Squirrel** *react.*

**Owl**   See you at the hollow. And Squirrel.

**Squirrel**   Yes, Owl?

**Owl**   Get Dunnock to call a crisis meeting!

**Squirrel** *starts to climb.* **Owl** *prepares for take-off, grasping* **Rabbit** *firmly.*

*The lighting fades and the scene changes back to half-way up the tree. Meanwhile, noises increase and become more menacing. Regular beat of the generator. Then voices.*

**Voice One**   Ready for the main action, Tom?

**Voice Two**   Ready, boss.

**Voice One**   Got enough cable?

**Voice Two**   Reckon so.

**Voice Three**   Where do we start, boss?

**Voice One**   Small ones first. Work up to the big one, eh?

**Voice Three**   Right.

*Laughter.*

*The lights fade up.* **Bat** *is snoring, asleep in* **Owl**'s *hollow.* **Jay** *is stuffing acorns into his suitcase. Suddenly,* **Mistlethrush** *bursts into song.*

**Mistlethrush** (*hidden*)
  La la la la laaaaah!

**Jay** *and* **Bat** *react.*

**Mistlethrush**   (*appearing, jubilant*)

  La la la la laaaaah!
  Spring, spring

Makes me sing
A celebration song.

**Jay** (*wincing*)    Wish I had your headphones, Bat!

*But* **Bat** *is asleep again.*

**Mistlethrush**
Spring, spring
My eggs are laid
And they'll hatch before too long.

**Dunnock** *appears by the nest.*

**Dunnock**    Congratulations, Mistlethrush. Four eggs!

**Mistlethrush**    Ta, dearie. And thanks for all your help.

**Dunnock**    Fancy a bite to eat?

**Jay** (*who has been listening*)    How's about some fresh mistletoe berries, Mistlethrush?

**Mistlethrush**    Oo, my favourites. How much?

**Jay**    No charge, Mistlethrush. My present to congratulate you on a safe delivery.

**Mistlethrush**    Oo, ta. (*Imitating him.*) Can't say fairer than that!

**Dunnock**    I'll get them for you.

*She starts to go down to* **Jay**, *who finds the berries.*

**Squirrel** *scampers up to the hollow.*

**Squirrel**    Right. Action stations, everyone!

**Dunnock**    You still at it, Squirrel? Up, down, up, down.

**Squirrel**    Dunnock, Owl says you're to call a meeting.

**Dunnock**    A meeting? Why?

**Squirrel**    You'll find out. It's an emergency.

**Dunnock**    Oh dear. Right. Come on, everybody. Meeting. (*She goes to* **Bat**.) Wake up, you smelly Bat. (*Lifting one of his earphones.*) Wake up! Meeting.

**Bat** *overbalances.*

**Bat**    OK, OK. Stay cool, Dunnock.

**Squirrel** (*to* **Jay**)    You still here?

**Jay**    Just on my way.

**Squirrel**    You'd better stay. (*Calling up.*) Mistlethrush!

**Dunnock**    She's just laid her eggs.

**Squirrel**    Can't help that. (*Calling.*) Mistlethrush! Down here.

**Mistlethrush** (*leaning out*)    Don't be daft, dearie. Can't leave my eggs.

**Squirrel**    Owl's orders.

**Mistlethrush**    But –

**Squirrel**    Emergency.

**Dunnock**    Cover the eggs up. Keep them warm.

**Jay** (*seeing the seriousness of the situation*)    Take her all this stuff. That'll help. (*He opens his coat, revealing the nesting material.*)

**Dunnock**    Thank you, Jay.

*She takes the nesting material and hurries up to* **Mistlethrush**. *During the next section we see both birds carefully covering the eggs in the nest.*

**Squirrel** (*to* **Bat**, *who has gone back to sleep*)    Bat!

**Bat**    I'm up! I'm up!

**Owl** *and* **Rabbit** *enter round the trunk to the hollow.* **Rabbit** *is conscious but weak. He crumples into the hollow, watched by the others.*

**Owl**    Everybody here?

**Squirrel**    Mistlethrush and Dunnock are on their way.

**Owl**    Now, you all know Rabbit.

**Bat**    He looks rougher than I feel.

**Owl**    He's in a bad way, I'm afraid.

**Jay**    Here. Try this. (*He produces a sprig from his suitcase, and puts it under* **Rabbit**'s *nose.*) Garlic mustard. Sniff this, Rabbit.

**Rabbit** *sniffs, then sneezes violently. He recovers somewhat.*

**Dunnock** *and* **Mistlethrush** *arrive in the hollow.*

**Mistlethrush**    What is all this? If my eggs don't hatch, Owl, there'll be trouble.

**Owl**    Hush, Mistlethrush.

**Mistlethrush** *sees* **Rabbit.**

**Mistlethrush**    What's that Rabbit doing here?

**Owl**    Hush! Rabbit, can you hear me?

**Rabbit** (*nodding*)    Where am I?

**Owl**    Safe. Up the tree. Among friends. Now tell us all what happened. Calmly.

**Rabbit**    Noises. Big Ones. Voices. Machines. Went to look. Met my friends and relatives other side of the field.

**Squirrel**    What did you see?

**Owl**    Quiet, Squirrel. Take your time, Rabbit.

**Rabbit**    Big machines. Sharp metal. With pointed teeth. Wire. Then one machine clears Big Ones' rubbish. I thought, 'Good. Rubbish dangerous.' But then . . . then . . .

**Owl** (*gently*)    Yes?

**Rabbit**    Another machine digs earth . . . and comes towards us. Panic. Fear. Down burrow. Then earth pouring down on us. Run through burrow. Scrabble to survive. Many friends and relatives can't make it. Buried alive . . . (*He breaks down.*)

*A shocked pause.*

**Mistlethrush**    But why?

**Owl**    Who can fully understand the Big Ones? Not us.

**Jay**    Butchers.

**Bat**    You stick with us, Rabbit, baby. You'll be OK.

**Dunnock**    You're safe up here.

**Rabbit**    No. White cross.

**Squirrel**    Yes! Tell them about the white cross.

**Rabbit**    On the tree. Paint. Still wet.

**Owl**    I saw it too.

**Mistlethrush**    What does it mean?

**Rabbit**    Others. Other white crosses. On the other trees. Danger! Danger!

**Owl**    All right, Rabbit, relax. (*To the others.*) We must find out more. Bat, how's your radar?

**Bat**    A-one, Owl. Shall I tune in? See what I can suss?

**Owl**    Please.

**Bat** *goes to his perch and 'tunes in'. A sudden noise interrupts.*

**Cuckoo** (*from behind the tree*)    Yoo-hoo! Yoo-hoo! Yoo-hoo!

**Cuckoo** *enters. She is loud and colourful and very tanned. She carries a travelling bag.*

Well, hi there, fans, I'm here to say
I've just flown in on my holiday
From Africa is many a mile

> So now I'm here I'll stay awhile
> Yoo-hoo!

**Mistlethrush** *springs up.*

**Dunnock**    Oh dear, oh dear. It's Cuckoo.

**Mistlethrush** (*fury rising*)    This is the last straw!

**Cuckoo**    Mistlethrush! Yoo-hoo!

**Mistlethrush** (*rushing to her nest*)    Get rid of her! Get rid of her!

**Cuckoo**    Aren't you glad to see me? I sure am glad to see you!

**Mistlethrush**    I bet you are.

**Owl**    Cuckoo. You've chosen a bad time. You're welcome, but –

**Mistlethrush** (*leaning out from her nest*)    Welcome? She's about as welcome as a bolt of lightning.

**Cuckoo**    That's not nice.

**Mistlethrush**    And you think what you did to me was nice? Last year? You sly bird. You dumped your egg in my nest, scarpered back off to the sun, and left me to bring up your brat.

**Cuckoo**    And a fine job you made of it. Then he flew right back to his momma in Africa.

**Mistlethrush**    And that's what you can do. Fly right back to Africa! Now!

*All try to placate* **Mistlethrush***. Suddenly a loud noise interrupts and freezes everyone into silence. The savage, harsh grating noise of a chainsaw.*

**Squirrel**    Shhhhhh!

*All look, horrified. After ten seconds or so, the sound of a falling tree.*

**Owl**    Bat?

**Bat** (*tuned in to his radar*)    No echo! I'm getting no echo!

**Owl**    Explain.

**Bat**    The tree the other side of the field. (*Realising.*) The Battery Disco Tree. Like it's gone. Disappeared.

*The noise of the chainsaw returns and increases to an almost painful level as the characters look at each other in fear and the lighting fades to blackout.*

*The noise of the chainsaw suddenly cuts out.*

*Curtain.*

# Act Two

*As the house lights fade, the screech of the chainsaw is heard. It rises in intensity.*

*Then the sound of another tree falling. Nearer than the earlier one.*

*The lights come up on the hollow. All except* **Mistlethrush** *are gathered as at a meeting, with* **Owl** *'in the chair'.* **Rabbit** *is recuperating.* **Mistlethrush** *is in her nest, visible. All listen, horrified.*

**Squirrel**   How many's that?

**Bat**   Five trees down. And they're getting nearer.

**Owl**   Bat, how many trees before they reach ours?

**Bat**   Two. Three. Depends on which direction they take.

**Cuckoo**   I don't see what all the fuss is about. We're quite safe here, aren't we?

**Squirrel**   Don't be stupid, Cuckoo. The Big Ones are clearing the land, the trees. *Our* tree, maybe.

**Mistlethrush**   Anyway, it's all right for her. She doesn't live here. This is our home, Cuckoo.

**Dunnock**   We'll have to move.

**Squirrel**   Why should we move? Mistlethrush is right. This is our home. It's always been our home.

**Owl**   There must be something we can do.

**Rabbit**   The white cross.

**Owl**   What about it?

**Rabbit**   The Big Ones painted white crosses on lots of trees. Why?

**Jay**   As a sign, if you ask me. To remind them which ones to remove, so to speak.

**Owl**   That means they wouldn't cut down our tree . . .

**Bat**   . . . if it didn't have a white cross on it! Yeah! Yeah!

**Owl**   Exactly. Dunnock, could you clean it off?

**Dunnock**   I could try.

**Jay**   Take my samples, Dunnock. Only the best. No rubbish. Clean off anything with that lot. (*He gives her his suitcase.*)

**Dunnock**   Thanks, Jay.

**Jay**   All part of the service.

**Rabbit**   Let me help. I'm better now, Owl. Take me down. I can do a bit of scouting too.

**Owl**    Good idea . . .

*Sudden interruption – nearer.*

**Voice One**    OK, Charlie. Turn on.

*The noise of the chainsaw. All freeze.*

**Owl**    Bat!

**Bat** (*tuning in*)    After this one, we're next in line.

**Owl**    Quick! Before it's too late.

**Owl**, **Rabbit** *and* **Dunnock** *(grabbing cleaning things) go behind the trunk, preparing to fly down, as the lighting fades and the chainsaw noise increases.*

*Then, in the blackout . . .*

**Voice Three**    Here she goes!

*Crashing noise of a tree falling.*

*The scene changes back to the base of the tree.*

**Dunnock** *and* **Rabbit** *are scrubbing out the cross. Already much of it has gone.* **Jay**'s *suitcase lies open.*

**Voice One**    OK, lads, chain her up.

*Noises of chains being attached to the next-door tree.* **Dunnock** *and* **Rabbit** *scrub furiously.* **Dunnock** *tires.*

**Dunnock**    Oh dear, oh dear.

**Owl** (*whispering*)    Keep going, Dunnock. Here, let me. (*She desperately joins in.*)

**Voice One**    Right, lads, take her away.

*The noise of a heavy vehicle dragging the tree away.*

Next one, Charlie.

*Heavy footsteps of two men approach. There is one area of white paint still visible, near the bottom of the trunk.*

**Dunnock**    I can't do it, Owl. This bit's dried solid. I can't . . .

**Owl**    Too late! Retreat!

**Owl** *and* **Dunnock** *escape behind the tree, remembering to take* **Jay**'s *suitcase.* **Rabbit** *starts to go, then, realising white paint is still visible, flings himself against it. He lies motionless.*

*The footsteps stop.*

**Voice Three**    Funny. Where's the cross?

**Voice One**    Let's have a bit more light on the subject.

*A sudden flash of light illuminates the trunk, moving up, down and across.*

Nothing.

**Voice Three**    This one staying, then, boss?

**Voice One**    Must be, Charlie.

*The light finds* **Rabbit**.

**Voice One**    What's that?

**Voice Three**    Rabbit. Dead by the look of it.

**Voice One**    Died of fright, I dare say.

*Laughter.*

Fancy a rabbit stew for your supper, Charlie?

**Voice Three**    No, no!

**Voice One**    I'll get it for you.

*Footsteps, plus shadows in the torchlight.*

*Suddenly, from behind the tree,* **Owl** *hoots menacingly.*

**Voice One**    Stone the crows, what's that?

**Owl** *hoots again.*

**Voice Three**    An owl, I reckon, boss.

**Voice One**    Don't like owls. Spooky creatures. Come on. We'll do the next one.

**Voice Three**    Right.

*The light and footsteps recede, as the* **Big Ones** *go.*

**Owl** *and* **Dunnock** *hurry round to see* **Rabbit**.

**Dunnock**    Well done, Rabbit! You really fooled them.

**Owl**    Congratulations, Rabbit. That was very brave.

**Rabbit**    Thanks, Owl. Your hoot really got 'em going . . .

*Footsteps returning.*

Look out, they're coming back!

**Owl** *and* **Dunnock** *dash behind the tree.* **Rabbit** *throws himself against the remains of the cross and feigns dead.*

**Voice Three** (*calling*)    It's over here somewhere!

**Voice Two** (*from a distance*)    Trust Charlie to leave the saw behind!

**Voice One** (*from a distance*)    Ha, ha.

**Voice Three**    I'll give you a sore behind in a minute! Here it is. Sorry, boss.

*The footsteps recede. Pause.*

**Rabbit** *gets up and looks tentatively off. Then . . .*

**Rabbit** (*in a loud whisper*)    All clear!

**Owl** *and* **Dunnock** *emerge.*

**Owl**    Thanks again, Rabbit.

**Rabbit**    A bit close that was, Owl.

**Dunnock**    I'd better finish scrubbing off this paint. (*She starts work again.*)

**Owl**    Good idea, Dunnock. Can't be too careful. Then we'd better go back up. Report to the others. A celebration is called for. You come too, Rabbit.

**Rabbit**    I don't think I'd better . . .

**Owl**    You must. You are the hero of the hour. Thanks to you, our home is safe. We are safe.

**Rabbit**    Well, it's very kind of you, Owl, but I'd rather not. I think I'd better see what's left of the burrow.

**Owl**    Of course. Very selfish of me. Your friends and relatives haven't been as lucky as us.

**Rabbit** (*quietly*)    No.

**Dunnock**    Finished!

**Owl**    Excellent. Up we go, then, Dunnock.

**Dunnock**    'Bye, Rabbit. Thanks again.

**Rabbit**    'Bye, Dunnock. 'Bye, Owl.

**Owl**    Goodbye, Rabbit.

**Rabbit** *starts to go.*

**Owl**    And Rabbit!

**Rabbit** *stops.*

**Rabbit**    Yes, Owl?

**Owl**    I hope you find at least some of your friends and relatives safe. I really do.

**Rabbit**    Thanks, Owl.

**Rabbit** *goes.*

*The noise of the chainsaw attacking the next tree makes* **Owl** *and* **Dunnock** *get moving.*
*They disappear, preparing to fly back up the tree, as . . .*

*The lighting fades and the noise intensifies.*

*The scene changes back to half-way up the tree. The noise continues as the lights come up.*

**Bat**, **Jay**, **Cuckoo** *and* **Squirrel** *wait tensely in the hollow.* **Mistlethrush** *looks down anxiously from her nest.*

*A tree is heard to fall. All react, nervous and powerless.*

**Cuckoo**    I don't understand your Big Ones. Why do they cut down your trees?

**Mistlethrush**    What's it matter to you, Cuckoo? You're only here a couple of weeks a year.

**Cuckoo**    It matters much. In Africa there are so few trees. They say Big Ones die because of this. Here they have trees. Why do they cut them down?

**Squirrel**    The Big Ones move in mysterious ways, Cuckoo. Who are we to reason why?

**Bat**    Cut the homespun philosophy, Squirrel, baby. I've got a sounding on the airwaves.

*All attend.*

(*Tuned in.*) Gotta work this out. The tree that's just fallen was west, right?

*He points. The others agree.*

The one that fell before was east, right?

*He points in the opposite direction. The others agree.*

Then, my, my, I think we've done it. The Big Ones have missed our tree out. Yippee!

*Relief and general cheers.*

**Jay**    Snack, anyone? (*He takes food from inside his hat or pockets and offers it round.*) Caterpillar, slug? First-class festive fare.

*They accept gratefully.*

**Squirrel**    I have to admit I misjudged you, Jay. I'm sorry. You've been very helpful.

**Jay**    That's big of you, Squirrel. I appreciate that. Fancy an acorn? (*He gives him one.*)

**Squirrel**    Thank you.

**Jay**    It's one of yours anyway.

**Squirrel** *goes to react, but thinks better of it and smiles. All laugh.*

**Cuckoo**    Come on down, Mistlethrush! It's party time!

**Mistlethrush**    Thanks, dearie, I'd love to, but I can't leave my eggs.

**Cuckoo**    I'll egg-sit for you. Very good egg-sitter I am.

**Mistlethrush**  Oh, would you? I could do with a stretch . . . (*Realising.*) . . . hang on, not blooming likely! Don't you come anywhere near my nest, Cuckoo. I know your game. Get up here, get rid of one of my eggs, lay one of your own and leave me to do the dirty work. Egg-sitter indeed!

**Cuckoo**  Only trying to help.

**Mistlethrush**  Ha!

**Bat** (*suddenly tuning in*)  Hey, hey! Cool it, you chicks. Something on the line.

*All attend.*

(*Eventually.*) It's OK. It's Owl.

**Owl** and **Dunnock** *enter from behind the trunk.*

**Owl**  Emergency over! Celebration!

*All cheer.*

**Squirrel**  What happened, Owl? Did you manage to clean off the white cross?

**Owl**  Well, yes . . .

**Jay**  Jay's classy cleaning products up to scratch, eh?

**Owl**  Yes, thank you, Jay. But it was Rabbit who truly saved the day.

**Dunnock**  We hadn't finished scrubbing off the paint, so Rabbit covered it up by pretending to be dead. And the Big Ones couldn't see it!

**Squirrel**  Good for Rabbit! Hip, hip, hip . . .

**All**  Hooray.

**Bat**  On with the party!

*Music starts.*

Come on, Owl baby, let's let it all hang out! (*He starts gyrating.*)

**Owl** (*looking shocked, then melting*)  Why not? Go, Bat, go! Groovy, groovy!

**Bat** *sings. The others pick up the song and dance with wild enthusiasm.* **Mistlethrush** *jogs about above.*

**Bat**
  You gotta keep hanging on

**All**
  Baby, gotta keep hanging on
  You gotta keep hanging on
  Baby, gotta keep hanging on.
  You gotta keep hanging on
  Baby, gotta keep hanging on

You gotta keep hanging on
Baby, gotta . . .

*Suddenly noises of the* **Big Ones** *make all freeze. First a loud whistle – a piercing human whistle to attract attention.*

*Then . . .*

**Voice One**    Oy! Charlie! Shift yourself.

*Running footsteps. Breathless arrival of* **Charlie**.

**Voice Three**    What is it, boss?

**Voice Two**    Look here.

*Rustle of paper.*

I thought there was something fishy going on.

**Voice Three**    What do you mean?

**Voice One**    Of course this tree has to come down. It's on the plan, see? Clear as daylight. No question.

**Voice Three**    Then why no white cross?

**Voice One**    Don't ask me. Administrative error. Who cares?

**Voice Three**    What do we do, then, boss?

**Voice One**    Don't be stupid, Charlie. It's marked on the plan so down it comes.

**Voice Three**    Right, boss.

**Voice One**    Now, it's the biggest of the lot, right? I want the chainsaw, the most powerful one we've got, with the yellow cable. And we'll need the generator. Tell Tom.

**Voice Three**    Right, boss.

**Voice One**    And get a move on. We don't want to be here all night.

*Footsteps recede.*

*A shocked hush on the tree. Eventually . . .*

**Squirrel**    That's it, then.

*Pause.*

**Owl**    We should have known. We can never beat the Big Ones.

**Jay**    Evacuate. Leave the tree. That's the answer. The only answer.

**Cuckoo**    You could all come home with me. To Africa.

**Mistlethrush**    I don't want to go to bloomin' Africa. This is my home.

**Squirrel**    I agree, Mistlethrush. If my home is to die, I will die with it.

**Mistlethrush**    Well. I didn't say *that*, dearie.

**Dunnock**    Forgive me, Squirrel, but that's a silly attitude. Dear oh dear, we can't just give up! (*She is embarrassed by her own vehemence.*)

**Bat** (*urgently*)    Turn down the volume, Dunnock, I'm picking up . . . hey, that's crazy!

**Owl**    What?

**Bat**    Cloud. Low cloud. Very low.

**Owl**    Cloud?

**Squirrel** (*sniffing the air*)    What's that smell?

*All sniff the air. Suddenly smoke begins to appear.*

**Jay**    That's not cloud, Bat. It's smoke!

**Dunnock** *and* **Cuckoo** *begin to cough. Sound of burning wood.*

**Owl**    They're burning the cut-down trees. (*She coughs.*) We've no choice now. We'll suffocate if we stay. Everybody leave. Abandon tree!

*The noise of flames increases. A red glow is seen to one side. More smoke.*

Meet down the bottom!

*Signs of panic as the creatures dash about.*

**Mistlethrush** (*screaming*)    No. No. My eggs. I won't leave my eggs!

**Dunnock**    Bring them with you!

**Mistlethrush**    I can't!

**Cuckoo**    You can, Mistlethrush! Let me help.

**Mistlethrush**    You?

**Cuckoo**    Please!

*All are affected by the smoke, which becomes thicker.*

**Squirrel** (*who has rushed to his drey*)    What about my acorns?

**Owl**    You'll have to leave them.

**Squirrel**    But we'll starve! And I've been storing them for days.

**Jay**    Take them with us, Squirrel. Drop them down the tree! Bat, give us a hand!

**Squirrel** *passes out acorns to* **Jay**, *who passes them to* **Bat**, *who throws them down the tree. Meanwhile,* **Mistlethrush** *hands down two eggs to* **Cuckoo**, *or even drops them down. Or maybe* **Dunnock** *works a relay system up and down. Two eggs go in* **Cuckoo**'s *bag, packed with nesting material that* **Mistlethrush** *flings down.* **Dunnock** *takes* **Jay**'s *'suitcase' for the other two eggs. In the confusion, perhaps an egg is mistakenly thrown to* **Bat** *as an acorn – then carefully passed back down to* **Cuckoo** *and* **Dunnock**. *In the midst of this hive of activity,* **Bat** *freezes.*

**Bat** (*tuning in*)    Big Ones returning! Big Ones returning!

**Owl**    Hurry! Hurry!

*Noises of vehicles, burning logs, and chainsaws intensify as the lighting fades on the scene of urgent activity.*

*The scene changes back to the base of the tree.*

*As the light fades up, there is still smoke, but not as much.*

*The evacuees arrive.* **Squirrel** *climbs down the tree.* **Owl, Dunnock, Mistlethrush, Bat, Cuckoo** *and* **Jay** *come round the trunk, having flown down.* **Bat** *uses his radar to check for safety.* **Cuckoo** *and* **Mistlethrush** *immediately improvise a nest in the root formations, checking that the eggs are well wrapped.* **Dunnock** *helps.*

**Owl**    All here? Mistlethrush?

**Mistlethrush**    Here.

**Owl**    Jay?

**Jay**    Here.

**Owl**    Bat?

**Bat**    Here.

**Owl**    Cuckoo?

**Cuckoo**    Here.

**Owl**    Dunnock?

**Dunnock** (*returning* **Jay**'s '*suitcase*' *to him*)    Here.

**Owl**    Squirrel?

**Squirrel**    Here.

**Owl**    Any sign of Rabbit?

**Squirrel**    No, Owl. Shall I go and look for him?

**Owl**    No. We stick together. Wait for Rabbit. He knows the field better than us.

*They huddle together.*

**Jay**    Anyone hungry?

**All** (*muttering*)    No, thank you, Jay.

**Mistlethrush** *perches on her improvised nest.* **Dunnock** *and* **Cuckoo** *fuss around her.*

**Mistlethrush**    I think the eggs are OK. Ta ever so, Dunnock. (*To* **Cuckoo**.) And you, dearie.

**Cuckoo**    Quiet, Mistlethrush. Try to rest.

**Mistlethrush**   No, I'm very grateful. And if we come through all this, Cuckoo, feel free to dump your rotten egg on me as usual.

**Cuckoo**   Thank you.

**Bat** (*tuned in*)   Owl! (*After a pause.*) Rabbit.

**Rabbit** *enters, breathless.*

*All listen eagerly.*

**Owl**   Well?

**Rabbit** (*not defeated*)   The field's a right old mess, Owl. They've filled in the burrow. Killed all my friends and relatives. They're burning the trees. Chaos it is, chaos.

**Bat** (*tuned in*)   Big Ones approaching.

*The rumble of a heavy vehicle approaching.*

**Owl**   We'd better move on.

**Rabbit**   No. There's nowhere to move on to. And this is the last tree. We can't let it die like the others.

**Squirrel**   Hear, hear!

**Owl**   But we can't stop the Big Ones.

**Rabbit**   Maybe not. But we can show a bit of resistance. Stand up for our home.

**Jay**   Go down fighting, eh?

**Bat**   Right on!

**Mistlethrush**   We can't fight them.

**Dunnock**   But we can't desert our home.

**Rabbit**   Good for you, Dunnock. What do you say, Owl?

*The heavy vehicle stops. Doors slam. As voices are heard approaching,* **Owl** *makes her decision. Standing centre, she stretches out her hands. The others, as if mesmerised, join her. They defiantly, bravely, form a chain in front of the tree.*

**Voice Two**   Right, boss. Let's get it down. Charlie, how are you doing?

**Voice Three**   Nearly ready.

*The sound of machinery being unloaded.*

**Voice Two**   Big one, this. What do we do, boss? Start up top?

**Voice One**   I reckon.

**Voice Two**   Polish this one off, be home in time for tea, eh?

*Laughter. Suddenly a yellow cable swings into view.*

**Voice Three**    Chainsaw ready, boss.

**Voice One**    Electrics ready?

**Voice Two**    Ready!

**Voice One**    OK, Charlie. Turn on.

*The ghastly noise of the chainsaw. Reflections from the savage metal glint on the faces of the tree folk. Suddenly, accompanied, as it were, by the noise of the chainsaw, they sing, loudly and defiantly.*

**Tree Folk**
　　Save our tree
　　Don't let it fall
　　Save our tree
　　Save us all.

　　Save its trunk
　　And leafy dome
　　Save our tree
　　Save our home.

　　Can't you see
　　This tree
　　Has a history
　　Its own traditions
　　And laws
　　Can't you see
　　This tree
　　Is a community
　　A world as alive
　　As yours.

　　Save our tree
　　Please set it free
　　Save our tree
　　Let it be.

　　This tree's ours
　　But it's your tree too
　　Share it, care for it
　　The way we do.

　　Save our tree
　　Don't let it fall
　　Save our tree
　　Save us all.

*The singing stops.*

**Voice Two**    What's all this, then?

**Voice One**    Some sort of demo?

*Laughter.*

Clear off, the lot of you. Vermin, that's what you are. Dirty, stinking vermin. Go on, Charlie, do your worst.

*The noise of the chainsaw increases. Suddenly* **Owl** *leaps forward as though to attack. She is followed by* **Jay** *and* **Cuckoo**. *But in vain. They mime being beaten back.* **Mistlethrush** *screams. The noise of the chainsaw attacking wood. The cable swings. The tree folk look upwards. A branch crashes down from above. The tree folk huddle against the trunk.*

*(Optional: More branches crash down, hopefully identifiable –* **Bat**'s *'perch', part of* **Owl**'s *hollow,* **Mistlethrush**'s *nest.)*

*Light increases to suggest that the chainsaw is coming lower. The wretched tree folk cower and maybe scream, clinging on to each other for dear life.*

*Suddenly* **Rabbit** *breaks out. As though in a trance of defiance. He moves to the cable, grabs it and bites it.*

*A flash. The fuse has blown. The noise of the chainsaw cuts out.*

**Rabbit** *shudders with the force of the electricity, then crumples in a heap. The others look on aghast.* **Squirrel** *approaches* **Rabbit**, *puts his ear to* **Rabbit**'s *heart, then turns to the others and shakes his head.* **Rabbit** *is dead.*

*The tree folk sadly hum the tune of their 'Save Our Tree' song, backing away, holding hands. The lighting narrows to a pin-spot on* **Rabbit**. *The others melt into the background.*

**Rabbit** *stirs, gets up and begins to take off the rabbit parts of his costume. He becomes* **Mr Bunn** *again.*

**Mr Bunn**    Will Mistlethrush's eggs ever hatch? Will Cuckoo lay her egg in Mistlethrush's nest and fly back to Africa? Will Bat find another Battery Disco? Will Owl, Dunnock and Squirrel ever lead a normal life again? Will Jay find other trees on which to carry out his business? Who knows? It's all in the imagination, anyway. Just a story. Who cares? Well, I care. And perhaps it *could* happen. It *will* happen if Mr Jay and Mr Batty have their way, if they do as they want and clear Turner's Field for their children's playground.

**Mr Bunn** *has wandered to the side of the stage, still in his pin-spot, as the scene is changed back to the public platform in the village hall.*

*The other characters return to take their places as at the beginning of the play –* **Mrs Wise**, **Mrs Dunnock**, **Mr Storer**, **Mr Jay**, **Mr Batty**, **Mrs Cook** *and* **Mrs Thrush**.

**Mr Bunn**    So, I put it to the meeting. What right have we to kill the See-Saw Tree, a tree that has lived longer than any of us? It would take three minutes, with a chainsaw, to destroy the work of three hundred years. And jeopardise the lives of all its inhabitants. Animals, birds, insects. And for what? So that Mr Batty and Mr Jay can line their pockets with the pocket money of our children.

*The lighting comes up on the meeting, and in the auditorium.*

**Mr Jay**    Madam Chairman, I object to that. We are providing a much-needed amenity in this area, and all this sentimental twaddle is totally irrelevant.

**Mr Batty**    Hear, hear.

**Mrs Thrush**    Hear, hear. We want that playground.

**Mrs Cook**    I agree. You can't stop the wheels of change. It's called progress.

**Mrs Wise**    Thank you. Well, we've heard the arguments. Earlier your votes suggested a children's playground was a good idea. But, please, let's vote again, this time on whether Mr Jay and Mr Batty should be allowed to cut down the See-Saw Tree. Please raise your hands if you want it cut down.

**Mrs Dunnock** *counts hands. They include* **Mr Jay***,* **Mr Batty***,* **Mrs Thrush** *and* **Mrs Cook***.* **Mrs Dunnock** *gives the number 'for'.*

**Mrs Wise**    Now please raise your hands if you do *not* want the See-Saw Tree cut down.

*Hopefully the audience unanimously raise their hands.* **Mrs Dunnock** *starts to count.*

**Mrs Wise**    The result, I think, can be said to be unanimous. The See-Saw Tree must stay.

**Mr Bunn** *and others lead applause. (For alternative endings to suit any eventuality on the voting, see end of play.)*

**Mr Jay**    Now hang on a minute. Earlier on you said you wanted the children's playground. Now you say you want the See-Saw Tree. You can't have it both ways.

**Mr Storer**    I think, if I may be allowed to speak, Madam Chairman, we *can.*

**Mrs Wise**    Go ahead, Mr Storer.

**Mr Storer**    Of course Mr Jay should have his children's playground – it's an excellent idea. But why can't the See-Saw Tree be part of it? For the children, indeed for all of us, to see and enjoy.

**Mrs Dunnock**    And why shouldn't Mr Batty provide a plank and give the tree a see-saw, as in the old days. Then today's children can play on it.

**Mrs Wise**    Well, Mr Batty?

**Mr Batty**    Ah. Well, it's not as simple as that. All the plans'll have to be redrawn. That costs money.

**Mr Jay**    I think it's fair enough, Batty. You've still got your video games and fruit machines, and they've got their tree.

**Mr Batty**    Well . . . I suppose . . . it's quite a neat idea . . . (*Visualising a sign over the entrance to the playground*.) 'The See-Saw Tree Children's Playground' . . . it's good! Yes! OK, I agree!

*Applause, led by* **Mr Bunn**.

**Mrs Wise**    Good. Thank you all for coming. I declare the meeting closed. And I suggest a celebration. To celebrate the saving of . . .

**Mr Bunn**    The rebirth of . . .

**All**    THE SEE-SAW TREE!

*All happily sing and dance, encouraging the audience to join in each chorus.*

SONG: **The See-Saw Tree**

*An actor accompanies the song on guitar or piano (the piano could be part of the village hall set).*

**All**
> Sing the story of
> The See-Saw Tree
> Standing proud and free
> Such a sight to see.
> May we always share
> With the creatures living there
> The story of
> The glory of
> The See-Saw Tree.

*The verses could be sung by all in unison, or solo lines could be allocated if required.*

**All** (*or solos*)
> A long time ago a squirrel found
> An acorn and buried it in the ground
> Came the rain and the sun
> On the fertile earth
> And the story had begun
> With an oak tree's birth.

*Using a song-sheet, the actors encourage the audience to join in the chorus.*

**All** (+ *audience*)
> So
> Sing the story of
> The See-Saw Tree
> Standing proud and free
> Such a sight to see.
> May we always share
> With the creatures living there
> The story of

The glory of
The See-Saw Tree.

**All** (*or solos*)

As the seasons changed and the years went by
The oak tree flourished and soared up high
So its trunk and its branches
And its roots could give
The animals and birds
A place to live.

**All** (+ *audience*)

So
Sing the story of
The See-Saw Tree
Standing proud and free
Such a sight to see.
May we always share
With the creatures living there
The story of
The glory of
The See-Saw Tree.

**All** (*or solos*)

The tree looked down on the old high street
The local landmark, the place to meet.
And ev'ry May Day
It set the scene
For the singing and the dancing
On the village green.

**All** (+ *audience*)

So
Sing the story of
The See-Saw Tree
Standing proud and free
Such a sight to see.
May we always share
With the creatures living there
The story of
The glory of
The See-Saw Tree.

**All** (*or solos*)

A tree with a future, witness of the past
Steadfast and stable in a world changing fast
Let the sun shine down
Let the see-saw sway
Long live our tree

As the children play.

**All** (+ *audience*)
So
Sing the story of
The See-Saw Tree
Standing proud and free
Such a sight to see.
May we always share
With the creatures living there
The story of
The glory of
The See-Saw Tree.

May we always share
With the creatures living there
The story of the glory of
The glory of the story of
The story of the glory of
The See-Saw Tree.

*The characters freeze at the end of the song. We hear the creak of a see-saw. The lights slowly fade.*

*Curtain.*

## Alternative endings

*Endings to suit (hopefully) any eventuality.*

*Each ending starts from* **Mrs Wise**'s *invitation to vote* against *the cutting down of the tree.*

*(1) If the vast majority of the audience vote* against:

**Mrs Wise**   The result is virtually unanimous. The See-Saw Tree must stay. (*Etc. as before.*)

*(2) If the audience are divided, but clearly more are* against *than* for:

**Mrs Wise**   The majority are against. So the See-Saw Tree must stay. (*Etc. as before.*)

*(3) If voting looks even:*

**Mrs Wise**   We are divided. No clear majority.

**Mr Storer**   If I may be allowed to speak, Madam Chairman.

**Mrs Wise**   Go ahead, Mr Storer.

**Mr Storer**   We may be divided on whether or not to cut down the See-Saw Tree, but we all agree a children's playground is a good idea. Now, why can't the See-Saw Tree be part of the children's playground?

**Mrs Dunnock**    And why shouldn't Mr Batty . . . (*Etc. as before.*)

(4) *If all the audience vote* for *cutting down the tree (hopefully unlikely):*

**Mrs Wise**    Well, the meeting clearly decides to cut down the See-Saw Tree. Mr Jay, Mr Batty – you have your go-ahead.

**Mr Jay** *and* **Mr Batty** *shake hands, delighted.*

**Mrs Wise**    Thank you all for coming to the meeting. Good day.

*All collect their papers and leave.*

(*NB: The play would therefore finish* without *the song.*)

# The BFG – Teacher Notes

*The BFG* is just brilliant isn't it?! Staging this well-known production in school will create a real buzz for actors and audiences alike due its familiarity and amazing characters. The playful nature is really fun to act and the storytelling, with its 'play within a play' style, is a good introduction for students to drama or theatre for the first time, using props and set in inventive ways. More experienced performers can develop their skills with puppetry and there are great opportunities here for design activities making the Giants' masks and the unusual props like snozzcumbers!

**Age range:** KS2/3
**Number of actors:** 8–30+
**Running time:** Approx. 60 minutes

## Characters
The original production has eight actors doubling up on several roles. Depending on the group size this can be increased or even decreased. Look out for opportunities for extra parts to be added as other giants at the BFG's cave and more students in the classroom dream scene, both in Act One; or in Act Two, the Queen can have several assistants, not just Mary, and the lines can be shared. All of the characters can be played unisex with some basic adaptations.

Clearly, Sophie and the BFG are the most substantial parts, with most lines to learn, and the actor playing Sophie requiring some basic puppetry skills (see activities). A simple doll can be used for Sophie to manipulate; to introduce this idea the actor could pick up a doll and say: 'This is Sophie! I'm Sophie, too!'

The BFG can be a normal-sized person, using movement and vocal skills, but to get the contrast in size I think the puppet or doll for Sophie is important. Make Sophie small not the Giant big, though you may wish to cast an adult or even a teacher to play the BFG!

When using a puppet it is important that actors fix their focus on the puppet, and not the other actor as the puppet 'speaks'.

## Costumes and props
Dressing all actors in one neutral colour, and then using one well-chosen piece of costume to represent each character may be suited to a school production – and will add to the storytelling nature of the piece. All the costume bits can be set on stage in a 'toy box' or 'clothes rail' in Sophie's playroom and taken on and off throughout the play. For example, an actor with a waistcoat becomes the BFG, a red scarf for Guy, a pair of glasses as Sophie, a crown for the Queen. Do not underestimate the power of movement, body language and accent, though, to differentiate character. The BFG should have a way of moving that makes him instantly recognisable throughout, rather than finding elaborate ways to make him physically enormous; so too the Queen does not need full regalia, but rather a decent accent and simply a crown, perhaps. In the scene at the Palace, you could imagine the BFG is offstage, and everyone looks up and off when

they speak to him, but for surprise effect a large cut-out BFG head on a long pole to appear at a window will look great for the final scene.

**Staging**

The action takes place in three locations: Sophie's playroom, the BFG's cave and Buckingham Palace, all of which can be re-created simply by the props in the playroom. Other spare actors can be used to move any set between scenes. A large picture or cardboard frame can be held to represent Sophie's window, while a dark sheet draped high across two hat stands makes a children's den in the playroom that then doubles up as the BFG's cave in the next scene. A red blanket becomes a red carpet, an upturned toy box the Queen's dinner table. It is reasonable to stage the dinner with the Queen as breakfast in bed to avoid a scene change or to have the Queen wake from her dream as though she had dozed off in a chair rather than in bed. In the script there is a raised platform at the back, upstage; this would be useful but not essential. With limited space there are several opportunities to act in the audience instead; for example, where the Giants are seen eating the children.

**Special props**

There are a number of special props that would be purpose made in a professional production – namely the BFG's suitcase, dream-blowing horn and the snozzcumbers – and these, along with the nasty Giants' masks (see activities), can be made as a part of a creative project in class if they are to be used.

Making the unusual props will enhance the otherworldly fun here but bear in mind that almost all the props can be represented by something else. The dream horn can be a hockey stick from the playroom, the dream jars empty shampoo bottles with watery shampoo in, the Queen's tea tray can be shown by using a pillow held reverentially or a board-game box.

**Music, sound effects and lighting**

If you have a musician, there is notation available on request, but all the scenes work fine without. All the special effects can be created by actors in the chorus, in the same way David has written 'an owl hooting noise' in the first scene. The other actors can create fanfares, wind, dramatic music or any other sounds that are needed, just using their voices. I feel there is much fun to be had re-creating the whizzpoppers!

**Lesson plan – Physical theatre monsters**

Working in a clear space:

*Starter activity*

Physical warm-up using 'Stop/Go/Clap/Jump'. Students find space in the room and follow the teacher's instructions. When 'Go' is called they move around individually; on 'Stop' they freeze. Add in 'Clap' and 'Jump'. After a while reverse the instructions so the opposite applies; for example, 'Go' means 'Stop'. You can add other instructions related to the play such as; 'BFG' or 'Queen' where students must freeze in an image of these characters.

Alternatively you can play Blind Man's Buff or Grandma's Footsteps as the children do in the story.

*Engaging*
Group the students into pairs, and set them the challenge of using just their bodies, arms and legs to create different shapes. A triangle, the letter 'H', the number '3', the letters 'B – F – G' perhaps. Give students 30 seconds to make each one.

*Developing*
Introduce the concept of storytelling theatre, where the actors perform a story using a limited set, props and costumes. One way to re-create things in drama is to use our bodies to make objects; we call this physical theatre or body as prop.

For the next activities again give the students a short amount of time to work, then share back half the class at a time. Take feedback on imaginative ideas.

In groups of around four or five challenge the students to make a cave, a window, a doll's house, a bed or anything else from the play.

*Developing*
Encourage the students to add movements and sounds to the next creations, a washing machine, a church, a windmill. They also appoint one group member to step out of the creation and narrate the features, such as the different speeds of the washing machine or the beautiful bells of the church.

Explain the main features of physical theatre are:

Imaginative ideas
Clear, exaggerated actions
Facial expressions
Sounds and movements

*Main task*
In groups the students should create their own ugly strange creature. It can be anything they like, with as many heads or feet as they wish. It should move and make noises. Again, they should have a narrator who tells us about the creature, its name, habitat, what food it eats and any notable features. Encourage the children to make up words for this, giving examples from *The BFG* as inspiration. This can be a follow-up writing/drawing task too.

**Other activities**

*Using props inventively*
The play-within-a-play storytelling style of *The BFG* allows director and actors to be playful and inventive with set and props. Here is a simple exercise to develop ideas for multi-use of props.

As a whole group take an everyday object and pass it a round the circle demonstrating different uses for the prop; for example, a sweeping brush becomes a fishing rod, a microphone, a walking stick, a metal detector. Actors should make a short mime and introduce: 'This is a . . .'

To develop this idea, in small groups actors are to create a short scene using one prop in as many different ways as they can. Suggested objects are a sheet of fabric, a suitcase, a chair, two hula hoops, etc.

Challenge the students to create some of the unusual props from the play using everyday items. For example, how might you represent a snozzcumber or a dream horn?

*Puppetry basics*

Watch the National Theatre YouTube tutorial on making basic brown paper puppets and have students play with making characters by experimenting how the puppets move and sit.

Using a doll, a shirt or a suit jacket as a puppet works too, where one person holds the neck and one arm and another person holds the lower back and another arm. Even sock puppets or balloons on a stick can be presented as characters.

Develop this idea by giving students a scene from the play to re-create using puppetry, or students could use devised narration to introduce the character(s). You could use puppetry to look into other famous stories too; perhaps re-creating Miss Trunchbull or the Iron Man.

*Mask making*

Of all the costumes and props arguably the most fun to produce are the nasty Giants' masks. They can be made in 2-D with card and colours or in 3-D with papier-mâché. Either way they will work best when mounted on a bicycle helmet or similar so the actors can move and speak freely while wearing them.

# The BFG

**Roald Dahl**

**adapted by David Wood**

By a sad coincidence, Mr Roald Dahl died while this play was being written. It is dedicated to him with great respect and admiration.

The BFG was first performed at Wimbledon Theatre on 19 February 1991 and on tour, followed by a West End season for Christmas at the Aldwych Theatre. The play was presented by James Woods and Justin Savage for Clarion Productions, and by Robert Cogo-Fawcett for Lyric Hammersmith Productions, by arrangement with Theatre Royal Presentations plc, with the following cast:

**Dad/BFG**                                        Anthony Pedley
**Mum/Childchewer/**
**Miss Plumridge/**
**Queen of England**                            Mary-Ann Coburn
**Sophie**                                           Fiona Grogan
**Guy (Sophie's brother)/**
**Bonecruncher/**
**Headmaster/Mr Tibbs**                         Adrian Phillips
**Daniel (Sophie's friend)/**
**Fleshlumpeater/Classmate/**
**Ronald Simkins/Head of the Army**        David Burrows
**Sam (Sophie's friend)/**
**Bloodbottler/Classmate/**
**Sam Simkins/Head of the Air Force**       Adam Stafford
**Katherine (Sophie's friend)/**
**Meatdripper/Classmate/Mary**               Janet Cost-Chrétien
**Rebecca (Sophie's friend)/**
**Gizzardgulper/Rebecca (dreamer)/**
**Undermaid/Queen of Sweden**               Josephine Baird

*Directed by* David Wood
*Designed by* Susie Caulcutt
*Lighting design by* Simon Courtenay-Taylor
*Movement by* Sheila Falconer
*Musical composition and supervision by* Peter Pontzen

The action of the play starts in Sophie's attic playroom/bedroom and moves to the BFG's cave in Giant Country, Dream Country and Buckingham Palace.

# Act One

**Sophie***'s attic playroom/bedroom.*

*This is an exciting space with colourful toys and books on shelves, a rocking horse, a doll's house, a toy grand piano, musical instruments including a trumpet/horn, a fishing net, a puppet booth, toy helicopters, a suitcase, a dressing-up chest, plus a rail of dressing-up clothes and masks, wigs, crown, etc. and cuddly toys. There is also a chest of drawers, a grandfather clock,* **Sophie***'s bed, a door to the landing and perhaps a door to a cupboard. A major feature of the room is a large studio window with curtains, in front of which is a platform, which can be used as a thrust stage. Small staircases lead up to it. Chairs have been placed to one side to give space for* **Sophie***'s birthday party.*

*As the curtain rises this is in full swing. A banner proclaims 'Happy Birthday, Sophie'. Hastily unwrapped presents lie around.*

**Sophie** *and her friends,* **Daniel**, **Katherine**, **Rebecca** *and* **Sam**, *are playing blind man's buff.* **Daniel** *is blindfolded and advances, arms outstretched, towards the others, who circle him. They giggle and shriek as he makes a few near-miss grabs. Eventually he grabs* **Sophie**, *who screams with delight.*

**Daniel**   Gotcha! Now who have we got here?

**Sophie** (*in a deep voice*)   It's me. Sam!

*Laughter.*

**Daniel**   No it's not. It's . . . Sophie!

*Laughter and applause.* **Daniel** *takes off the blindfold.*

**Sophie**   Very good, Danny. Now, let's play Grandmother's Footsteps!

**Rebecca**   Bags be Grandmother.

**Sophie**   Right. Becky's Grandmother.

**Rebecca** *turns her back as the others stand in a line.*

**Rebecca**   Ready.

**Sam**   No peeping.

*They advance on tiptoe.* **Rebecca** *suddenly turns, but can't catch anyone moving. Another go. This time she catches* **Daniel** *moving.*

**Rebecca**   Danny.

**Daniel** *goes back to the 'start'.* **Rebecca** *turns her back again. All advance towards her.* **Katherine** *rushes to* **Rebecca** *and taps her on the back.*

**Rebecca** (*with a jump*)   Katherine!

**Katherine**   OK. My turn.

*She takes* **Rebecca**'s *place. The others go back in line and the game starts again.*

*Suddenly loud, booming footsteps echo from outside.*

*All freeze in fright.*

**Katherine**   What's that?

**Daniel**   A very fat grandmother!

*They laugh nervously.*

*Suddenly a voice booms from outside.*

**Guy** (*off*)   Fee, fi, fo, fum. I'm coming to gobble you up!

*The children scream and cluster in a group watching the door, which bursts open.*

**Guy** *enters.*

**Guy**   It's only me! Fooled you!

**Sophie**   Guy! It's Guy, everyone, my boring big brother.

*All relax.*

**Guy**   Hi, everyone. Happy birthday, Sophie.

*He produces a present from behind his back.*

**Sophie** (*opening it*)   Thanks. (*Finding a book:* The BFG.) Hey! *The BFG*! My favourite book! I've borrowed it from the library three times!

**Guy**   You've got your very own copy now!

**Rebecca**   What's it about?

**Sophie**   A huge giant.

**Guy** (*advancing on the group*)   Fee, fi, fo, fum!

**Sophie**   Shut up, Guy. And thanks!

**Mum** *and* **Dad** *enter, rather flustered.*

**Mum**   Hallo, everyone.

**All**   Hallo.

**Sophie**   Look what Guy's given me, Mum.

**Mum** (*not really noticing*)   Lovely, Sophie. Now, listen, everyone. I don't know quite how to tell you, but . . .

**Dad**   You see, for Sophie's party we booked an entertainer . . .

*The children cheer.*

No, no, listen. He's just phoned to say he's very sorry but he's been taken ill. A tummy bug or something.

**Mum**   So . . . no entertainer. Sorry, folks.

*Silence.*

**Guy**   Oh, come on, kids, it's not that bad. We'll just have to make our *own* entertainment.

**Sophie** (*suddenly*)   I know! We'll do *The BFG*!

**Dad**   Do the what?

**Sophie**   Tell the story. Act it out! Please! We've got the dressing-up box. I'll be Sophie, the girl in the story. (*To the children.*) You can all be giants. Guy can be Fleshlumpeater.

*The children all rush excitedly to the dressing-up box.*

**Dad**   Well, that's settled then. Have fun!

*He and **Mum** start to go.*

**Sophie** (*stopping him*)   Dad, you can't go. You're the BFG!

**Dad**   Me?

**Sophie**   You. And there's a great part for Mum later.

**Mum**   Really?

**Dad**   All right, then.

*The children cheer.*

We'd better get ready.

**Mum** *and* **Dad** *join the children preparing, finding props and bits of costume.* **Sophie** *finds her nightie under her pillow, plus a 'Sophie' doll.*

**Sophie** (*putting her nightie on over her other clothes*)   Stand by, everyone. Music! Lights!

*One of the children tinkles on the toy grand piano. Eventually the musical director takes over. Another child lowers the lights.*

(*Announcing.*) The BFG!

*Holding a toy trumpet, one of the children sounds a loud fanfare.*

(*Starting the story.*) It was late at night . . .

*Someone makes an owl hooting noise.*

. . . in the orphanage.

**Sophie** *looks around and sees the doll's house. She motions to* **Guy**, *who places it in a prominent position. From now on, the cast 'makes the story happen', improvising props, setting up scenes and also acting as an audience.*

**Sophie**   In the dormitory. Sophie couldn't sleep. (*She opens the doll's house and places the 'Sophie' doll inside.*) A brilliant moonbeam was shining right on to her pillow.

*Someone shines a torch on the doll's house.*

She slipped out of bed to get a drink of water.

**Mum** (*a voice from the darkness*)   Sophie! Back to bed this instant. You know the rules.

**Sophie**   Mrs Clonkers. Sophie went back to bed. She tried very hard to doze off. The time ticked by. The house was absolutely silent. Perhaps, thought Sophie, this is what they call the witching hour, that special moment in the middle of the night when everyone is in a deep, deep sleep, and all the dark things come out from hiding and have the world to themselves. She crept to the window. And suddenly she saw . . . a giant!

*Sinister music as **Dad**, in a cloak and carrying a suitcase, appears as the **BFG**. He looms over the doll's house, then proceeds to another part of the room, acting out the narration.*

**Sophie**   He stopped at the house opposite, bent down to look in a bedroom window and then . . .

*The **BFG** opens his suitcase, takes out a jar and pours its contents into the end of a horn-like trumpet. Then he blows through it into the imaginary window. He replaces the jar and trumpet in his case. He turns towards the doll's house.*

**Sophie** (*with a gasp*)   He saw Sophie. She pulled back from the window, flew across the dormitory and jumped into her bed and hid under the blanket, tingling all over.

*The **BFG** approaches the doll's house as the music intensifies. He peeps in the window, and, with a growl, pushes his hand through the window and snatches the 'Sophie' doll.*

**Sophie**   Aaaaaaaah!

*The **BFG** tucks the 'Sophie' doll inside his cloak and goes up on to the platform stage.*

*The curtains are drawn, revealing the window. The area is suddenly filled with back light, in which the **BFG** begins slow-motion, on-the-spot, running.*

*A howling wind blows.*

**Actors**   Running, striding, leaping through the night. Over fields, over hedges, over rivers, each stride as long as a tennis court. Faster, faster, feet scarcely touching the ground. Over oceans, over forests, over mountains. To a land unknown to human beings.

*The **BFG** slows down and walks off the platform stage. The curtains close and the lighting fades.*

**Sophie** *swings round a wall of bookshelves or a wardrobe to reveal the **BFG**'s cave with a rough-hewn table and stool and shelves covered with a sack-cloth curtain.*

*The* **BFG** *enters the cave, puts down his suitcase, removes his cloak, then carefully brings out the 'Sophie' doll. He puts it on the table.*

**Sophie** *enters the scene and manipulates the doll like a puppet, while providing* **Sophie***'s voice.*

**BFG**    Ha! What has us got here?

*He looks carefully at* **Sophie***. At first he should not appear to be very friendly.*

**Sophie** (*nervously*)    Where am I?

**BFG**    This is my cave.

**Sophie**    Why did you snatch me and bring me here?

**BFG**    Because you *saw* me. If anyone is ever *seeing* a giant, he or she must be taken away hipswitch.

**Sophie**    Why?

**BFG**    Human beans is not believing in giants, is they? Human beans is not thinking giants exist.

**Sophie**    I do.

**BFG**    Ah, but that is because you has *seen* me. If I hadn't snitched you, you would be scuddling around yodelling the news on the telly-telly bunkum box that you were actually *seeing* a giant, and then a great giant-hunt, a mighty giant look-see would be starting up all over the world, and human beans would be trying to catch me and put me in the zoo with all those squiggling hippodumplings and crocadowndillies.

**Sophie**    So what's going to happen to me now?

**BFG**    You will just have to be staying here with me for the rest of your life.

**Sophie**    Oh no!

**BFG**    Oh yes! Now, I is hungry!

**Sophie** (*gasping*)    Please don't eat *me*!

**BFG** (*bellowing with laughter*)    Just because I is a giant, you think I is a man-gobbling cannybull! No!

**Sophie**    Oh, good.

**BFG**    Yes, you is lucky. If one of the *other* giants is snitching you, they is crunching you up for sure. In one scrumdiddlyumptious mouthful. Bones crackety-crackety-cracking. Gobble, gobbledy, gone!

**Sophie**    Other giants? You mean there are more of you?

**BFG**    Of course! This is Giant Country! (*He picks up the 'Sophie' doll.*) Be peeping out over there, little girl, and be seeing a brain-bogglingsome sight.

*He carries her to the cave entrance.*

*Lights come up on the platfom stage, where the other* **Giants** *appear (***Mum**, **Guy**, **Katherine**, **Daniel**, **Rebecca** *and* **Sam** *wearing giant headdresses).*

*The* **Giants** *lumber about, looking menacing and hungry, grunting and occasionally threatening one another. They make themselves identifiable as the* **BFG** *mentions them.*

**Sophie**    Gosh!

**BFG**    Is you believing your gogglers?

**Sophie**    What on earth are they doing?

**BFG**    Nothing. They is just moocheling and footcheling around and waiting for the night to come. Then they will be galloping off to places where human beans is living to find their suppers.

**Sophie**    Where?

**BFG**    All over the world.

**Bonecruncher**    I is fancying a gallop to Turkey to guzzle some tasty Turks.

**BFG**    That's the Bonecruncher. He is thinking Turkish human beans is juiciest beans. They is tasting of . . .

**Sophie**    Turkey?

**BFG**    No! Turkish delight!

**Sophie**    Of course. Who's that big, fierce one?

**BFG**    That's the Fleshlumpeater.

**Fleshlumpeater**    I is fancying getting my chompers round a handful of human beans from Wellington!

**Sophie**    Where's Wellington?

**BFG**    Your head is full of squashed flies. Wellington is in New Zealand.

**Sophie**    What do people in Wellington taste of?

**BFG**    Boots, of course.

**Sophie**    But boots taste horrid.

**BFG**    Rubbsquash! Boots taste bootiful!

**Sophie**    Ha ha.

**Bloodbottler**    I could be murdering some human beans from England!

**Sophie**    England?

**BFG**    That's the Bloodbottler. He is thinking the English is tasting ever so wonderfully of crodscollop.

**Sophie**    I'm not sure I know what that means.

**BFG**    Meanings is not important. I cannot be right all the time. Quite often I is left instead of right.

*A row breaks out among the* **Giants**. *They grunt and push, arguing about where to go.*

**BFG**    Let's go back. You will be coming to an ucky-mucky end if any of them should ever be getting his gogglers upon you. You would be swallowed up like a piece of frumpkin pie, all in one dollop.

*They return inside the cave.*

*The lights dim on the* **Giants** *and they exit.*

**BFG**    There. You is safe in here.

**Sophie**    I think eating people is horrible.

**BFG**    I has told you. *I* is not eating people. Not I! I is a freaky giant! I is a nice and jumbly giant! I is the BFG!

**Sophie**    The BFG?

**BFG**    The Big Friendly Giant! What is *your* name?

**Sophie**    My name is Sophie.

**BFG**    How is you doing, Sophie. (*He shakes hands with the doll.*) Is you quite snuggly in your nightie, Sophie? You isn't fridgy cold?

**Sophie**    I'm fine.

**BFG**    I cannot help thinking about your poor mother and father. By now they must be jipping and skumping all over the house shouting, 'Hallo, hallo, where is Sophie gone?'

**Sophie**    I don't have a mother and father. They died when I was a baby.

**BFG**    You is a norphan?

**Sophie**    Yes.

**BFG**    Oh you poor little scrumplet. You is making me sad.

**Sophie**    Don't be sad. No one at the orphanage will be worrying much about me.

**BFG**    Was you happy there?

**Sophie**    I hated it. Mrs Clonkers locked me in the cellar once.

**BFG**    Why?

**Sophie**    For not folding up my clothes.

**BFG**    The rotten old rotrasper!

**Sophie**    It was horrid. There were rats down there.

**BFG**    The filthy old fizzwiggler! You is making me sadder than ever. (*He sobs.*)

**Sophie**    Don't cry, BFG. Please. Listen, tell me – if you don't eat humans, what *do* you eat?

**BFG** (*pulling himself together*)    That, little Sophie, is a squelching tricky problem. In this sloshflunking Giant Country, happy eats like pineapples and pigwinkles is simply not growing. Nothing is growing except for one extremely icky-poo vegetable. It is called the snozzcumber.

**Sophie**    The snoozzcumber? There's no such thing.

**BFG**    Is you calling me a fibster?

**Sophie**    Well . . .

**BFG** (*getting cross*)    Just because you has not *seen* something isn't meaning it isn't existing. What about the great squizzly scotch-hopper?

**Sophie**    I beg your pardon?

**BFG**    And the humplecrimp?

**Sophie**    What's that?

**BFG**    And the wraprascal? And the crumpscoddle?

**Sophie**    Are they animals?

**BFG**    They is *common* animals. Swipe my swoggles! I is not a very know-all giant myself, but it seems to me you is an absolutely know-nothing human bean. Your brain is full of rotten-wool.

**Sophie**    You mean cotton-wool.

**BFG** (*grandly*)    What I mean and what I say is two different things. (*He stands.*) I will now show you the repulsant snozzcumber.

*The **BFG** finds a huge black and white striped, knobbly, cucumber-shaped vegetable, rather like a giant's club.*

**Sophie**    Gosh. It doesn't look very tasty.

**BFG**    It's disgusterous! It's sickable! It's maggot-wise! (*He breaks it in two.*) Try some.

**Sophie**    Pooh! No, thank you.

**BFG**    There's nothing else to guzzle. Have a go.

*The 'Sophie' doll nibbles some.*

**Sophie**    Uggggggh! Oh no! It tastes of frogskins. And rotten fish.

**BFG** (*roaring with laughter*)    Worse than that! To me it is tasting of clockcoaches and slimewanglers.

**Sophie**  Do I really have to eat it?

**BFG**  Unless you is wanting to become so thin you will be disappearing into a thick ear.

**Sophie**  Into *thin air*. A thick ear is something quite different.

**BFG** (*going to answer back, but checking himself*)  Words is oh such a twitch-tickling problem to me. I know exactly what words I is wanting to say, but somehow they come out all squiff-squiddly.

**Sophie**  That happens to everyone.

**BFG** (*sadly*)  Not like it happens to me. I is speaking the most terrible wigglish.

**Sophie**  I think you speak beautifully.

**BFG** (*brightening*)  You do? You is not twiddling my leg?

**Sophie**  No. I love the way you talk.

**BFG**  How wondercrump. How whoopsey-splunkers. Thank you, Sophie.

*Sudden thumping and shouting interrupts them.*

**Bloodbottler** (*off*)  Runt! Runt?

**Fleshlumpeater** (*off*)  What is you up to, runt?

**BFG**  Quick, Sophie, hide.

**Sophie** (*narrating as she hides the 'Sophie' doll behind the snozzcumber on the table*)  Sophie hid behind the snozzcumber.

**Bloodbottler** and **Fleshlumpeater** *enter.*

**Bloodbottler**  Aha!

**Fleshlumpeater**  Aha!

*They stand threateningly over the* **BFG**, *who sits at the table trying to look calm.*

**BFG**  Hallo, Bloodbottler. Good day, Fleshlumpeater.

**Bloodbottler**  Don't hallo good day us, runt.

**Fleshlumpeater**  We is hearing you jabbeling.

**Bloodbottler/Fleshlumpeater**  Who is you jabbeling to, runt?

**BFG**  I is jabbeling to myself.

**Bloodbottler**  Pifflefizz!

**Fleshlumpeater/Bloodbottler**  You is talking to a human bean!

**BFG**  No, no!

**Bloodbottler**    Yus!

**Fleshlumpeater**    Yus!

**Bloodbottler**    We is guessing you has snitched away a human bean and brought it back to you bunghole as a pet!

**Fleshlumpeater**    So now we is winkling it out and guzzling it as extra snacks before supper!

*They start sniffing and searching. The* **BFG** *tries to conceal* **Sophie**.

**BFG** (*nervously*)    There's no one here. Why don't you leave me alone?

**Bloodbottler** (*threateningly*)    Piffling little swishfiggler!

**Fleshlumpeater**    Squimpy little pogswizzler!

**Bloodbottler/Fleshlumpeater** (*sniffing and searching*) Where is it? Where is it?

*They freeze.*

**Sophie** (*narrating, and manipulating the doll*)    Terrified, Sophie scooped out some slimy snozzcumber seeds and, unseen by the BFG, crawled inside the pongy vegetable.

**Bloodbottler** *and* **Fleshlumpeater** *see the snozzcumber.*

**Bloodbottler**    So this is the filthing rotsome clubbage you is eating!

**Fleshlumpeater**    You must be cockles to be guzzling such rubbsquash!

**BFG**    Snozzcumbers is scrumdiddlyumptious.

**Bloodbottler**    Human beans is juicier.

**BFG**    Try some. It's glumptious.

**Fleshlumpeater**    You is not switchfiddling us, is you?

**BFG**    Never. Vegitibbles is very good for you.

**Bloodbottler**    Mmm. Just this once we is going to taste these rotsome eats of yours.

**Fleshlumpeater**    But if it is filthsome, we is smashing it over your sludgy little head!

*They each pick up half the snozzcumber. Music as the action goes into slow-motion.*

**Sophie** (*narrating*)    Sophie felt herself being lifted up and up and up. She clung on desperately to stop herself falling out.

**Bloodbottler** *and* **Fleshlumpeater** *mime taking a bite.*

**Sophie**    Suddenly there was a crunch as the Bloodbottler bit a huge hunk off the end. Sophie saw his yellow teeth clamping together. Then, utter darkness. She was in his mouth. Terrified, she waited for the next crunch . . .

*In slow motion,* **Bloodbottler** *and* **Fleshlumpeater** *splutter with the horrible taste.*

**Bloodbottler**    Eeeeeowtch!

**Fleshlumpeater**    Ughbwelch!

*They spit.*

**Sophie** (*narrating*)    All the great lumps of snozzcumber, as well as Sophie herself, went shooting out across the cave.

*She manipulates the 'Sophie' doll, slowly wheeling it in an arc from the* **Bloodbottler**'s *mouth to the floor.*

**Bloodbottler** *and* **Fleshlumpeater** *snap out of slow-motion.*

**Bloodbottler**    You little swinebuggler!

**Fleshlumpeater**    You little pigswiller!

**Bloodbottler/Fleshlumpeater**    It's disgusterous!

*They hit the* **BFG** *on the head with the snozzcumber halves.*

**BFG** (*rubbing his head*)    You is not loving it?

**Bloodbottler**    You must be buggles to be swalloping slutch like that!

**Fleshlumpeater**    Every night you could be galloping off happy as a hamburger and gobbling juicy human beans.

**BFG**    Eating human beans is wrong and evil. You is revoltant!

**Bloodbottler**    And you is an insult to the giant peoples! You is not fit to be a giant!

**Fleshlumpeater**    You is a pibbling pitsqueak! You is a . . . a . . . a cream puffnut!

**Bloodbottler** *and* **Fleshlumpeater** *exit, bellowing.*

*The* **BFG** *checks they have gone.*

**BFG** (*whispering*)    Sophie! Where is you, Sophie?

**Sophie**    I'm here.

*The* **BFG** *finds the 'Sophie' doll on the floor and tenderly picks her up.*

**BFG**    Oh, I is so happy to be finding you all in one lump.

**Sophie**    I was in the Bloodbottler's mouth!

**BFG**    What?

**Sophie**    I hid in the snoozzcumber.

**BFG**    And I was telling him to eat it! You poor little chiddler, forgive me. Oho! You is needing some frobscottle to make you better.

*He brings the 'Sophie' doll to the table.*

**Sophie**    Frobscottle?

**BFG**    Frobscottle. (*He proudly finds a bottle of green liquid.*) I drink it lots. Delumptious, fizzy frobscottle.

*He removes the stopper. There is a fizzing sound. Bubbles are seen going downwards.*

**Sophie**    Hey, look! It's fizzing the wrong way!

**BFG**    What is you meaning?

**Sophie**    Downwards. In our fizzy drinks, like Coke and Pepsi, the bubbles go upwards.

**BFG**    Flushbunking rubbsquash!

**Sophie**    They do!

**BFG**    Upwards is the wrong way.

**Sophie**    Why?

**BFG**    If you is not seeing why, you must be as quacky as a duckhound! Upgoing bubbles is a catasterous disastrophe.

**Sophie**    But why?

**BFG**    Listen. When you is drinking this cokey drink of yours, it is going straight down into your tummy. Is that right? Or is it left?

**Sophie**    It's right.

**BFG**    And the *bubbles* is going also into your tummy. Right or left?

**Sophie**    Right again.

**BFG**    If the bubbles is fizzing upwards, they will all come swishwiffling up your throat and out of your mouth and make a foulsome belchy burp!

**Sophie**    That's often true. But what's wrong with a little burp now and again? It's sort of fun.

**BFG**    Burping is filthsome. Us giants is never doing it.

**Sophie**    But with *your* drink . . .

**BFG**    Frobscottle.

**Sophie**    With frobscottle, the bubbles in your tummy will be going *downwards* and that could have a far nastier result.

**BFG**    Why nasty?

**Sophie**    Because they'll be coming out somewhere else with an even louder and ruder noise.

**BFG**    A whizzpopper! Us giants is making whizzpoppers all the time! Whizzpopping is a sign of happiness. It is music in our ears!

**Sophie**   But it's . . . it's rude!

**BFG**   But you is whizzpopping, is you not, now and again?

**Sophie**   Everyone is . . . whizzpopping. Kings and queens, film stars, even little babies. But where I come from, it's not polite to talk about it.

**BFG**   Redunculous! If everyone is making whizzpoppers, then why not talk about it? Now, let's be having a swiggle and seeing the result!

*The* **BFG** *drinks from the bottle. Pause. Then ecstasy fills his face. A very loud whizzpopper nearly shoots him in the air.*

Whoopee!

*And another.*

Wheeee!

*And another.*

Wheeeeeeee!

**Sophie** *laughs, in spite of herself.*

**BFG**   Have some yourself.

**Sophie**   Well. . .

**BFG**   Go on. It's gloriumptious!

*He holds the bottle to the 'Sophie' doll's mouth. Pause.*

**Sophie**   It's lovely.

**BFG**   Just wait!

*Suddenly a whizzpopper propels the 'Sophie' doll into the air. Then a succession of whizzpoppers send her somersaulting up and over, over and up.*

**Sophie**   Wheeee! Wheeeeee!

*The* **BFG** *roars with laughter.*

*Eventually both settle, the 'Sophie' doll in the* **BFG**'s *arms. Night-time music as the lights fade.*

**BFG** (*yawning*)   Time for a snoozy sleep. Goodnight, Sophie.

**Sophie** (*sleepily*)   That was fun. Goodnight, BFG.

*The lights fade.*

*Elsewhere, dim lighting fades up on the other* **Giants** *entering.*

**Fleshlumpeater**   'Tis the witchy hour!

*The others grunt their agreement and all begin a kind of war-dance. Suddenly they all freeze.*

**Meatdripper**    'Tis time for supper!

*All excitedly agree and lumber round again. They suddenly stop.*

**Bloodbottler**    Human beans . . .

**All**    Here we come!

*There is a strobe-type lighting effect and exciting music as the* **Giants** *run towards the audience, pounding along on the spot. Eventually they stop and the lights change as they menacingly look about them, hungrily sniffing. Suddenly, with a whoop, they swoop on dolls on* **Sophie**'*s bed, and savagely mime eating them. Having gorged themselves, they happily return to their former positions on the platform stage, and, as though in a drunken stupor, start snoring.*

*Music suggests time passing.*

*The lights fade down on the* **Giants***, then slowly up as dawn breaks in the cave.*

*The* **BFG** *wakes, carefully puts the sleeping 'Sophie' doll on the table, and moves to his shelves. He quietly draws the sack-cloth curtain, revealing rows and rows of glass jars, all magically flickering with different coloured lights. He puts three empty jars in his suitcase, closes it, then puts on his cloak. He picks up his fishing net and starts to tip-toe from the cave.*

*Suddenly the 'Sophie' doll wakes up.*

**Sophie**    BFG?

**BFG** (*stopping*)    Yes.

**Sophie**    Where are you going?

**BFG**    I is going to work?

**Sophie**    Back where I live? Blowing your trumpet thing?

**BFG** (*shocked*)    You is seeing me blowing?

**Sophie**    Yes. What were you doing?

**BFG**    Is I trusting you?

**Sophie**    Of course.

**BFG**    Well, then. I, Sophie, is a dream-blowing giant. I blows dreams into the bedrooms of sleeping chiddlers. Nice dreams. Lovely golden dreams. Dreams that is giving the dreamers a happy time.

**Sophie**    Gosh.

**BFG**    See these jars? I is keeping the dreams in them.

*He carries the 'Sophie' doll to look.*

**Sophie**    These are all dreams? But where do you get them?

**BFG**    I collect them.

**Sophie**   Collect them? That's impossible.

**BFG**   You isn't believing in dreams?

**Sophie**   Well, of course, but . . .

**BFG**   Listen. Dreams is very mysterious things. They is floating around in the air, like wispy misty bubbles, searching for sleeping people. Come on. I is showing you. You is coming dream-collecting with me!

**Sophie** (*loudly*)   Really? Yes, please!

**BFG**   Shhh! Hold your breaths and cross your figglers. Here we go!

*He tucks the 'Sophie' doll in his cloak, and sets off from the cave. The 'shelves door' is closed by* **Sophie***, who then observes the action.*

*The lights come up on the platform stage, where the other* **Giants** *are still snoring.*

*The* **BFG** *creeps past them, treading carefully between their sprawled limbs. Just as we think he has negotiated them:*

**Fleshlumpeater**   Ho-ho there, runt!

**Bloodbottler**   Ho-ho there, little grobsquiffler!

**BFG** (*trying to be casual*)   Ho-ho there, has you had a good feasting?

*The other* **Giants** *are waking.*

**Fleshlumpeater**   We has had a glumptious gorging!

**Bloodbottler**   In Sweden!

**Bonecruncher**   We is liking the Sweden sour taste!

*The* **Giants** *laugh.*

**Fleshlumpeater**   Where is you going, runty one?

*He grabs the* **BFG** *(on stage level) from above.*

**Bloodbottler**   Where is you splatch-winkling away to?

*He too grabs the* **BFG***.*

**BFG** (*nervously*)   Be so kind as to be letting go.

*The other* **Giants** *advance.*

**Bonecruncher**   Let's be having him!

**Fleshlumpeater**   To you, Bonecruncher!

*He pushes him towards* **Bonecruncher***. The* **Giants** *roughly push him one to another.*

**Bonecruncher**   To you, Meatdripper!

**Meatdripper**   To you, Gizzardgulper!

**Gizzardgulper**   To you, Childchewer!

**Childchewer**   To you, Bonecruncher!

*They laugh as the* **BFG**, *feverishly hanging on to his suitcase and fishing net, and, of course, the 'Sophie' doll, is shoved to and fro.*

**Sophie** (*narrating*)   Inside the BFG's cloak, Sophie clung on for dear life. At last the other giants tired of their game.

**Fleshlumpeater**   Run away, little runt!

*Stunned, the* **BFG** *starts to stagger away.*

**Bloodbottler**   Troggy little twit!

**Bonecruncher**   Shrivelly little shrimp!

**Meatdripper**   Mucky little midget!

**Gizzardgulper**   Squaggy little squib.

**Childchewer**   Grobby little grub!

*Laughing, they retire.*

*The* **BFG** *checks the 'Sophie' doll is all right under his cloak, then escapes through the door.*

*There is music and the sound of a whistling wind as swirls of mist envelop the stage. Coloured lights glow and dance on the smoke. Eventually:*

**Sophie** (*plus optional offstage echoes; narrating*)   The BFG, clutching Sophie tight to his chest, ran and ran, leaped and galloped and flew . . . till at last . . .

*The* **BFG** *enters through the mist.*

*He takes the 'Sophie' doll from his cloak.* **Sophie** *takes the doll and manipulates it once more.*

**BFG**   We is here!

**Sophie**   Where?

**BFG**   We is in Dream Country. Where all dreams is beginning.

*Electronic sounds create a mysterious mood.*

*The 'Sophie' doll looks on as, to music, the* **BFG** *opens his suitcase, then watches, waits, and suddenly spies a floating dream. He slowly advances with his net, takes aim, then, with a swooping motion, leaps in the air and 'catches' the dream. Delighted, he transfers the dream to a jar, which lights up with a golden glow as he corks it.*

*Another watchful wait, then a sighting. An energetic chase, at first 'missing' the dream, starting again, then triumphantly 'catching' it and transferring it to a jar, which glows pink.*

*The 'Sophie' doll watches as the* **BFG** *waits once more, the colours still swirling against the misty background. A third dream is sighted. Having caught it, the* **BFG** *has a struggle as it tries to escape the net. He tames it finally, and transfers it, using all his strength, to a jar, which glows green.*

*Placing the jars in the suitcase and snapping it shut, the* **BFG** *takes the 'Sophie' doll, puts it under his cloak and disappears through the mist.*

*There is the sound of whistling wind, as the lights change, and* **Sophie** *re-opens the 'shelves door' to reveal the* **BFG**'s *cave once more. The jars on his shelves glimmer and glow.*

**Sophie** (*narrating*)    By the time the BFG and Sophie arrived back at the cave, darkness was beginning to fall.

*The* **BFG** *enters the cave, puts his suitcase on the table, and carefully takes the 'Sophie' doll from under his cloak.* **Sophie** *takes her and manipulates her once more, making her stand on the table, watching as the* **BFG** *removes his cloak, then opens his suitcase.*

**BFG**    Let us see what dreams we is catching! (*He holds up the golden jar.*) Oh my! It's a phizzwizard! A golden phizzwizard!

**Sophie**    Is that good?

**BFG**    The best. This will be giving some chiddler a very happy night when I is blowing it in.

**Sophie**    How can you tell?

**BFG**    I is hearing the dream's special music. I is understanding it.

**Sophie**    Gosh.

**BFG**    Shall I be showing Sophie this dream?

**Sophie**    Oh, yes please. But how?

**BFG**    Concentratiate. Watch and be listening!

*As they stare at the jar, the lights fade from the cave and come up in another area. But the jar's golden glow continues to shine.*

*On* **Sophie**'s *bed lies* **Rebecca** *asleep. Suddenly, to eerie music, her head starts to turn from side to side.*

**Rebecca**    I'm dreaming . . . I'm dreaming . . . I'm (*She opens her eyes, then gets off the bed. She acts out her dream.*) at school . . . in class . . . and my teacher, Miss Plumridge, is droning on in a very boring way about William the Conqueror and the Battle of Hastings . . .

**Mum** *acts the teacher, as though talking to the class and writing on the blackboard.* **Daniel**, **Sam** *and* **Katherine** *play other children in class.*

**Rebecca**    . . . when suddenly I can't help myself humming a little tune. (*She hums.*)

**Mum/Miss Plumridge**   Rebecca, cease that humming this instant!

**Rebecca** . . . but I can't help myself humming my little tune, and I hum it louder . . . (*She hums it louder.*)

**Mum/Miss Plumridge**   Rebecca, how *dare* you! I said stop . . .

**Rebecca** *'fluences'* **Miss Plumridge**, *who suddenly freezes. The other children have joined in the humming.*

**Rebecca**   Suddenly she freezes, then slowly but surely she starts to dance!

**Mum/Miss Plumridge** *slowly starts to dance, unsure of what is happening to her. This builds into a wild, uncontrolled rock'n'roll kind of shake, arms flailing, legs kicking. The class hums and 'la las' louder, thoroughly enjoying the fun.*

*Suddenly the door opens and the* **Headmaster** *(***Guy***) bursts in.*

*The humming stops but* **Miss Plumridge** *goes on dancing.*

**Rebecca**   The Headmaster!

**Guy/Headmaster**   What's going on in here? (*He sees* **Miss Plumridge**.) Miss Plumridge! How dare you dance in class. Go fetch your coat and leave this school for ever! You are sacked! You are a disgrace!

**Rebecca** *'fluences' the* **Headmaster**. *He freezes as* **Rebecca** *starts to hum again. The others join in.*

*Suddenly the* **Headmaster** *starts to dance too. Unable to resist, he too starts jigging around, and builds up into a wild explosion of movement. The class enjoy it even more when he starts jiving with* **Miss Plumridge**. *Both still look shocked. The class clap in rhythm and join in the dance, still humming and 'la la-ing'.*

*During this,* **Rebecca** *returns to bed.*

*Everything reaches a climax, then suddenly stops. All clear to reveal* **Rebecca** *on the bed.*

**Katherine/Mummy** (*off*)   Rebecca!

**Rebecca**   Then suddenly I hear Mummy's voice . . .

**Katherine/Mummy** (*off*)   Wake up! Your breakfast is ready!

**Rebecca** *jolts upright, and looks disappointed, then, remembering her dream, roars with laughter.*

*The lights fade and come up again in the cave, where the* **BFG** *and* **Sophie** *gaze at the golden jar, and laugh.*

**Sophie**   What a funny dream!

**BFG**   It's a ringbeller! A whoppsy!

*He places the golden jar on the shelf.*

**Sophie**    Can we see another one? Please?

**BFG**    We can.

*He takes the pink one from the suitcase. They stare at it.*

Oho! This is a pink dinghummer! Concentratiate! Watch and be listening!

*The lights fade, leaving the pink jar glowing. The lights come up in another area.*

**Sam** *lies on the bed. Suddenly, to eerie music, his head starts to turn from side to side.*

**Sam**    I'm dreaming . . . I'm dreaming . . . I'm . . . (*He opens his eyes☐then gets out of bed. He acts out his dream.*) doing my homework, trying to work out a nasty bit of algebra, when suddenly . . .

*A telephone rings and there is a voice from off stage –* **Father** *(***Daniel***).*

**Daniel/Father** (*off*)    Sam! Answer that, will you?

**Sam** (*calling*)    I'm doing my homework, Dad.

**Daniel/Father** (*off*)    I'm in the bath. Answer it!

**Sam** (*calling*)    You said I had to do my homework, Dad.

*A growl from* **Father***, who enters from the platform stage as though coming downstairs. His hair is wet and he is dressed in a bath towel. He is very pompous.*

**Daniel/Father**    You'll pay for this, Sam. (*He finds the telephone receiver and picks it up. The telephone stops ringing. Fiercely.*) Hallo. Simpkins here. (*In amazement.*) What . . . *who?* (*When he hears the reply, he stands to attention and tries to smarten himself up.*) Good evening sir . . . yes, sir, how can I help you, sir? . . . Simpkins, sir . . . *Ronald* Simpkins . . . no, sir, *Ronald*, how can I help? . . . Who? . . . Well, yes sir, there *is* a *Sam* Simpkins on this number, but surely it is *me* you wish to speak to, sir, not my little son? . . . Yes, sir, very well, sir, I will get him, sir. (*Turning to* **Sam**.) Sam, it's for you.

**Sam**    Oh. Who is it, Dad?

**Daniel/Father**    The er . . . the President of the United States.

**Sam** (*matter-of-factly*)    Oh, right. (*He takes the receiver.*)

**Daniel/Father** (*staggered*)    Do you *know* the President of the United States?

**Sam** (*with a smile*)    No, but I expect he's heard of me.

*As he speaks on the telephone,* **Father** *watches, eyes wide, mouth open in disbelief.*

**Sam** (*casually*)    Hallo . . . Oh hi! . . . What's the problem? . . . OK, Mr President, leave it to me, I'll take care of it . . . No, no, you'll bungle it all up if you do it your way . . . A pleasure, Mr President. Now I must get on with my algebra homework! Bye! Have a nice day!

**Father** *watches, bemused, as* **Sam** *puts down the telephone and returns to lie on the bed, asleep.*

**Father** *exits.*

**Daniel/Father** (*off*)    Sam!

**Sam**    Then suddenly I hear Dad's voice.

**Daniel/Father** (*off*)    Get up, you lazy slob, or you'll be late for school!

**Sam** *jolts upright, and looks disappointed, then, remembering his dream, roars with laughter.*

*The lights fade and come up again in the cave, where the* **BFG** *and* **Sophie** *gaze at the pink jar, and laugh.*

**Sophie**    That was good too!

**BFG**    A dumhinger, I is telling you! (*He places the pink jar on the shelf and then takes the green one from his suitcase.*) Now, what has we here? (*He looks at it. Suddenly.*) Aaaaaaah!

**Sophie**    What's the matter?

**BFG** (*in alarm*)    Oh no! I is catching . . . a trogglehumper!

**Sophie**    A trogglehumper?

**BFG**    Yes. A bad, bad dream. A nightmare!

**Sophie**    Oh dear. What will you do with that?

**BFG**    I is never blowing it! If I do, then some poor little tottler will be having the most curdbloodling time! (*He puts it in his suitcase.*) I is taking it back tomorrow. (*With a shudder.*) Uggh! I is hating trogglehumpers.

*Suddenly a roar startles them, the roar of the other* **Giants**.

**BFG**    Quick! Let's go look-see!

*As he and the 'Sophie' doll go to the cave entrance, the lights cross-fade to the platform stage, where the other* **Giants** *assemble, with energy and evil intent.*

**Bloodbottler**    'Tis the witchy hour. And I is starveling!

**Fleshlumpeater**    I is starveling rotten too!

**Giants**    And I! And I! And I!

**Bonecruncher**    Let us go guzzle human beans!

*The* **Giants** *cheer their agreement.*

**Childchewer**    Let us flushbunk to England!

**Gizzardgulper**    England is a luctuous land and I is fancying a few nice little English chiddlers!

*The* **Giants** *cheer.*

**Sophie**    Oh no!

**BFG**    Shhh!

**Meatdripper**    I is knowing where there is a gigglehouse for girls and I is guzzling myself full as a frothblower!

**Fleshlumpeater**    And I knows a bogglebox for boys. All I has to do is reach in and grab myself a handful! English boys is tasting extra lickswishy!

*The* **Giants** *cheer.*

**Bloodbottler**    Be following me . . . to England!

*The* **Giants** *cheer and freeze.*

*The* **BFG** *and* **Sophie** *return inside the cave as the lights cross-fade.*

**Sophie**    It mustn't happen! We've got to stop them! We must chase after them and warn everyone in England they're coming!

**BFG**    Redunculus and umpossiple. They is going twice as fast as me and they is finishing their guzzle before we is halfway. Besides, I is *never* showing myself to human beans. I is telling you, they will be putting me in the zoo with all the jiggyraffes and cattypiddlers.

**Sophie**    Nonsense.

**BFG**    And they will be sending *you* straight back to the norphanage. Grown-up human beans is not famous for their kindnesses. They is all squifflerotters and grinksludgers.

**Sophie**    That simply isn't true. Some of them are very kind indeed.

**BFG**    Who? Name one.

**Sophie**    The Queen of England. You can't call her a squifflerotter or a grinksludger.

**BFG**    Well . . .

**Sophie**    I've got it! Listen, BFG, we'll go to the Queen and tell her about the giants. She'll do something, I know she will.

**BFG**    She will never be believing in giants.

**Sophie** (*with a sudden idea*)    Then we'll make her *dream* about them. Can you make a person dream absolutely anything in the world?

**BFG**    Well, yes, I could be mixing any such dream but . . .

**Sophie**    Then mix a dream fit for a Queen!

*The* **BFG** *thinks, then springs into action.*

**BFG**    Fit for a Queen!

*Exciting music as he leaps to his shelves, taking down jars, and pours small amounts from them into one larger jar. He mixes the dream with a mechanical whisk, then transfers it into a smaller jar. He puts it in his suitcase, grabs his cloak and the 'Sophie' doll.*

*He exits at speed.*

**Sophie** *closes the 'shelves door' as:*

*The* **Giants** *break their freeze and lumber up to the platform stage. The curtains open and light pours in on the* **Giants**, *who 'rev' themselves up in formation.*

**Giants**    England!

*All exit, menacingly.*

*The* **BFG** *enters, now wearing his cloak, and, silhouetted in the window, starts running on the spot, carrying his suitcase and the 'Sophie' doll.*

*Suddenly he turns, his back to the audience, and continues running.*

**Sophie**    The BFG arrived in England. Sophie directed him to London. To Buckingham Palace!

*Slowly the back wall of the set flies out. Buckingham Palace, its windows lit up, appears in glory upstage, as the* **BFG** *continues his progress towards it.*

*Curtain.*

## Act Two

**Sophie**'s *attic playroom/bedroom. A little later.*

*Family and friends are gathered round* **Sophie**'s *birthday cake with lighted candles. The remains of the birthday tea are on a cloth, picnic-style on the floor.*

*They all sing 'Happy Birthday' to* **Sophie**, *and cheer and applaud.*

**Mum**   Blow!

*Encouraged by the others,* **Sophie** *takes a deep breath and blows out the candles. More cheering.*

**Dad**   Make a wish!

**Sophie**   I wish . . .

**Guy**   You're not supposed to tell us!

**Sophie**   Why not! I wish . . . we could start part two of the play!

*Cheers and laughter. Preparations start and the tea things are cleared.*

**Mum**   Do you need me? If not I'll do the washing-up.

**Sophie**   Of course we need you! This is your big moment, Mum! (*She runs to the dressing-up box and brings back a cardboard crown.*) You're the Queen! (*She puts the crown on* **Mum**'s *head.*)

*All cheer and bow to* **Mum**.

**Mum**   Well, I never! (*Queen voice.*) It gives me great pleasure . . .!

*Laughter.* **Sophie** *helps her mother into a dressing gown.*

**Sophie**   Right, you're in bed, asleep.

*The bed is positioned.*

**Mum** (*getting into bed*)   Oh. Don't I have anything to say?

**Sophie**   Just wait, Mum. Ready everyone? Music!

*Someone tinkles on the toy piano.*

Lights!

*Someone lowers the lights.*

**Mum** (*springing up*)   Hey, hang on!

**Sophie**   What?

**Mum**   Where's my corgi! I never sleep without my corgi!

**Sophie** *grabs a soft toy animal and throws it to* **Mum**.

**Sophie**    You'll have to make do with this. (*She steps forward.*) *The BFG*, Act Two.

*A child sounds a fanfare.*

Buckingham Palace.

*The musical director takes over the music as the narration progresses.*

Carefully holding Sophie, the BFG crept along the back wall of the Palace, peering into the upstairs bedroom windows. Suddenly, through a crack in the curtains, they saw, in the moonlight, a sleeping face. A female face that Sophie had seen on stamps and coins and in the newspapers all her life.

*A beam of light picks out the* **Queen***'s (***Mum***'s) face.*

**Sophie**    With great care, the BFG raised the Queen's bedroom window, and then . . .

*The lights come up on the curtain as, slowly, a giant-sized* **BFG** *trumpet slides through them, pointing towards the* **Queen***, and a loud blowing sound is heard.*

**Sophie** *climbs the steps to the platform stage. The trumpet recedes.*

**Sophie**    Then the BFG placed Sophie inside the window, behind the curtains . . . (*She goes behind the curtains, with her head still in view.*) . . . closed the window, and, waving goodbye and good luck to Sophie, strode into the garden and hid among the trees.

**Sophie** *disappears behind the curtains.*

*The other actors remaining now exit.*

*After a pause, the* **Queen***'s head tosses from side to side as she dreams.*

**Queen** (*talking in her sleep*)    Oh no! No! Don't! Someone stop them! Don't let them do it! It's horrible! Please stop them! It's ghastly! No! No! No!

*As she drifts back to peaceful sleep, music suggests the passing of time, and lighting suggests the coming of dawn.*

*There is a sudden knock on the door.*

**Mary***, the* **Queen***'s maid (***Katherine***), enters, carrying a tray with breakfast things and a newspaper. She is dressed in a complete maid's costume; from now on, all the characters are 'real' rather than openly 'acted' by the family and guests.*

**Mary**    Good morning, your Majesty. Your early morning tea.

*The* **Queen** *wakes up.*

**Queen**    Oh, Mary! I've just had the most frightful dream! It was awful!

**Mary**    Oh, I *am* sorry, ma'am. But don't be distressed. You're awake now.

**Queen**    I dreamt, Mary, that girls and boys were being snatched out of their beds at boarding school and were being eaten by the most ghastly giants!

**Mary** *pays attention.*

**Sophie**    The giants were putting their arms in through the dormitory windows and plucking the children out with their fingers. It was all so . . . so vivid, Mary. So real.

**Mary** *has been staring in amazement. The crockery on the tray rattles.*

**Queen**    Mary! What is it?

*Suddenly* **Mary** *drops the tray with a clatter.*

**Queen**    Mary!

**Mary**    Sorry, your Majesty . . .

**Queen**    I think you'd better sit down at once. You're as white as a sheet.

**Mary** *sits on the edge of the bed.*

**Queen**    You mustn't take it so hard, Mary, just because I've had an awful dream.

**Mary**    That . . . that isn't the reason, ma'am . . . (*She reaches for the newspaper.*) Look, ma'am! Look at the front page! The headlines!

**Queen** (*unfolding the newspaper*)    Great Scott! (*She reads.*) 'Children vanish mysteriously from boarding-school beds. Bones found underneath dormitory windows!' (*She gasps as she scans the small print.*) Oh, how ghastly! It's absolutely frightful! Those poor children!

**Mary**    But ma'am . . . don't you see, ma'am . . .

**Queen**    See what, Mary?

**Mary**    Those children were taken away almost exactly as you dreamt it, ma'am.

**Queen**    Not by giants, Mary.

**Mary**    No, ma'am. But the rest of it. You dreamt it and . . . and . . . and it's happened. For real! Ooh, it's spooky, ma'am. That's why I came over all queer.

**Queen**    I'm coming over a bit queer myself, Mary.

**Mary**    It gives me the shakes, ma'am, when something like this happens, it really does. (*She tidies up the tray.*)

**Queen**    I *did* dream about those children, Mary. It was clear as crystal.

**Mary**    I'm sure you did, ma'am.

**Queen** (*lightening the mood*)    I don't know how *giants* got into it. That was rubbish.

**Mary**    Shall I draw the curtains, ma'am? Then we shall all feel better. It's a lovely day.

**Queen**    Please do.

**Mary** *ascends the platform stage and draws the curtains.* **Sophie** *is revealed.*

**Mary**    Aaaaaaah!

**Sophie** *looks frightened. The* **Queen** *looks frightened.* **Mary** *looks frightened, but recovers first.*

**Mary**    What in the name of heaven do you think you're doing in here?

**Sophie**    Please, I . . . (*She looks beseechingly towards the* **Queen**.)

**Queen**    I don't believe it. I simply don't believe it.

**Mary**    I'll take her out, ma'am, at once.

**Queen** (*sharply*)    No, Mary, don't do that. Tell me, is there really a little girl in a nightie by the window, or am I still dreaming?

**Mary**    You're wide awake, ma'am, and there's a little girl in a nightie by the window, though heaven only knows how she got there.

**Queen** (*remembering*)    But I *know* how she got there. I dreamt that as well. A giant put her there.

**Mary** *reacts with a gasp.*

**Queen**    Little girl, am I right?

**Sophie**    Yes, your Majesty.

**Mary**    Well, I'll be jiggered. It can't be true!

**Queen**    And your name is . . .

**Sophie** *goes to speak.*

**Queen**    Don't say it! Mary, come here.

**Mary** *goes to the* **Queen**.

**Queen**    Her name is . . . (*She whispers in* **Mary**'s *ear.*)

**Mary**    Impossible, ma'am, how could you know that? (*To* **Sophie**.) What's your name, girl?

**Sophie**    My name is Sophie.

**Mary**    Aaaaaaah! (*She clutches her heart, looking, mouth open in amazement, from* **Sophie** *to the* **Queen** *and back again.*)

**Queen**    Told you. Come here, Sophie.

**Sophie** *approaches.*

**Queen**    Sit down, dear.

**Sophie** *sits on the* **Queen**'s *bed.*

**Queen**    Are you real?

**Sophie**    Yes, your Majesty.

**Queen**    And did a giant really bring you here?

**Sophie**  Oh yes, your Majesty. He's out there in the garden now.

**Mary** *shudders.*

**Queen**  Is he indeed? In the garden?

**Sophie**  He's a *good* giant, your Majesty. The Big Friendly Giant. You needn't be frightened of him.

**Queen**  I'm delighted to hear it.

**Sophie**  He is my best friend.

**Queen**  How nice.

**Sophie**  Shall I call him for you?

**Queen** (*after a pause*)   Very well.

**Sophie** *runs to the window.*

**Mary**   Is this wise, ma'am?

**Queen**  Slippers, Mary.

**Mary** *fetches them, as the* **Queen** *gets out of bed. She puts them on.*

**Sophie** (*calling from the window*)   BFG! Her Majesty the Queen would like to see you.

*Pause.*

**Mary** *and the* **Queen** *look at each other, not really expecting anything to happen.*

**Queen**  I don't see any giant.

**Sophie**  Please wait.

**Mary**   Shall I take the girl away now, ma'am?

*Sudden heavy footsteps echo from outside the window.* **Mary** *and the* **Queen** *look in fearful anticipation.*

*The footsteps stop. A voice booms.*

**BFG** (*off*)   Your Majester, I is your humbug servant.

*Suddenly a huge puppet* **BFG** *head appears at the window.*

**Mary** *screams 'silently' and faints, unseen by the* **Queen**.

**Queen** (*taking things in her stride*)   We are very pleased to meet you. Mary, ask Mr Tibbs to prepare breakfast for our two visitors. In the ballroom, I fancy. (*Pause.*) Mary? (*She turns to see* **Mary** *flat out on the floor.*) Oh.

*Blackout, followed by scene change 'blue wash' light.*

*Regal music sounds, to accompany a transformation scene change.*

**Mr Tibbs**, *the* **butler** *(***Guy***), is found by a follow spot (optional). In butler fashion, he conducts the scene change, assisted by* **Mary** *and the* **Undermaid** *(***Rebecca***).*

*Gradually the attic room disappears, as trucks revolve and the back wall flies out. The scene transforms into a ballroom, with high pillars and a red-carpeted staircase leading to an archway entrance. A breakfast table and two chairs are set to one side.*

*When all is ready,* **Mr Tibbs** *signals for a royal fanfare and waits by the entrance. The lights come up.*

*The* **Queen** *enters in full rig – ballgown, sash and glittering crown, leading a real corgi.*

*She is followed by* **Sophie***, wearing the* **Queen***'s dressing gown, which is a little large for her.*

*They descend the stairs.*

**Mr Tibbs** *deferentially shows them to their table, and sits them down.*

*Another fanfare is signalled by* **Mr Tibbs***.*

*He leads on a truck consisting of a grand piano topped by a chest of drawers, on which sits a huge* **BFG** *puppet, the arms of which are manipulated by* **Dad** *(a miniature version of the puppet). The puppet* **BFG***'s arms rest on a large tabletop supported by grandfather clocks as legs. (NB: In the original production,* **Dad** *operated the giant puppet from inside; a radio microphone made his speech audible.)*

*The music continues as* **Mr Tibbs** *summons an* **Undermaid** *(***Rebecca***).*

*She enters in full uniform, and brings a breakfast tray to the* **Queen** *and* **Sophie***, who start to mime eating.*

*The* **Undermaid** *exits.*

*Then* **Mr Tibbs** *fetches a stepladder, places it by the* **BFG***'s table, and summons* **Mary***, who carries a very large breakfast tray with a giant mug and a heap of food.*

**Mr Tibbs** *takes the tray and carefully climbs the stepladder, deposits the tray on the tabletop, then descends.*

*The puppet* **BFG** *mimes eating.*

**Mr Tibbs** *and* **Mary** *stand formally in the background as the music finishes.*

**BFG**   By goggles, your Majester, this stuff is making snozzcumbers taste like swatchwallop.

**Queen**   I beg your pardon?

**Sophie**   He has never eaten anything except snozzcumbers before, your Majesty. They taste revolting.

**Queen**   They don't seem to have stunted his growth!

**BFG**   Where is the frobscottle, Majester?

**Queen**   The *what*?

**BFG**   Delumptious fizzy frobscottle! Everyone must be drinking it. Then we can all be whizzpopping happily together!

**Queen**   What *does* he mean? What is whizzpopping?

**Sophie**   Excuse me, your Majesty. (*She goes to the* **BFG**.) BFG, there is no frobscottle here and whizzpopping is strictly forbidden.

**BFG**   What? No whizzpopping? No glumptious music?

**Sophie**   Absolutely not.

**Queen**   If he wants to make music, please don't stop him.

**Sophie**   It's not exactly music . . .

**BFG**   Listen, I can whizzpop perfectly well *without* frobscottle if I is trying hard enough.

**Sophie**   No! Don't! Please!

**Queen**   When I'm up in Scotland, they play the bagpipes outside my window while I'm eating. (*To the* **BFG**.) Do play something.

**BFG**   I has her Majester's permission!

*After a moment's concentration a very loud and long whizzpopper rents the air, causing the lighting to flicker and everyone to jump, then react.*

Whoopee! How's that, Majester?

**Queen**   I think I prefer the bagpipes!

*But she smiles, to* **Sophie**'s *relief.*

**Queen**   Now, to business. Sophie, you have told me of your visit to Giant Country and of the Giants' ghastly night-time children-eating raids. But before we decide what is to be done, I must confirm the facts. Big Friendly Giant, last night your . . . er . . . colleagues raided England. Where did they go the night before?

**BFG**   I think, Majester, they was galloping off to Sweden. They is liking the Sweden sour taste.

**Queen**   Right. Mr Tibbs, the telephone.

**Mr Tibbs** *approaches with a portable telephone on a silver tray.*

**Queen**   Thank you. (*She presses the dialling buttons and waits.*)

*A telephone rings. The lighting changes, staying on the* **Queen** *and coming up on an area the other side of the stage.*

*The* **Queen of Sweden** *(*Rebecca*) enters in full ceremonial dress. She holds a telephone.*

**Queen of Sweden** (*on the phone*)    Hallo, Queen of Sweden here.

**Queen**    Good morning, it's the Queen of England. Is everything all right in Sweden?

**Queen of Sweden**    Everything is terrible! Two nights ago, twenty-six of my loyal subjects disappeared. My whole country is in a panic!

**Queen**    They were eaten by giants. Apparently they like the sweet and sour taste of Swedes. So says the BFG.

**Queen of Sweden**    I don't know *what* you're talking about. It's hardly a joking matter when one's loyal subjects are being eaten like popcorn.

**Queen**    They've eaten mine as well.

**Queen of Sweden**    Who's *they*, for heaven's sake?

**Queen**    Giants.

**Queen of Sweden**    Look here, are you feeling all right?

**Queen**    It's been a rough morning. First I had a horrid nightmare, then the maid dropped my early morning tea and now I've a giant on the piano.

**Queen of Sweden**    You need a doctor quick!

**Queen**    I'll be all right. I must go now. Thanks for your help.

*The lights fade on the* **Queen of Sweden***, who exits.*

*The* **Queen** *hands the telephone back to* **Mr Tibbs***.*

**Queen**    That proves it. Mr Tibbs, summon the Head of the Army and the Head of the Airforce immediately.

**Mr Tibbs** *bows, clicks his fingers and points to the entrance.*

*Military music plays as, immediately, the Heads of the Army (***Daniel***) and Air Force (***Sam***), in full military uniform, enter, carrying batons. They march in step down the stairs, not seeing the* **BFG***. They arrive at the* **Queen***'s table, stand to attention and salute.*

**Queen**    Good morning, gentlemen.

**Head of the Army**    What ho, your Majesty!

**Head of the Air Force**    Toodle pip, your Majesty!

**Queen**    We have a job for you.

**Head of the Army**    Jolly good show, your Majesty!

**Head of the Air Force**    Whizzo prang, your Majesty!

**Queen**    Now, you've read about the disappearing children?

**Head of the Army**    Jolly bad show, your Majesty.

**Head of the Air Force**    Bally disgrace, your Majesty.

**Queen**    They were eaten.

**Head of the Army** and **Head of the Air Force** (*scandalised*)    Eaten?

**Queen**    By giants.

*Pause.*

**Head of the Army**    Hold fire, your Majesty.

**Head of the Air Force**    Giants?

**Head of the Army**    No such fellas, your Majesty.

**Head of the Air Force**    Except in fairy tales.

**Head of the Army**    Except in fairy tales.

**Head of the Army** and **Head of the Air Force**    Ha, ha, ha, ha, ha!

**Head of the Army**    Jolly good joke, your Majesty.

**Head of the Air Force**    Not April the First, is it?

**Head of the Army** and **Head of the Air Force**    Ha, ha, ha, ha, ha!

**Queen**    Gentlemen, allow me to present the Big Friendly Giant. (*She indicates behind them.*)

**Head of the Army** and **Head of the Air Force**    Big Friendly Giant! Ha, ha, ha, ha, ha! (*They turn. They see the* **BFG**.) Aaaaaaaaaaah! (*They cling to each other in terror.*)

**BFG**    How is you doing, gentlebunglers?

**Head of the Army** and **Head of the Air Force**    A giant!

**Queen**    Indeed. Luckily a friendly one. His colleagues are not. Tonight those bloodthirsty brutes will be galloping off to gobble up another couple of dozen unfortunate wretches. They have to be stopped. Fast.

**Head of the Army**    Message received, your Majesty!

**Head of the Air Force**    Message understood, your Majesty!

**Queen**    They must be brought back. Alive.

**Head of the Army**    But how, your Majesty? I mean, giants . . .

**Head of the Air Force**    They'd knock us down like ninepins!

**Head of the Army**    Absolutely.

**Head of the Air Force**    Absolutely.

**Head of the Army**    Indisputably.

**Head of the Air Force**    Indisputably.

**BFG**    Wait! Keep your skirts on! I has the answer.

**Queen**    Let him speak.

**BFG**    Every afternoon all these giants is lying on the ground snoozling in the Land of Noddy.

**Head of the Army**    Land of Noddy? What's he prattling about?

**Sophie**    Land of Nod. Asleep. It's pretty obvious.

**BFG**    All you has to do is creep up on them and tie them up.

**Head of the Air Force**    But how do we get the brutes back here?

**BFG**    You is having bellypoppers, is you not?

**Head of the Air Force**    Are you being rude?

**Sophie**    He means helicopters.

**Head of the Air Force**    Then why doesn't he say so? Of course we have bellypoppers . . . er, helicopters.

**Queen**    Then, gentlemen, get cracking.

**Head of the Army**    Yes, your Majesty. Forward!

**Head of the Air Force**    Chocks away! Roger and out!

*The Heads of the Army and Air Force turn inward and bump into each other.*

*Blackout.*

*The roar of helicopter engines echoes through the darkness, fading as a screen flies in for a shadow-puppet sequence, to music and sound.*

*(1) A bird flies happily from left towards right. Helicopter engine noises are in the distance. The bird sees something and squawks, flapping its wings and opening its beak in amazement.*

*(2) The **BFG**, running, enters from right towards left. He carries a tiny **Sophie**.*

**BFG** (*echoing*)    Follow, follow!

*The bird flies upward to avoid being hit by the **BFG** as he runs across the screen and disappears.*

*(3) The helicopter engine noises grow louder. The bird flies lower again, then has another shock. It squawks, flaps its wings and flies upwards, narrowly avoiding the entrance of three helicopters, one by one.*

*The bird exits.*

*(4) The helicopters fly in formation, in a circular pattern. The helicopter engine noises fade to background hum as voices are heard, as though through headphones.*

**Head of the Army**    Where the devil are we going?

**Head of the Air Force**    I haven't the foggiest idea. We've flown clear off the map!

**Head of the Army**    Look! Look down!

*Loud snoring noises sound over the hum of the helicopter noises.*

Giants!

**Head of the Air Force**    Stand by, chaps!

*(5) Three soldiers slowly descend from the helicopters on ropes, eventually dropping behind the limit of the screen.*

*The snoring continues.*

*The colour on the screen changes to suggest the passage of time.*

**Head of the Air Force**    Winch away!

*(6) The ropes rise, pulling up two **Giants** each, trussed up, with the occasional moving limb. The soldiers are balanced on top.*

*(7) When all are visible, the voices of the **Giants** are heard, and continue as the helicopters move off and exit, carrying their giant cargo.*

**Fleshlumpeater**    I is flushbunkled!

**Childchewer**    I is splitzwiggled!

**Bonecruncher**    I is swogswalloped!

**Meatdripper**    I is gunzleswiped!

**Gizzardgulper**    I is slopgroggled!

**Bloodbottler**    I is crodsquinkled!

*(8) The helicopter engine noises fade, as the **BFG** enters, bringing up the rear, carrying **Sophie**.*

**BFG**    Sophie, we has diddly diddly done it!

**Sophie**    Yes, BFG. We diddly diddly has!

*They disappear and the lighting on the screen fades to black.*

*Music plays as the screen flies out to reveal the attic playroom back to normal.*

**Sophie**, *alone, is lit as she narrates.*

**Sophie**    Meanwhile, back in England, a tremendous bustle and hustle was going on. Every earth-digger in the country had been brought in to dig a colossal hole in Regent's Park, near London Zoo, where the giants would be on view to the public. Ten thousand men and ten thousand machines worked ceaselessly through the night under powerful arc-lights. The hole was twice the size of a football field and the depth of fifty swimming pools. When the helicopters triumphantly arrived home, the giants were lowered into the hole.

*The lights come up on the* **Giants**, *who, with a roar, tumble forward, below the platform, as though landing in the hole.*

**Sophie**    The BFG watched the complicated operation, then peered down into the Giant-pit.

*The* **BFG** *stands above, looking down at the* **Giants**.

**Fleshlumpeater**    Why is they putting us in this grobsludging hole?

**BFG**    Because, Fleshlumpeater, here you is never eating human beans no more. From now on you is eating only these. Snozzcumbers! (*He throws some down.*)

**Giants** (*in disgust*)    Snozzcumbers!

**BFG**    Oh yes! I is bringing snozzcumber plants from Giant Country and the Royal Gardener is growing them special for you.

**Fleshlumpeater**    You is paying for this, runt. You is paying for this!

*The other* **Giants** *bellow threateningly.*

**Sophie**, *carrying the 'Sophie' doll, climbs the steps to the platform stage. She is met by the* **BFG**.

**Sophie** (*narrating*)    That afternoon, the BFG brought Sophie to look at the giants.

*The* **BFG** *lies down for a better view.* **Sophie** *manipulates the doll.*

*The* **Giants** *have gone to sleep – having their usual afternoon nap. They snore.*

**BFG**    They is asleep, Sophie. You know, I is almost feeling sorry for them. (*He hangs his arm over the edge.*) Now they is harmless.

*Suddenly* **Fleshlumpeater** *leaps up and grabs the* **BFG**'*s arm.*

**Fleshlumpeater**    Harmless? I isn't harmless, runt! But you is going to be armless! (*He tries to pull the* **BFG** *into the pit.*)

**Sophie** *screams.*

**BFG**    Aaah! Help! Help!

**Fleshlumpeater** *roars as he struggles with the* **BFG**, *who appears to be losing the struggle.*

**Fleshlumpeater**    You grobbly little grub! You is a traitor!

*Suddenly* **Sophie** *pushes the 'Sophie' doll perilously near the edge.*

**Sophie** (*with a shriek*)    Let him go, you great bully, do you hear me? Let him go!

*With a roar,* **Fleshlumpeater** *loosens his grasp on the* **BFG** *and grabs the 'Sophie' doll.* **Sophie** *screams.*

**Fleshlumpeater**    You squiggling, incy human bean. You has had it! I is eating you!

**Sophie**    No, no! Help!

*The* **BFG** *has recovered himself.*

**BFG**    Sophie! No! (*He cries out.*) What can I be doing? (*He has a sudden idea.*) The trogglehumper!

*In slow motion,* **Fleshlumpeater** *holds the 'Sophie' doll high and steadily brings her towards his open mouth.*

*Meanwhile, the* **BFG** *opens his suitcase and brings out the jar, glowing green. He pours its contents into his trumpet, and just as the 'Sophie' doll is about to be eaten, blows the trumpet towards* **Fleshlumpeater**.

*The lights snap to green as* **Fleshlumpeater** *freezes with a roar, at the same time throwing the 'Sophie' doll up to the* **BFG**, *who catches her and gently cradles her.*

**Fleshlumpeater**, *stunned, suddenly jerks his head from side to side, as the nightmare trogglehumper starts to take effect. He picks up a snozzcumber to protect himself.*

**Fleshlumpeater**    Save me! It's Jack! It's the grueful, gruncious Jack! Jack is after me! Have mercy, Jack! Have mercy on this poor little giant! The beanstalk! He is coming at me with his terrible spikesticking beanstalk! Take it away! Don't hurt me, Jack! I is begging you!

*He starts lashing out with the snozzcumber, which hits the other* **Giants**, *waking them up. They pick up a snozzcumber each and, in unison, accompanied by angry roars, smash them three times onto the cowering* **Fleshlumpeater**.

*All freeze. The* **BFG** *and* **Sophie** *pose triumphantly above.*

*The lights fade on the* **Giants**.

*The actors prepare for the final scene, removing their giant headdresses and collecting their puppets –* **Mum** (*Queen puppet*), **Guy** (*Mr Tibbs puppet*), **Daniel** (*Head of the Army puppet*), **Sam** (*Head of the Air Force puppet*), **Katherine** (*Mary puppet*), **Rebecca** (*Undermaid puppet*).

**Sophie** (*narrating*)    Sophie soon felt better, and, with the BFG, returned to Buckingham Palace.

*Music plays as the cast assemble. The* **BFG** *remains on the platform stage, alongside* **Sophie** *and the 'Sophie' doll.*

*On stage level the others manipulate their puppets.*

*The puppets 'act' on the platform stage above, looking up at the* **BFG**.

**Queen**   BFG, on behalf of England, on behalf of the whole world, we thank you, and gladly present you with the Queen's Medal for Gigantic Courage.

*Cheers.*

*The* **BFG** *stoops to collect his medal.*

**BFG**   Thank you, Majester.

**Queen**   To Sophie, too, we owe our gratitude, and announce that her orphanage has been closed and Mrs Clonkers dismissed.

*Cheers.*

We invite Sophie and her orphan friends to live with us at Buckingham Palace.

*Cheers.*

**Sophie**   Thank you, your Majesty.

**Queen**   BFG, we invite you to stay too, in a new wing of the palace, to be built specially for you.

*Cheers.*

**BFG**   Thank you, Majester. But no. I must be returning to Giant Country, to my wopsey cave and to my dream-blowing.

**Queen**   Very well, but you must visit us at least once a year. On Sophie's birthday.

**BFG**   Majester, I will, (*He bows to her, then gently picks up the 'Sophie' doll.*) Goodbye, little Sophie. I is going to miss you.

**Sophie**   Goodbye, dear BFG. I is going to miss you too.

*The* **BFG** *kisses the 'Sophie' doll, and returns her to* **Sophie**. *He puts on his cloak and picks up his suitcase.*

**BFG**   Goodbye, human beans.

**All**   Goodbye, BFG.

*The* **BFG** *turns. The curtains open. Light pours through the window.*

*The* **BFG** *walks on the spot in slow motion, his back to the audience.*

*The puppets wave.*

*The music builds.*

*Blackout.*

# Save the Human – Teacher Notes

*Save the Human* is a deliciously clever play that really makes us think about animal rights. There are some great opportunities for introducing mask theatre here and playing around with the roles of narrators. You can also stage a real life rock concert!

**Age range:** KS2/3
**Number of actors:** 8–25+
**Running time:** Approx. 60 minutes

## Characters
The main characters are:

> The Bear Family × 4 (Father, Mother, Becky and Ben)
> Becky's friends × 3 (Chas Chimp, Freda Ferret and Patch Badger)
> Professor Rhino
> Securiboar × 2/3
> Newshound
> Norman

There are several other characters including: narrators, human refugees, Mrs Mole and her guide-human, Dr Beagle, Nurse Rat, Sister Guinea Pig and various crowd/extra characters; for example, in Act Two, Scenes Four and Five there are lots of 'human' extras needed.

## Casting notes
The original production has eight actors playing multiple roles including the narrators but you can create extra, more manageable parts easily by casting most roles individually and using some actors as narrators only. I would say, though, that the narrators should have some sort of identity, such as 'human-spotters' with binoculars and notebooks, or students of the year 2150 in school uniform telling a story of the past, or indeed as 'actors' in a rehearsal as written in by the playwright. The narration should be an integral part of the story and should move seamlessly in and out the action. To keep away from long pauses in between scenes, try and avoid the narrators sitting/standing to the side until it is 'their turn' and then shuffling on and off to speak their lines; instead they should be on stage all or most of the time, reacting to the action, moving position, quietly changing scenery and interacting occasionally with characters. One part where the narrators can certainly be used is to create the slow-motion rolling of Ben's pram, by moving and manipulating the pram, the Ben Bear bundle and anything else as needed.

There are also opportunities to include further actors/musicians as the band/crowd in the 'Human Aid' scenes.

All of the characters can be played unisex with some basic adaptations.

Becky Bear is the lead role, with the most lines and being in every scene bar one or two. The actor playing Becky will also require some basic singing skills. Similarly, Becky's friends are pretty much constantly on stage.

Newshound is a great role and could be split into two or perhaps pre-recorded if technology allows.

Norman the pet human is a really interesting role with quite a bit of stage time, but no actual speaking lines, so this actor must be proficient acting with facial expression, movement and gestures alone (see activities).

### Costumes and props

The original production saw all actors wearing simple tracksuits, with animal roles signified by a headdress – they will work best when they do not obstruct the actors' faces; so mounted on a bicycle helmet or similar so performers can move and speak freely while wearing them. Stick-masks (animal head cut-outs on sticks are another option, double sided ideally) are an option, though again caution should be taken to not act with the masks fully covering the face, but rather held slightly aloft with lines spoken from underneath more like a puppet. The main concern is that the 'animal' characters should behave very much normally, so no crawling on the floor or hopping, etc. Similarly, the human pets should not act like animals.

There are a number of props you should not do without, the 'Pigeon Post' springs to mind, and these can be made using the stick-puppet technique above. Along with the headdresses, and other things like 'Top Secret' files and protest banners, they can make a fun art and design activity for a class.

### Staging

The action takes place in three main locations, the Bears' house, the playground and H.A.R.M. laboratories, with several other smaller scenes/locations throughout. There is no need to use lots of set and scenery here, and all the locations can be shown simply with one or two select items. Projections or slides can be used or the main locations could be represented in the same or similar style to the original production, using giant cut-out card scenery. These can be made from light card and should be made free standing so actors can move and set easily. If time, space or budget means you need something simpler, then I would suggest some versatile items that can be used and re-used in several scenes. For example, a table for the Bears' house becomes Professor Rhino's desk by removing a tablecloth and adding a name plate. The same blue tablecloth can be a pond or the sea later on. Similarly, chairs can be become podiums and prams – though avoid scraping chairs across the stage. A taped/chalked square on the floor can be a general stage marker to determine playing space (if you have no back- or off-stage area available anyone stood outside the box is 'off-stage') and with the addition of a basketball net becomes the playground. A simple free-standing sign saying 'H.A.R.M. – Keep out' and a filing cabinet is enough for the laboratory. Some items will have to be made; an individual cardboard frame with bars can be held by the actors up to their faces to signify a cage, for example.

If nothing else you can use actors themselves to make the scene. Two parallel lines with their backs turned can make a good long corridor, and an actor with arm outstretched becomes an effective door or a 'key hook'!

### Music, sound effects and lighting

The play is described as a 'play with music' and has three main songs: 'Save the Human', 'I Love my Human' and 'Rock 'n' Roar'.

The 'Human Aid' scene would benefit from live musicians to create that real concert feel. I would say 'Save the Human' and 'I Love my Human' *could* be adapted to poems with music underneath if needed, as the sentiment in the lyrics is what is important here. 'Save the Human' in Act One, Scene Eleven can also draw on the call and response with the audience used in the conference of the animals and introduce some protest-style chants. Overall, the songs should be included where possible as they are important as protest songs or celebratory songs.

Lighting and special effects are detailed in the script and can be used as little or as much as resources allow – at the director's discretion.

## Lesson plan – Mime, movement and mask
Many of the roles in *Save the Human* require actors to perform with masks, and there are a number of mimed sequences too. These exercises can introduce the basics of both skills.

### Starter activity
Everyone sits in a circle. Each pupil mimes in turn opening a parcel and taking something out – perhaps a hat or scarf, perhaps something else they can remember from the play; they should try and make it clear what it is by using clear gestures, actions and facial expressions. Others then guess the item.

### Engaging tasks
As a whole class using Act Two, Scene Three, students should mime everyday human activities, such as sunbathing, picnicking, shopping, playing games or meeting friends.

As a contrast you should then ask them to mime a 'caged human' in a cell, curled up or pacing, banging on the walls or clinging onto bars.

In pairs students develop a mimed activity using an imaginary ball: a bowling ball, basket ball, beach ball, football, rugby ball etc. Pupils need to practise their own short routine and be able to repeat it perfectly including throwing, catching, bouncing, missing, heading, etc.

In pairs one person plays a Securiboar, the other one of the animals trying to sneak into the H.A.R.M. laboratory. The Securiboar should mime patrolling the corridors, checking locks, shining a torch, etc., while the animal mimes opening windows, picking locks, walking sneakily, etc. When the Securiboar spins round with the torch light the animal can freeze in various positions. You can introduce *Pink Panther* music, *Mission Impossible* or similar.

Spotlight good examples of clear actions, big movements, facial expressions and imagination – remember, no sounds!

### Developing – Slow motion
Introduce the idea of slow-motion mime – discuss the moments in the play that use or could use slow motion.

With a small group of volunteers, stage a slow-motion race – the winner is the slowest! Highlight the key skills again, and above all go slow! The biggest mistake people make is moving too quickly when attempting slow motion.

For the next activities, give the students a short amount of time to work on a slow-motion sequence from the play; perhaps Ben's buggy incident Act One, Scene Four, the chase in Act One, Scene Nine, H.A.R.M. rounding up the humans in Act Two, Scene Four, a rock concert like 'Human Aid', or any other scene. Then share back one group at a time; a bit of *Chariots of Fire* music works well here.

*Developing – Mask work*
There are many different types of mask available including half masks, headdresses and stick masks. These activities are designed for a full mask, they can be simple white plain masks, or a specific set for use in drama workshops such as the Trestle mask collections.

Give each student a mask and either ask them to describe the character in adjectives, or for a plain mask to invent a character. They should consider how the character might move and stand – what would they do with their hands?

Explain the golden rules of mask work are:

Put your mask on and take your mask off, away from (back turned to) the audience
Don't touch the mask whilst wearing
No speaking in a full mask
Clear and exaggerated actions
'Clock' (notice) the audience

To practise movement for their character, in turns, students should put their mask on, enter the space, clock or notice the audience, react, and then leave, take off mask.

For example a character may walk in big strides confidently, stop, turn and look at the audience, shake fist angrily, then leave. Or, shuffle in slowly with hands in pockets, stop, look at audience, lower head down and walk slowly away. Watch various examples from the actors.

In groups the students should eventually create their own scenes in mask; for example, an exam, a disco, a protest, a weightlifting competition. The audience should be able to tell character, emotions and storyline just through the use of movements and mime.

# Save the Human

**from a story**
**by Tony Husband and David Wood**

**Book and lyrics by David Wood**
**Music by Peter Pontzen and David Wood**
**Lyrics for 'Rock 'n' Roar' by Tony Husband**

*Save the Human* was commissioned by Cambridge Theatre Company, who first performed it at the Arts Theatre, Cambridge, on 15 February 1990, followed by a short tour. The production was subsequently toured by Whirligig Theatre, including a season at Sadler's Wells Theatre, London. The original cast was:

| | |
|---|---|
| **Actor One (Father Bear, Securiboar)** | David Bale |
| **Actor Two (Norman)** | Neil Smye |
| **Actor Three (Patch Badger, Newshound)** | Robert McKewley |
| **Actor Four (Professor Rhino, Securiboar)** | David Burrows |
| **Actor Five (Becky Bear)** | Jenny Galloway |
| **Actor Six (Ben Bear, Norma)** | Mandy Lassalles |
| **Actor Seven (Chas Chimp, Securiboar)** | Adam Stafford |
| **Actor Eight (Mother Bear, Freda Ferret)** | Wendy Holland |

All other parts played by the company.

*Directed by* Ben Forster and David Wood
*Designed by* Susie Caulcutt, based on the cartoons of Tony Husband
*Choreography and movement by* Sheila Falconer
*Musical co-composition and supervision by* Peter Pontzen
*Musical direction by* Cliff Atkinson
*Lighting by* Robert Ornbo

The action of the play takes place in the town and house where the Bear Family lives, outside Becky Bear's school, outside and inside the H.A.R.M. Headquarters, at the Human Aid Concert, at the United Creations Assembly and at the seaside.


With sincere thanks to Robin Midgely, James Williams and everyone at Cambridge Theatre Company for commissioning this play, and for their encouragement, their enthusiasm and their splendid premiere production

David Wood, Tony Husband, Peter Pontzen

# Act One

## Prologue

*The stage is bare as the audience enter.* **Actors,** *in rehearsal clothes, welcome them. Other* **Actors** *do warm-up exercises.*

*With the house lights still up, the cast assembles on stage to a musical pulse.*

**Actors** (*chanting*)
S-A-V-E
T-H-E
H-U-M-A-N
Save the Human!

*Music punctuates.*

**All**
I
We
You
Are all proud members of the human race.

**Actor Five**   We share the Earth with other creatures but we make the rules. We are in control. We are all-powerful.

**Actor One**   But let's suppose . . .

**Actor Six**   Let's imagine . . .

**Actor Eight**   Let's pretend . . .

*Lighting changes as some* **Actors** *leave the stage.*

**Actor Four**   . . . that way, way in the future, hundreds of years in the future, times have changed.

*Sound effect.*

The human beings who ruled the world made a terrible mess of it. They kept having wars and killing each other. And the cleverer they became, inventing things and trying to make a better world, the more they polluted the Earth and changed the balance of Nature. The weather got too hot for them. The seas rose and drowned many of them. Crops wouldn't grow and humans starved.

*Sound effect.*

Now, other creatures have taken over.

**Actor Seven**   Animals –

**Actor Two**   Birds –

**Actor Three**   And fish –

**All**   Now rule the world.

**Actor Seven**   And in an ordinary home . . .

**Actor Four**   . . . an ordinary family –

*The* **Actors** *playing the* **Bear** *family enter, showing their bear heads.*

**Actor Five**   Becky Bear, . . .

**Actor Six**   Ben Bear, her little brother, . . .

**Actor Eight**   Their mother, . . .

**Actor One**   And their father, . . .

*The* **Bears** *put on their heads, to music.*

**Actors Two, Three, Four,** *and* **Seven**   Begin an ordinary day.

*The* **Bears** *greet each other.*

*Other* **Actors** *bring on a table, kennel and television.*

**Norman** *conceals himself behind the kennel.*


**Scene One**

*The* **Bears**' *living room.*

*The* **Bears** *are at the table.* **Father** *reads a newspaper.*

**Becky**   Can I get down, Mum?

**Mother**   Finished your breakfast, dear?

**Becky**   Yes, thanks. Can I turn the telly on?

**Mother**   All right.

**Father**   Ben, what are you doing?

**Ben**   Making a mountain with my cornflakes.

**Father**   Eat them, don't play with them.

**Ben** *starts to sob, as* **Becky** *turns on the television.*

**Mother**   Quiet, Ben. I want to hear the news.

**Newshound** *has collected his mask and appears on the television screen. We hear a news signature tune.*

**Newshound**   Good morning, good morning, this is Newshound with the latest update. Three more tower blocks have been pulled down to make way for a young animals' adventure forest and play area. Many humans who had refused to evacuate the buildings were finally forced out of their homes. Carrying a few hastily packed belongings they fled screaming from the advancing bulldozers. Child humans got trampled in the stampede. And now the latest pop video from the Funky Monkies.

**Mother** *turns off the television.*

**Mother**    I don't know what the world's coming to.

**Becky**    Oh Mum, the Funky Monkies aren't that bad!

**Mother** (*returning to the table*)    Not the Funky Monkies, silly. That news report. How could we animals be so cruel to those defenceless humans? Eat up, Ben.

**Becky**    What will happen to them all, Mum?

**Mother**    Well, some may find somewhere else to live. But lots won't make it.

**Becky**    You mean they'll die?

**Mother**    Of course. The more we take away their natural habitat, all those housing estates and blocks of flats we keep destroying, the less chance of survival the humans have. Before long they'll become extinct.

**Ben**    *I* want a drink.

**Mother**    Please.

**Ben**    Please.

**Becky**    Why do we do it?

**Father** (*folding his newspaper*)    It's called progress, Becky. Animals need adventure forests to play in and there aren't enough of them. So the human homes have to go.

**Becky**    But it's not fair. I wouldn't treat Norman like that.

**Father**    That's different, Norman's our pet human.

**Becky** (*calling into the kennel*)    Norman! Come on, good boy.

*Music as* **Norman** *emerges sleepily from the kennel, then smiles at the* **Bears**.

**Ben**    I love Norman.

**Mother**    Of course you do, darling. We all love Norman. Is Norman hungry? Does he want his brekky?

**Norman** *reacts pleased.*

**Becky**    I'll get it.

*She places an imaginary bowl by* **Norman**, *who tucks in hungrily.*

**Father**    Of course, not everyone loves their pet human as much as we do. Look how many animals are given baby pet-humans as birthday presents or Christmas presents, play with them for a few days, and then decide they don't want them after all. They dump them on the motorway or throw them in the river.

**Becky**    Come on, Norman, walkies! (*She puts a lead on* **Norman**.)

**Mother**, **Father** *and* **Ben** *exit.*

*The scene is cleared.*

*Narration:*

**Actor Two**    Becky was thoughtful as she took Ben and Norman for a walk.

**Mother** *pushes* **Ben** *on in a buggy, kisses him goodbye and hands him to* **Becky**.

**Mother** *exits.*

**Actor Two**    They set off down the street towards the park.


**Scene Two**

*Street with shops.*

**Becky**, *with* **Ben** *in his buggy, and* **Norman**, *pass two human refugees helping each other sadly along.*

*Narration:*

**Actor Two**    They passed some human refugees, tired and hungry, searching desperately for a new home.

**Becky**    It can't be right, Ben, it can't be right.

**Mrs Mole** *enters, led by her guide-human.*

**Becky**    Look, there's old Mrs Mole. She's blind, Ben. Her guide-human keeps her safe. He's her best friend. Humans can be useful.

**Mrs Mole** *and her guide-human exit.*

**Becky**    And fun too! Do you remember the Humans' Tea Party at the Zoo?

**Ben** *laughs.*

**Becky**    The little one . . .

**Ben**    Sploshed custard on the big one's face!

**Becky**    And the Great Rabbito? Remember him? Doing magic tricks at my party? Nothing up my sleeve! Abracadabra! . . . Then out of his hat he pulled . . . a baby human!

**Ben**    That was fun.

**Norman** *pulls at his lead.*

**Becky**    All right, Norman. We're coming!

*They exit.*

*Narration:*

**Actor Seven**    In the park, down by the lake, three of Becky's best friends were playing. (*He puts on* **Chas***'s mask.*) Chas Chimp . . .

**Actor Three** (*putting on* **Patch***'s mask*)    Patch Badger . . .

**Patch** *and* **Chas** *mime kicking a ball.*

**Actor Eight** (*putting on* **Freda***'s mask*)    And Freda Ferret.

**Freda** *traps the imaginary ball with her foot.*


**Scene Three**

*The park/lake.*

**Chas** *and* **Patch** *collect their two pet-humans, while* **Freda** *bounces the ball.* **Chas** *and* **Patch** *unleash their pet-humans.* **Freda** *throws the imaginary ball to* **Chas**, *who shows it to the pet-humans.*

**Chas**    Look.

**Chas** *invites the pet-humans to catch the ball but 'throws' it to* **Patch**.

**Chas**    Fetch!

*The pet-humans chase it.* **Patch** *'throws' it to* **Freda**. *The pet-humans chase it.*

**Patch**    Fetch!

**Freda** *'throws' it to* **Chas**. *The pet-humans chase it.*

**Freda**    Fetch!

*Meanwhile,* **Becky**, **Ben** *and* **Norman** *enter.*

**Chas**    Fetch!

**Chas** *'throws' it to* **Patch**. *This time the pet-humans chase and one catches the 'ball'. The other wants it. A fight ensues. The friends close round the pet-humans, enjoying the tussle.*

**Chas**    Go on, boy, get it!

**Patch**    Quick! Grab it! Grab it!

**Freda**    Fight! Fight!

**Becky** *intervenes.*

**Becky**    Stop them! Stop them at once!

*The others laugh.*

**Chas**    Run away, Becky!

**Patch** (*to his pet-human*)    Get it! Get it!

**Freda**    Fight! Fight!

**Norman** *shrinks back.*

**Becky**    It's all right, Norman. I won't let you join in.

*One pet-human gets the 'ball'. The chums cheer.*

**Ben** *cries.* **Becky** *parks the buggy a few paces back.*

**Becky**    Don't cry, Ben. (*She pushes back to the fray.*) Stop them please! It's not fair, teasing them like that.

**Chas**    Come off it, Becky. It's only a bit of fun.

**Becky**    Not for the humans, it's not.

**Freda**    Don't interfere, Becky. They enjoy fighting, anyway.

**Becky**    That's no reason to encourage them. It's cruelty to dumb humans, don't you see that?

*Suddenly* **Ben** *screams as the buggy rolls towards the lake.*

**Chas**    Becky, look!

*Sound effect as the scene goes into slow motion. The four animals turn helplessly and look towards the lake. The buggy tips over.* **Ben** *flounders in a blue pool of light.*

*A loud splash. The animals freeze with horror.* **Becky** *moves to the front, then stops.*

**Becky** (*crying out*)    I can't swim!

**Others**    Nor can we!

**All**    Help! Help!

*Still in slow motion,* **Norman** *determinedly steps forwards and gallantly wades into the lake, then 'swims'.*

*Narration:*

**Actor Two**    Suddenly Norman strode to the lake, waded in and swam strongly towards the floundering Ben.

**Actor Six**    Bravely he took him in his arms,

**Actor Two**    And keeping his head above water, carried him safely back to shore.

**Norman** *hands* **Ben** *to* **Becky**. *The slow motion finishes. All cheer.*

**Becky**    Thank you, Norman.

**Chas**    Good boy.

**Freda**    Brave Norman.

**Patch**    You're a hero!

*The animals retrieve the buggy and gently put* **Ben** *in it.*

*The other pet-humans advance menacingly on* **Norman**, *whose pride turns to fear.*

*Narration:*

**Actor Two**    But the other pet-humans didn't think Norman was a hero.

**Actor One**    'Animal-lover' –

**Actor Two**    – they seemed to say –

**Actor One** and **Actor Four**    – 'dirty animal-lover'.

**Becky**    Come on, Norman.

**Norman** *evades the pet-humans as the scene breaks up.*

**Chas** *and* **Patch** *retrieve their pet-humans and exit.*

**Freda** *leaves too.*

**Becky**, *putting* **Ben** *in the buggy, and* **Norman** *prepare to go home.*

**Becky**    Come on, Ben. Let's go home.

*They set off.*

*They are stopped in their tracks as the lighting darkens, and a loud siren sounds which continues throughout the next episode.*

*A van marked H.A.R.M. speeds on.*

*The van stops and from it emerge two* **Securiboars**. *In almost silent-film style they roughly push* **Becky** *and* **Ben** *to one side, grab* **Norman** *and unceremoniously drag him towards the van and bundle him in.* **Becky** *tries to intervene but is pushed back.*

*The* **Securiboars** *drive off in their van, at the last minute throwing out* **Norman**'*s lead.*

**Becky**, *with* **Ben**, *stands helplessly. She picks up the lead and looks sadly at it.*

**Mother** *and* **Father Bear** *enter, setting the television and kennel.*


**Scene Four**

*The* **Bears**' *living room.*

*The siren stops.*

**Becky** *is explaining to her parents.*

**Becky** (*on the verge of tears*)    It all happened so quickly. They took him. The Securiboars.

**Father**    Securiboars?

**Mother**    Poor Norman. He saved Ben, and then . . .

**Becky**    If only I could have saved *him*.

**Ben**   Where's Norman?

**Mother**   Oh, Ben.

**Becky**   Will we ever see him again, Dad?

**Father**   Tell me about the Securiboars' van, Becky. What was it like? It's important you remember.

**Becky**   It had a word written on the side. HARM.

*Tension music.*

**Father**   HARM?

**Becky** *nods.*

**Father**   Then I'm afraid, my girl, we may have lost dear old Norman for good. You see, Becky, the letters H.A.R.M. stand for 'Human Analysis and Research Ministry'.

*A sound effect pierces the air as the scene breaks up.*

**Ben, Mother** *and* **Father Bear** *are replaced by* **Patch, Chas** *and* **Freda**.

**Becky** *remains.*

*The television and kennel exit.*

*Narration:*

**Actor Five**   Next day, in the school playground, Becky reported the news to her friends.


**Scene Five**

*The school playground.*

**Chas**, **Patch** *and* **Freda** *play ball.*

**Becky**   'Human Analysis and Research Ministry'.

**Chas**   Never heard of it.

**Becky**   They do tests and things on humans. New medicines. Antibiotics, that kind of thing.

*The ball game stops.*

**Patch**   They couldn't give new medicines to us animals without testing them first. Stands to reason.

**Becky**   But why test them on poor Norman? It's not fair.

**Freda**   Especially after he saved your little brother.

**Becky**   Exactly. Norman's one of the family. He's an honorary animal.

**Chas**   I can't see there's much you can do, my old mate.

*The school bell rings.*

Hey up. Back to the grindstone.

*They start to go.*

**Becky**    Listen. Will you help? I've got a plan.

*Music as the scene clears.*

*The H.A.R.M. gatehouse is set.*

*Narration:*

**Actor Seven**    The Human Analysis and Research Ministry, was a dark, unwelcoming building surrounded by a high wall crowned with barbed wire. After school, Becky and her friends nervously approached the gatehouse.

**Scene Six**

*Outside H.A.R.M.*

*The four animals approach.*

*Suddenly a **Securiboar** appears at the gatehouse.*

**Securiboar**    What do you lot want? You're not thinking of trespassing, are you? 'Cos if you are, I might be thinking of persecution.

**Chas** (*cheekily*)    Don't you mean prosecution?

**Securiboar**    Both if necessary.

**Becky**    Sorry to bother you, sir, but we're doing a project at school. All about health and research into disease, that sort of thing . . .

**Securiboar**    Well?

**Becky**    Well, our teacher suggested we might interview the Director of this Ministry.

**Freda**    Get some facts and figures.

**Patch**    Straight from the horse's mouth.

**Securiboar**    The Director's not a horse. You want to get your facts right.

**Becky**    Exactly, sir. That's why we've come here.

*The **Securiboar** considers, then presses numbers on a portable phone.*

**Securiboar**    Hallo? Director, sir?

*The friends react.*

Security here. Group of school animals want to view you . . .

**Chas**    *Inter*view, dummy.

**Becky** *shushes him.*

**Securiboar** (*to* **Chas**)    Watch it! (*On the phone.*) Interview you. For a reject.

**Patch**    Project, stupid.

**Becky** *shushes him.*

**Securiboar** (*to* **Patch**)    Watch it! (*On the phone.*) No, sir, not you. Er . . . project. (*Pause.*) Right, sir. (*To the others.*) First left. Across the courtyard. In the main entrance.

**Becky**    Oh, thank you.

*They start to go through the gatehouse.*

**Securiboar**    And . . .

*They turn.*

Watch it!

*The scene starts to clear. Tension music.*

*Narration:*

**Actor Seven**    Once inside, Patch, Freda and Chas headed straight for the Director's office.

*The three bid farewell to* **Becky** *and exit.*

**Actor Five**    But Becky tiptoed warily down a corridor.


**Scene Seven A**

*H.A.R.M. corridor.*

**Nurse Rat** *scuttles through.* **Becky** *hides.*

*A door marked 'office' opens and* **Dr Beagle** *emerges.* **Nurse Rat** *returns with* **Sister Guinea Pig.**

**Dr Beagle**    Sister Guinea Pig. A moment, if you please.

**Sister Guinea Pig**    Coming, Dr Beagle.

*They exit, past the hiding* **Becky.** **Nurse Rat** *leaves, in the other direction.*

**Becky** *tiptoes further along the corridor.*

*Suddenly* **Nurse Rat** *returns.*

**Becky** *dives into the door in the nick of time.*

**Nurse Rat** *passes and exits.*

**Becky** *emerges from the door. She carefully checks the coast is clear, then exits.*

*Music continues as the door moves, to become the Director's door.*

**Dr Beagle** *and* **Sister Guinea Pig** *emerge from it and exit.*

**Chas**, **Freda** *and* **Patch** *enter and knock on the door.*

**Professor Rhino** (*off*)    Enter!

*They enter the door, which then exits.*

*Meanwhile* **Professor Rhino**'s *desk is set.*

*Narration:*

**Actor Four**    Chas, Freda and Patch found themselves in the presence of . . .

*An* **Actor** *enters and puts on his* **Professor Rhino** *mask.*

**Actor Four**    . . . Professor Rhino.

*He goes behind his desk.*


**Scene Seven B**

**Professor Rhino**'s *office.*

*Narration:*

**Actor Four**    He welcomed his visitors and described to them the work of the Ministry.

**Professor Rhino**    Have any of you suffered from ringworm? Rabies? Foot and mouth disease? Scurvy? Distemper? Mixamatosis?

*The animals shudder and shake their heads.*

**Freda**    No, sir.

**Professor Rhino** (*triumphantly*)    Of course not! I and my colleagues have thoroughly researched these diseases and wiped them from the face of the Earth. Impressive, eh?

*The animals nod.*

**Chas**    Yes, sir.

**Patch**    We quite understand, sir, that some experiments are necessary on humans . . .

**Professor Rhino**    Indeed they are! If we animal scientists were to experiment on animals, just imagine the howls of protest we would receive from the general animal public.

*Music. The action freezes and the lighting changes.*

*On the other side of the stage, two cages appear.* **Norman** *is in one, a female human – at present concealed – is in the other.*

*A* **Securiboar** *enters. He locks the cage door, placing the keys on a visible hook.*

**Scene Seven C**

*Inside the laboratory.*

*The action follows the narration.*

*Music continues.*

*Narration:*

**Actor One**    After locking Norman up, the Securiboar gave him an injection to make him sleep.

**Norman** *crumples.*

*The* **Securiboar** *leaves.*

*Lighting changes to suggest the passage of time.*

**Actor Two**    When he awoke some hours later, Norman took stock of his surroundings. The low roof of the cage didn't allow him to stand up straight. And the straw on the floor was damp and dirty.

*A sudden tapping sound.* **Norman** *reacts.*

**Actor Two**    A tapping sound.

*More tapping.*

From the cage next door. Pressing his face tight to the bars, Norman saw two frightened eyes staring into his.

**Actor Six**    A female human face, pale and nervous as Norman's. A flicker of a smile, a flash of hope at finding a fellow victim.

*Slowly the female human stretches her arm through the bars.*

**Norman** *does the same. Their hands meet and clasp.*

**Becky** *enters.*

**Actor Five**    Becky found the laboratory.

**Becky** *looks along the cages.*

**Becky** (*whispering*)    Norman! Norman!

*She finds him. The female human drops his hand and nervously retreats.* **Norman** *smiles at* **Becky**.

**Becky**    Come on. We're going home.

**Norman** *points to the keys.* **Becky** *finds them and unlocks the cage door.* **Norman** *comes out, but remembers the female human, takes her hand and looks imploringly at* **Becky**. **Becky** *sees the female human.*

**Becky** (*understanding*)    I see. Come on then.

*She unbolts the female human's cage. The female human emerges and hugs* **Norman**. *They look gratefully at* **Becky**, *who, replacing the keys, bids them follow.*

*They all exit.*

**Actors** *follow the narration.*

*Narration:*

**Actor One**   As they left, hundreds of arms pressed through the bars of hundreds of cages as hundreds of humans, hands outstretched, begged to be saved too.


**Scene Seven D**

**Professor Rhino**'s *office.*

*Music as the lighting unfreezes the scene.* **Professor Rhino, Chas, Freda** *and* **Patch** *resume their conversation.*

**Freda**   But, Professor Rhino, sir, do the humans suffer much pain?

**Professor Rhino**   Of course not. Our scientists are trained to damage them as little as possible. We value them too much. You see, (*Confidentially.*) the fact is humans are getting rather scarce. Quite difficult to come by.

**Chas**   Is that why you send out vans looking for them?

**Patch**   We saw one the other day.

**Professor Rhino**   Really? Most observant of you. Yes, we are allowed to pick up, er . . . stray humans wandering the streets.

**Freda**   But not pet humans?

**Professor Rhino**   Pet humans? (*He laughs.*) Of course not, my dear. Of course not.

*The animals look at each other.*

*Suddenly a loud alarm bell rings.* **Professor Rhino** *jumps.*

Excuse me. Emergency!

*The Director's door 'enters' and he dashes through it as the scene begins to change.*

*The animals exit.*


**Scene Seven E**

*H.A.R.M. corridor.*

**Nurse Rat** *dashes on.*

**Professor Rhino** (*roaring*)   Nurse Rat! What's going on?

**Nurse Rat**   An escape, Professor, an escape!

**Professor Rhino** *and* **Nurse Rat** *exit in confusion.*

*The alarm continues to ring.*

*The Director's door retreats.*

*Music as a stylised chase sequence begins.*

**Becky**, **Norman** *and the female human gingerly enter and cross, but have to retreat when spotted by* **Professor Rhino**. *All chase off.*

*The three animals enter the other side and cross, but are spotted by* **Professor Rhino**, *who chases them off again.*

*The door approaches, becoming the office door.*

**Becky**, **Norman** *and the female human enter and start to escape. But they see* **Professor Rhino** *advancing, and take refuge in the office.*

**Professor Rhino** *passes the office, stops, scratches his head, and looks off to see the three animals advancing. He chases them off.*

**Becky**, **Norman** *and the female human come out of the office.* **Becky** *clutches a file marked 'Top Secret'. They escape.*

*The three animals also escape. Then* **Becky**, **Norman** *and the female human cross once again, leaving a frustrated* **Professor Rhino** *shaking his fists.*

*The lighting changes as:*

**Professor Rhino** *exits.*

*A clock begins to strike nine.*


**Scene Eight**

*The* **Bears**' *living room.*

*The kennel and television are set.*

*Lights up on* **Father** *and* **Mother Bear** *anxiously waiting. The clock finishes striking.*

**Mother**    It's late, Dad. I'm worried.

**Father**    Dammit, where is she?

**Becky** *rushes in.*

**Becky**    Oh Mum, Dad.

*They embrace.*

**Mother**    Where have you been, Becky?

**Becky**    I'm fine, Mum, really. Look.

**Norman** *enters.*

**Mother**    Norman. (*She makes a fuss of him.*)

**Father**    You found him! Good boy, Norman. Welcome home.

*The female human enters nervously.*

**Mother**    Who's this?

**Becky**    Norman's friend. Mother, say she can stay.

**Norman** *looks imploringly at* **Mother**.

**Becky**    Please.

**Mother**    Well, I . . . of course she can.

*Delighted,* **Norman** *shows the female human to his kennel.*

**Father**    What's her name?

**Becky**    No idea, Dad.

**Mother**    We'll call her . . . Norma.

**Norma** *pops her head out and smiles.*

**Mother**    All right, Norma? Good.

**Father** (*turning on the television*)    Just catch the late night news.

*News signature tune.*

**Newshound** *appears on the screen.*

**Newshound**    Good evening, good evening! This is Newshound with the latest update. Two humans escaped from the Human Analysis and Research Ministry tonight. Professor Rhino, the Director, has ordered a Securiboar search. It is thought that human rights activists were responsible. Here ends this update.

**Father** *turns off the television.*

**Mother**    Oh, Becky, you didn't.

**Becky**    I had to, Mum.

**Father**    We'll have to keep Norman and Norma indoors for a while. During the day, anyway. Maybe take them for walks at night, when it's dark. Those Securiboars mean business.

*Music.*

*The scene clears around* **Becky**.

**Chas**, **Freda** *and* **Patch** *enter.*

*Narration:*

**Actor Five**    After school dinner next day, Becky and her friends met as usual in the playground.

**Scene Nine**

*The school playground.*

**Freda** *plays hopscotch.* **Chas** *and* **Patch** *play conkers.*

**Becky** *enters with the 'Top Secret' file.*

**Becky**   Thanks for yesterday. You were all brilliant.

**Chas**   Our pleasure.

**Freda**   We enjoyed it.

**Patch**   It was exciting.

**Chas**   How's Norman?

**Becky**   Fine. And his friend. We've called her Norma. Now, everyone. Look at this. (*She shows them the file.*) 'Top Secret'.

*The others stop playing and join* **Becky**.

I found it in an office at H.A.R.M.

**Patch**   A bit dangerous stealing it.

**Becky**   Maybe. But just as well I did. (*She opens the file.*) Listen. (*Reading.*) 'Confidential memo. Because of the growing worldwide shortage of humans a regular supply for experimental research is becoming harder to obtain.'

**Patch**   He told us that . . .

*The others 'shush' him.*

**Becky** (*reading*)   'From now on, all Securiboars have the power to arrest or capture not just strays but *any* humans they can find. Signed Professor Rhino, Director.'

**Freda**   So he was lying.

**Becky**   Of course. And don't you see? The more tower blocks they demolish, the more humans become homeless, and the more likely they are to end up in H.A.R.M.

**Chas**   They'll soon be extinct anyway. We learned that in history.

**Patch**   There's nothing anyone can do, I reckon.

**Becky**   But there must be. And we're the animals to do it. We've got to tell the world . . . to save the humans before it's too late.

**Patch**   Save the humans? Us?

**Becky**   Why not? (*Her voice rises.*) Are you with me? A campaign! Save the human! Save the human!

*Music heralds a burst of activity as the scene changes.*

**Scene Ten**

*The campaign.*

SONG: **Save the Human**

**Becky**
Save the Human
He won't die
If we try
To

**Becky**, **Freda**, **Patch** *and* **Chas**
Save the Human
Let him be
Set him free.

*They are joined by* **Ben** *in his buggy,* **Father** *and* **Mother Bear**.

**All**
Save the Human
Let's be fair
Show we care
And
Save the Human
End this crime
While there's time.

Save the Human
Save him now
Save the Human
Somehow.

**Newshound** *enters.*

**Newshound (Actor Four)**    Hallo, viewers, hallo. It's your roving reporter
Newshound here, with a special report. Becky Bear's campaign to 'Save the Human'
is hitting the headlines. Tell us, Becky, how did you start?

*(He holds an imaginary microphone near* **Becky**.*)*

**Becky**    With a petition.

**Chas**, **Freda** *and* **Patch** *hold up clipboards.*

**Becky**    My friends and I asked other animals to sign it.

*The animals mime approaching other animals, and, out front, almost invite the
audience to sign.*

**Chas**, **Freda** *and* **Patch** (*variously*)
Save the Human.
Save the Human.
Save the Human.

**Becky**   We got thousands of signatures.

**Chas**, **Patch** *and* **Freda** *exit.*

**Newshound**   What then, Becky?

**Becky**   We needed money. So we decided to sell our old toys.

**Ben** *holds up toys as* **Father Bear** *wheels him along.*

**Ben**   Save the Human! Save the Human! Save the Human!

**Newshound**   Anything else, Becky?

**Becky**   Well, yes, we put on a concert at school.

*Lights brighten and music changes to music-hall-type accompaniment.*

**Chas** *enters miming juggling,* **Patch** *enters dancing and* **Freda** *enters miming singing (or other similar activities).*

*They finish their brief entertainment with a flourish and a chord. Loud applause.*

*All except* **Becky** *and* **Newshound** *exit.*

**Becky**   Soon we had enough money to print hundreds of thousands of leaflets to spread the word about Save the Human. The Pigeon Post Office Union agreed to deliver the leaflets free, worldwide.

*Actors carry across puppets of pigeon postal officers on sticks. They exit.*

**Newshound**   And what was the response, Becky?

**Becky**   Overwhelming! Animals everywhere organised fund-raising events for Save the Human.

*Actors prepare to take up their masks and act out* **Becky**'s *speech.*

In Africa the animals held jungle sales. In Australia . . .

*A* **Kangaroo** *enters.*

**Kangaroo**   Boing.

**Becky**   Kangaroos . . .

**Kangaroo**   G'day.

**Becky**   . . . held sponsored hops.

**Kangaroo**   Save the Human! Ninety-five, ninety-six, ninety-seven! Save the Human!

*He exits.*

**Becky**    In the oceans of the world, sea creatures held sponsored swims.

*The* **Dolphin***, carried by two actors, swims across.*

**Becky**    And in America pigs held sponsored slims.

*A* **Pig** *is offered a box of chocolates, and stealthily goes to eat one.*

**Pig**    Oo! Choccychocs! No, no! I mustn't! I mustn't be tempted. Save the Human!

**All**    Save the Human!

*They cheer and exit to collect banners.*

**Newshound**    Congratulations, Becky, congratulations.

**Newshound** *leaves.*

*The music swells.*

SONG: **Save the Human** (*cont.*)

*During the first chorus,* **Becky** *welcomes on* **Patch, Freda, Chas, Mother, Father** *and* **Ben***. They all carry 'Save the Human' banners.*

**All**
Save the Human
Bang the drum
His time's come
Let's
Save the Human
Spread the word
Make it heard.

Save the Human
Take a stand
Shake his hand
And
Save the Human
Make amends
All make friends.

Mammals and reptiles
Birds of a feather
The moment has come
To stand together
Hot-blooded, cold-blooded,
Insects, fish
Join as one to make this wish.
Save the Human . . .

*The music continues.*

**Newshound** *brings on the television.*

**Becky** *appears on screen. The others watch; most in evidence are the proud* **Bear** *family.*

**Becky**   I wish to announce Save the Human's first Annual Conference, to be attended by delegates from all corners of the globe.

*All cheer.* **Becky** *waves.*

*The television exits.*

**All** (*singing*)
  Save the Human
  Save him now
  Save the Human . . .

*The music continues as the scene clears.*

*Narration:*

**Actor Four**   The Conference was held at the seaside, so that every kind of animal could attend, creatures of the earth, the sky, and the sea.

*Music as the delegates assemble for the conference, collecting their stick masks. Each actor can have two masks, thus increasing the number of delegates.*

(*To the audience.*) You and I are invited to attend as special delegates. Please, imagine you are an animal, any animal. And if you have a mask, please put it on. Now.

*The house lights come up as, hopefully, the audience put on their masks, led by the* **Narrator** *(***Actor Four***), holding a dolphin mask.*


**Scene Eleven**

*The seaside conference.*

*Narration:*

**Actor Four**   The Conference of the Animals!

*The actors use their stick masks as puppets.*

**Becky** *arrives and stands centre.*

**Becky** (*to the audience*)   Welcome. Thank you all for taking part in our conference today. Your representatives are ready to speak. Please, if you agree with their statements, show your support by answering, 'Hear, Hear'. The Dolphin.

*Animal delegates respond to each statement with 'Hear, Hear', to lead the audience.*

**Dolphin**   The human should be a protected species.

**All**   Hear, hear!

**Becky**    The Tiger.

**Tiger**    No more hunting humans for sport.

**All**    Hear, hear!

**Becky**    The Goose.

**Goose**    Fattening up humans for food must stop!

**All**    Hear, hear!

**Becky**    The Crocodile.

**Crocodile**    Hunting humans for their skins should be a crime!

**All**    Hear, hear!

**Becky**    The Ape.

**Chas**    Save the human habitat!

**All**    Hear, hear!

**Becky**    The Polar Bear.

**Polar Bear**    Close the zoos and create special Wild Human Estates!

**All**    Hear, hear!

**Becky**    The Elephant.

**Elephant**    Give humans back their dignity. No more circuses!

**All**    Hear, hear!

**Becky**    And I say: Ban all research experiments on humans.

**All**    Hear, hear!

*Cheers.*

Let every creature (*Taking in the audience.*) join in our anthem. Let the world hear our cry.

SONG: **Save the Human**

**All**
Save the Human
He won't die
If we try
To
Save the Human
Let him be
Set him free.

Save the Human
Let's be fair

Show we care
And
Save the Human
End this crime
While there's time.

Mammals and reptiles
Birds of a feather
The moment has come
To stand together
Hot-blooded, cold-blooded,
Insects, fish
Join as one to make this wish.

Save the Human
Bang the drum
His time's come
Let's
Save the Human
Spread the word
Make it heard.

Save the Human
Take a stand
Shake his hand
And
Save the Human
Make amends
All make friends.

*All encourage the audience to join in.*

Save the Human
Save the Human
Save the Human
Save the Human
Save the Human
Save the Human.

Let's unite
Fight and strive
For man's right
To stay alive
We pray
We may
Save the Human
Today.

*The house lights go out. The actors remain.*

*Narration:*

**Actor Two**   At home . . .

**Actor Six**   . . . Norman and Norma . . .

**Actors Two** *and* **Six**   . . . proudly watched their caring young owner on television. They smiled.

**Norman** *and* **Norma** *sit to one side of the stage.*

**Actors One, Three, Five, Seven** *and* **Eight**   Someone else was watching the jubilant scene on television. He was *not* smiling.

*On the other side,* **Professor Rhino** *enters, reacting with slow fury, plotting revenge.*

*Tension music swells until the . .*

*Blackout.*

*Curtain.*

# Act Two

*A darkened stage.*

*A cacophony of applause and excited cheering.*

*A pin-spot hits* **Patch**, *who is a DJ/presenter.*

**Patch**  Creatures of the world. A big, big welcome to the greatest, grooviest rock concert in Earth's history.

*Applause and cheering.*

Featuring all your favourite, fabulous artistes live by TV satellite to every corner of the globe, it's Human Aid!

*Applause and cheering.*

## Scene One

*The Human Aid concert.*

*Disco-style flashing lights.*

**Patch**  And who dreamed the whole thing up. Our own, one and only, Becky Bear!

*Screams and applause as* **Becky** *enters and takes a bow.*

**Becky**  Thank you, thank you. And now it's time to meet the Kings of the latest Jungle Sound . . . The Pride!

**The Pride** – *a group of lions with guitars, drums etc. – enter to cheers and screams, waving a greeting to the audience.*

**Becky** *stays at the side as a member of the audience, joining in when asked.*

*The* **Lead Lion** *comes forward, encouraging the audience to join in.*

**Actors** *as animals (*Chas, Patch, Freda*) go into the audience to lead them.*

**Lead Lion**  Are ya all right?

**Audience**  Yeah!

**Lead Lion**  I said, are ya all right?

**Audience**  Yeah!

**Lead Lion**  Every animal, let me hear ya! Are ya all right?

**Audience**  Yeah!

**Lead Lion**  Then let's rock 'n' roar. What are we gonna do?

**Audience**  Rock 'n' roar!

**Lead Lion**    Animal babies, I can't hear you! What are we gonna do?

**Audience**    Rock 'n' roar!

**Lead Lion**    One more time!

**Audience**    Rock 'n' roar!

SONG: **Rock 'n' Roar**

**The Pride**
>I wanna rock 'n' roar
>I wanna rock 'n' roar
>I wanna get back to the jungle
>Like I did before.
>
>I wanna rock 'n' roar
>I wanna rock 'n' roar
>I wanna turn back the clock
>An' do it some more.
>
>People are strange
>But they ain't bad
>An' makin' 'em extinct
>Just makes me sad.
>
>I wanna rock 'n' roar
>I wanna rock 'n' roar
>I wanna get back to the jungle
>Like I did before.
>
>I wanna rock 'n' roar
>I wanna rock 'n' roar
>I wanna turn back the clock
>An' do it some more.

*Instrumental break.*

>Come on hold out your paws
>To this thing called man
>Show him we love him
>Let him understand.
>
>I wanna rock 'n' roar
>I wanna rock 'n' roar
>I wanna get back to the jungle
>Like I did before.
>
>I wanna rock 'n' roar
>I wanna rock 'n' roar
>I wanna turn back the clock
>An' do it some more.

Come on let's make a move
While we're in the groove
And save mankind
While it's on our mind.

(*Chant.*)

I wanna rock 'n' roar
I wanna rock 'n' roar
I wanna rock 'n' roar
I wanna rock 'n' roar
I wanna rock 'n' roar
I wanna rock 'n' roar
I wanna turn back the clock
And do it some more.

*Audience roars of applause.*

**Lead Lion**   Thank you! An' goodnight y'all!

*More wild screams as* **The Pride** *exit.*

*The scene clears as* **Actors** *prepare to play news reporters, using stick masks.*

**Scene Two A**

*Newspaper headlines.*

**Chas** *mimes handing newspapers out.*

*Narration:*

**Actor Seven**   The world's press clamoured to proclaim the news! 'The News of the Earth. The News of the Earth.'

**Newshound**   Human Aid rocks the world.

*Narration:*

**Actor Seven**   'The Animal. The Animal.'

**Tiger**   Human Aid raises fortune for Save the Human.

*Narration:*

**Actor Seven**   'The Eagle. The Eagle.'

**Goose**   Becky Bear Megastar. Collect your coupons for 'I love my human' T-shirts.

*Narration:*

**Actor Seven**   'Mammals Monthly. Mammals Monthly.'

**Elephant**   Becky Bear entertained by world leaders.

*Narration:*

**Actor 7**   'Underwater Weekly. Underwater Weekly.'

**Dolphin**   World leaders' special meeting on Saving the Human.

*Narration:*

**Actor 7**   'Tortoise Express. Tortoise Express.'

**Crocodile**   Becky Bear invited to address United Creations.

*Music as the scene changes. A podium stands centre.* **Actors** *become listeners.*


**Scene Two B**

*The United Creations Assembly.*

**Becky** *ceremoniously steps to the podium. As she talks, her youthful enthusiasm should appear to have been overtaken by a professional gloss and awareness of presentation.*

**Becky**   Friends. You, world leaders all, have the power. I, a humble schoolbear, have the will. You are just. I seek justice. You are wise. I seek wisdom. Friends, I humbly and heartily beg you to get your act together and Save the Human NOW!

SONG: **I Love My Human**

> I love my human
> I'll stick by him till the end
> I treat him kindly
> And I find he
> Is my friend.
>
> I love my human
> Won't you love him too?
> Love your human
> And your human will love you.

*Loud applause, in which* **Becky** *basks.* **Actors**, *hands above their heads, clap in slow motion and surround her.*

*Then music picks up the 'I Love My Human' theme as the actors turn, as humans, realising their situation has improved.*

*Narration:*

**Actor 5**   Slowly but surely things began to improve. The human became a protected species. Hunting humans for sports, food or their skins became a thing of the past.

**Scene Three**

*A street with housing.*

*During this section, the lighting fades up slowly to suggest the dawn of the new human age.*

*Humans portray in mime their new freedom and peace. They demonstrate everyday human activity – sunbathing, picnicking, shopping, meeting friends, etc.*

*Narration:*

**Actor Five**    Humans were allowed to keep their tower blocks, and splendid Wild Human Estates were created, showing humans living in specially designed re-creations of their own habitat. Animal families and school parties flocked to see them, and enjoyed learning about these beings, whom they now accepted had a right to share the earth with them. Some animals joined 'Adopt-a-human' schemes and many stray humans were rescued and given good homes. And as the world became a safer place for humans, so their numbers began to increase.

*The lighting has reached its full intensity. A few relaxed humans bask happily in its warmth.*

**Becky** *proudly surveys the scene.*

SONG: **I Love My Human** (*cont.*)

**Becky**
    I love my human
    Won't you love him too?
    Love your human
    And your human will love you.

**Becky** *exits.*

*An insistent pulse to suggest imminent danger.*

*The humans, unsuspecting, relax.*

*The lights lower as* **Professor Rhino** *enters and surveys the scene. He laughs cruelly.*

*Seeing the humans in repose,* **Professor Rhino** *gives a signal.*

**Professor Rhino**    Now!

*Music as, almost in silent-film style, the H.A.R.M. van enters at speed. Out pop two* **Securiboars**, *who, in slow motion, bundle two humans inside and drive off, as other humans run for safety.*

**Professor Rhino** *rubs his hands in glee and, laughing a bloodcurdling laugh, exits.*

**Scene Four**

*The school playground.*

*Sad music and the sound of an electronic game introduce the scene.* **Patch** *and* **Chas** *sit, morose and silent.* **Freda** *plays with the electronic game.*

**Freda**   Want a game?

**Patch** *and* **Chas** *shake their heads.*

**Becky** *enters.*

**Freda** (*seeing* **Becky** *approach*)   Hi, Becky.

**Becky**   Hallo, Freda. Can't stop. Got a meeting.

**Freda**   Another meeting?

**Becky**   About the new Centre for Human Studies. (*Seeing* **Chas** *and* **Patch**.) What's the matter with them?

**Freda**   The Securiboars snatched their pet-humans yesterday.

**Becky**   Oh. (*She goes to them.*) I'm sorry.

**Chas**   H.A.R.M. should be closed down.

**Becky**   No chance, I'm afraid. Not yet anyway. I had a meeting with Professor Rhino.

*The others are surprised.*

**Patch**   What did he say?

**Becky**   Nothing new. He believes his work benefits all animal life. I suppose we have to respect that.

**Freda**   Nonsense. You don't really believe that. If you do, why did you rescue Norman?

**Becky**   That was different. He was my pet.

**Chas**   What's so special about *your* pet? Why aren't we rescuing other people's pets?

**Patch**   *Our* pets.

**Chas**   And all the other wretched humans suffering under Rhino?

**Freda**   Come on, Becky. We helped you, please help us.

**Patch** *and* **Chas**   Yes! Please!

**Becky**   I'm sorry. 'Save the Human' has never committed crimes to plead its cause. Peaceful persuasion is still the right way. Believe me. Now, if you'll excuse me . . .

*She leaves.*

**Freda**    Becky's changed.

*Narration:*

**Actor Seven**    The three friends decided to go it alone.

*They put their heads together, plotting.*

**Actor Three**    Secretly they planned and plotted.

**Actor Eight**    Late into the night.

*Lights fade as the scene changes.*

*The H.A.R.M. gatehouse enters.*

## Scene Five A

*Outside H.A.R.M. Night.*

*Through the shadows,* **Patch**, **Chas** *and* **Freda** *gingerly approach the gatehouse.* **Chas** *shines a torch.*

*Suddenly a* **Securiboar** *pops out of the gatehouse. After a 'Grandmother's Footsteps' attempt to get past him, the friends are spotted.*

*The* **Securiboar** *grabs* **Patch** *and* **Freda** *and makes to cosh them.* **Chas** *tries to intervene, and, grabbing the cosh from behind, unintentionally, in self-defence, coshes the furious advancing* **Securiboar**, *who sways, stunned.*

*The friends slip in through the gatehouse.*

*The scene clears.*

## Scene Five B

*H.A.R.M. corridor.*

**Chas**, **Patch** *and* **Freda** *creep along the corridor.*

*The door to the laboratory enters, then opens.* **Dr Beagle** *and* **Nurse Rat** *emerge. The friends hide as they exit.*

*Then the friends tiptoe through the door, which clears as the scene changes.*

## Scene Five C

*Inside the laboratory.*

*Two cages with pet-humans in. Rows of cages could be visible or imagined.*

*The friends see their pet-humans, find the keys and set them free. They replace the keys, and all start to leave. The pet-humans stop and indicate the other cages. The friends understand and start miming opening all the cages. A flow of humans escape, joyfully drinking in the fresh air.*

**Actors** *exit and reappear several times to give the impression of a mass escape.*

*The scene clears as humans celebrate.*

*Sinister music leads to . . .*

**Scene Six**

**Professor Rhino** *'s office.*

**Professor Rhino** *and a* **Securiboar***.*

**Professor Rhino**    You fool! You incompetent fool!

**Securiboar**    Yes, sir. Sorry, sir. They were too quick for me, sir.

**Professor Rhino**    My life's work ruined. Not one research human left! Who did it? Who?

**Securiboar**    Don't ask me, sir. I never saw them. But they stuck these stickers all over the lab.

**Professor Rhino**    I might have guessed! 'Save the Human'. It's that Bear. That meddling little Bear!

*Music as the scene clears.*

*Narration:*

**Actor Five**    All this time, Becky had been at home, in bed asleep. Next morning, when she had finished her breakfast, she turned on the television as usual.

**Scene Seven**

*The* **Bears**' *living room.*

**Becky** *turns on the television.* **Mother, Father** *and* **Ben** *are at the breakfast table.* **Norman** *and* **Norma** *are not visible but are in their kennel. We hear the news signature tune.*

**Newshound**    Good day, good day! This is Newshound with the latest update.

**Ben**    I want a drink, please.

**Mother**    Quiet, Ben.

**Ben**    I said please.

**Father** Shh.

**Newshound** News is coming in of a mass escape of research humans from the laboratory of H.A.R.M.

*All take an urgent interest.*

It is suspected that members of the 'Save the Human' campaign were responsible.

**Becky** (*turning off the television*) Oh, no. Chas, Patch and Freda. I tried to warn them.

*Suddenly there is an urgent knocking on the door and off-stage cries of 'open up'. Music for tension.*

*Two* **Securiboars** *rush in.*

*The* **Bears** *leap up.* **Ben** *cries.*

**Securiboar One** You're coming with us. Professor Rhino's orders. Subversive suspection. I mean, Suspertive subvection. Or something like that.

**Mother** You can't take my daughter! It was nothing to do with her.

**Securiboar Two** We're not taking your daughter, missis. We're taking all of you.

*The* **Securiboars** *bundle the* **Bears** *off.*

**Norman** *and* **Norma** *emerge warily and look off.*

*Narration:*

**Actor Two** Norman awoke, to see his caring owners bundled roughly into a Securiboar van, the very van in which he had been captured before.

**Norman** *clasps* **Norma***'s hand.*

**Actor Six** Norma owed her life to the Bears. As she watched them driven away, she wondered if she and Norman would ever see them again.

*Short freeze. Then the lighting fades. Music as the scene clears.*

*In semi-darkness, two cages are set. A* **Securiboar** *leads the* **Bears** *on and roughly locks them up –* **Ben** *and* **Becky** *in one cage,* **Mother** *and* **Father** *in the other. He returns the keys to their hook and exits.*


**Scene Eight**

*Inside the laboratory.*

*Lights up on the* **Bears** *huddled sadly in their cages.*

**Ben** Mummy!

**Ben***'s hand stretches through the bars. From the other cage* **Mother** *extends a hand and squeezes* **Ben***'s hand.*

**Professor Rhino** *enters.*

**Professor Rhino**    Aha! The 'Save the Human' mob! Welcome!

**Father**    Listen, you can't treat us like this. How dare you!

**Professor Rhino**    How dare your wretched daughter ruin my life's work? Without humans to test on, how can I make the world a better place?

**Becky**    I want to make the world a better place too.

*Sinister music.*

**Professor Rhino**    In that case, I'm quite sure you will not mind sacrificing your family and yourself to the cause of my animal welfare research. Tomorrow we will commence experiments. On you. (*He laughs evilly.*)

*The lighting fades.*

*The scene clears.*

*Narration:*

**Actor Three**    Meanwhile, what had happened to the research humans? Chas, Patch and Freda had set them free thinking they would be happy, thinking they would be grateful.


**Scene Nine**

*Street with housing.*

*Humans start to enter.* **Actor Three** *joins them.*

*Narration:*

**Actors One, Two, Four, Five** *and* **Six**    But in their hundreds they roamed the city in packs, angry with the animal kingdom, determined and thirsting for . . .

*Lights brighten as the humans chant.*

**Humans**    Revenge! Revenge! Revenge!

*A stylised, slow-motion mime, in semi-silhouette, echoes the narration. Perhaps the 'revenge' chant continues under.*

*Narration:*

**Actor Seven**    They rampaged through the streets, smashing windows and breaking into animals' homes. They destroyed property, set fire to buildings and terrified innocent animals.

*Smoke appears. The lighting begins to turn red with flames.*

**Actor Eight**    News of the human riots spread. Other humans decided to join the rebels. Pet-humans attacked their animal owners, performing humans refused to perform, working humans stopped working and joined their colleagues on the streets.

**Actor Seven**   They stormed the Wild Human Estates, encouraging the humans living there to revolt.

**Chas** *and* **Freda** *enter.*

**Chas** *and* **Freda**   The animals pleaded with them to stop.

**Chas** *and* **Freda** *appeal for mercy to the humans. Tense pause. Then the humans, in slow motion, knock over* **Chas** *and* **Freda** *and come forward chanting.*

**Humans**   Revenge! Revenge! Revenge! (*They freeze.*)

**Newshound** *appears.*

**Newshound**   Update! Update! Following the mysterious disappearance of their leader, Becky Bear, 'Save the Human' announce a Crisis Conference at the seaside.

*The humans begin to advance.*

(*Urgently, terrified, seeing the humans advancing.*) The world is in chaos!

**Humans**   Revenge!

**Newshound**   Animals are dying.

**Humans**   Revenge!

**Newshound**   Is history repeating itself?

**Humans**   Revenge!

**Newshound**   Will humans take over the world?

**Humans**   Revenge!

**Newshound** *is chased off in terror.*

*Narration:*

**Actor Two**   But through the chaos crept two humans who still loved their animal owners.

**Norman** *and* **Norma** *appear, and pick their way through other humans.*

**Actor Six**   They had a new mission.

**Actors Two** *and* **Six**   To 'Save the Bears'.

*Music changes to accompany a stylised journey.*

*The scene clears.*

**Scene Ten A**

*Outside H.A.R.M.*

*A* **Securiboar** *is on duty by the gatehouse.*

**Norman** *and* **Norma** *manage to evade him as he parades.*

*But he suddenly sees them. He tries unsuccessfully to cosh them. A short chase ensues. The* **Securiboar** *trips and falls.*

**Norman** *and* **Norma** *manage to escape the* **Securiboar** *and slip through the gatehouse.*

*The* **Securiboar** *picks himself up, blows a whistle and exits in the wrong direction.*

*The scene clears. The laboratory door enters.*

## Scene Ten B

*H.A.R.M. corridor.*

**Norman** *and* **Norma** *dart down the corridor searching for the right door. As they reach it, the door opens and* **Professor Rhino** *emerges.*

**Norman** *and* **Norma** *flatten themselves against the wall.*

**Professor Rhino** *passes them and exits.*

**Norman** *and* **Norma** *slip through the door.*

*The* **Securiboar** *enters, searching for them.*

*He cannot find them. He blows his whistle.*

**Professor Rhino** *returns. They exchange an animated mimed conversation, then exit.*

*The scene clears. Two cages enter with the* **Bears** *inside.*

## Scene Ten C

*Inside the laboratory.*

**Norman** *and* **Norma** *reach the cages, find the keys and release the delighted* **Bears***. Greetings, embraces. As they replace the keys and turn to leave,* **Professor Rhino** *and the* **Securiboar** *suddenly enter and confront them.*

*A struggle ensues, in which* **Professor Rhino** *grabs* **Norma** *and the* **Securiboar** *grabs* **Norman***.*

**Norma** *manages to kick the* **Securiboar***'s rear. He lets go of* **Norman** *and furiously goes to cosh* **Norma***, who ducks.* **Professor Rhino** *receives a hard blow instead. He releases* **Norma***.*

**Norman** *and* **Norma** *escape.*

**Professor Rhino** *furiously coshes the* **Securiboar** *and sends him off in pursuit.*

*The* **Securiboar** *exits.*

**Professor Rhino** *forces the* **Bears** *back into one cage, locks it and replaces the keys.*

**Norman** *and* **Norma** *return and nearly bump into* **Professor Rhino**. *They turn to escape, but are trapped by the arrival of the* **Securiboar.**

**Professor Rhino** *and the* **Securiboar** *advance at speed.* **Norman** *and* **Norma** *separate.* **Professor Rhino** *and the* **Securiboar** *collide head on and fall over.*

**Norman** *and* **Norma** *escape.*

**Professor Rhino** *and the* **Securiboar** *stagger to their feet and exit in pursuit.*

**Norman** *and* **Norma** *enter.*

*They fetch the keys and release the* **Bears**. *They all hide as* **Professor Rhino** *and the* **Securiboar** *return.*

**Professor Rhino** *and the* **Securiboar** *find the cage empty, and, bemused, enter it in disbelief, searching for their prisoners.* **Norman** *and* **Norma** *dash out then lock the cage door in triumph.*

*Lighting fades as the* **Bears** *and* **Norman** *and* **Norma** *make their triumphant escape.*

**Professor Rhino** *shakes his fists, defeated.*

*The scene clears to a bare stage.*

*Narration:*

**Actor Three**    With great care, Norman and Norma led the Bears through war-torn streets where animal-hating humans lurked, ready to attack. At last they reached the seaside.


**Scene Eleven A**

*The seaside.*

**Norman, Norma** *and the* **Bears** *arrive and huddle together.*

*Narration:*

**Actor Three**    The 'Save the Human' Crisis Conference was due to start, but no animals had arrived to take part. Many would not risk the journey. And, in the light of recent developments, many no longer felt able to support the campaign.

**Becky** (*desolate*)    It's all over.

**Father**    You tried, Becky. You did your best. And we're safe.

**Chas, Patch** *and* **Freda** *rush on.*

**Chas**    They're here!

**Becky** (*tiredly*)    Hallo, Chas, Freda, Patch.

**Patch**    You made it then!

**Becky** *nods.*

**Freda**    And so did we!

**Becky**    But nobody else, Freda.

*Pause.*

**Chas**    Becky, we're sorry. It was our fault.

**Becky**    No, it was mine. I got big-headed. Carried away. Forgot who my real friends are. I'm the one who's sorry.

**Patch**    But we should never have broken into H.A.R.M. and saved those humans. That's what started it.

**Becky**    Maybe we should never have started it in the first place. Maybe the humans weren't ready to be saved. Maybe they shouldn't have any freedom. Maybe they'll make a mess of things like they did last time. Maybe this time they'll destroy themselves.

*They all turn to look inland. A flame effect. Smoke.*

*The 'I Love My Human' theme starts under:*

*Narration:*

**Actor Five**    Becky, her family, her friends and her pet humans looked sadly at a world once more in turmoil.

**Becky** *whispers an idea to* **Chas**, **Patch** *and* **Freda**. *They fetch a boat and all board it.*

**Actor Five**    They set off in a boat, leaving the smoky battleground behind them.


**Scene Eleven B**

*The sea.*

*The boat slowly sails away, then comes to a stop.*

*Narration:*

**Actor Five**    They found an empty desert island, miles from anywhere. Together animals and humans started again. Together they lived in peace.

SONG: **I Love My Human** (*reprise*)

**Animals**
    I love my human
    I'll stick by him till the end
    I treat him kindly
    And I find he
    Is my friend.

**Norman** *and* **Norma** *leave the boat and look at their new land.*

**Animals**
> I love my human
> Won't you love him too?
> Love your human

**Norman** *and* **Norma**
> And your human will love you.

*The lights fade to blackout.*

*Curtain.*

*As the light brighten, the* **Actors** *remove their masks for the curtain call.*

**Suggested curtain call reprises:**

**All**
> I wanna rock 'n' roar
> I wanna rock 'n' roar
> I wanna get back to the jungle
> Like I did before.
>
> I wanna rock 'n' roar
> I wanna rock 'n' roar
> I wanna turn back the clock
> And do it some more.
>
> Come on let's make a move
> While we're in the groove
> And save mankind
> While it's on our mind.
>
> I wanna rock 'n' roar
> I wanna rock 'n' roar
> I wanna rock 'n' roar
> I wanna rock 'n' roar
> I wanna rock 'n' roar
> I wanna rock 'n' roar
> I wanna turn back the clock
> And do it some more.
>
> Save the Human
> Bang the drum
> His time's come
> Let's
> Save the Human
> Spread the word
> Make it heard.

Save the Human
Take a stand
Shake his hand
Let's
Save the Human
Make amends
All make friends.

Save the Human
Save the Human
Save the Human
Save the Human
Save the Human
Save the Human
Let's unite
Fight and strive
For man's right
To stay alive
We pray
We may
Save the Human today.

# Mother Goose's Golden Christmas – Teacher Notes

**Age range:** KS2 (could make a good teachers' show for KS1!)
**Number of actors:** 12+
**Running time:** Approx. 90 minutes

This is a 'proper' pantomime with lots of physical comedy, traditional characters, fairy-tale fun, audience interaction and brilliant songs to be sung. You can be inventive and creative making set and costumes, and you might even be able to find some real live sheep for the ending . . .

## Characters

The original casting has some doubling up on the roles Monster of the Moat and Spider; though these would provide fun non-speaking roles for a school performance. There is also plenty of opportunity here for stage hands to move set, place props and manipulate puppets.

Due to the fairy-tale origins of most of the characters they will be more recognisable as their intended gender, and the playwright suggests a Victorian look to them and the play. I would say there is some potential fun in 'modernising' the characters (see costume) which might allow gender swaps too. Humpty Dumpty, the Giant, Goose and Wolves can be unisex.

Mother Goose, the five fairy-tale characters and the two Wolves are the main parts, and actors will require enough confidence to facilitate audience interaction – one of the best bits about this play! Fairy Lethargia is a smaller part, appearing sporadically, and I would allow this character to appear when needed from offstage.

Good roles to involve reluctant speakers are Gertie the Goose, a non-speaking part that relies on movement and mime, but could also be shown as a puppet; the Monster of the Moat will need to be operated as a giant puppet, perhaps by several people; and the Spider can be a puppet or a person, but again with no dialogue.

The Giant speaks mostly offstage, and where he would appear in the last scene you can continue to speak offstage if you wish – meaning we never see the Giant but this perhaps adds to the mystery – but might have to sacrifice the Act Two, Scene Five sequence where Jack fights the Giant (see below). You could imagine the Giant is offstage, and everyone looks up and off when they speak to him.

Having the Giant speaking offstage using a microphone adds an ominous volume, and there are also possibilities to green-screen and project the Giant when he appears if you have the technology.

## Costumes and props

The playwright suggests a Victorian theme, and given the pantomime nature of the play an authentic attempt at the characters' costumes as we know them from the fairy tales would certainly suit. It could be fun to 'modernise' the traditional characters, so Mother Goose is a kind of 2020s mum, Tommy Tucker a teenager eating crisps, Bo Peep on her mobile phone and is 'losing' sheep on an app or game. Perhaps the Wolves are in leather jackets and bovver boots and the Fairy is a YouTuber.

If you choose to use an actor to play the Spider, dress all in black with black tubing attached, perhaps.

The Monster of the Moat could be a fun one to build in the style of a Chinese dragon/Loch Ness Monster with numerous cardboard sections. Four or five people dressed in green with simple masks works fine, though, providing they rehearse moving as one or at least in unison to give the effect of singularity.

The scene that requires Mother Goose to be in her underwear might be best as a nightie!

Some characters need specific personal props that you will probably need to stick to: Bo Peep with her crook/mobile phone, Fairy's wand, Miss Muffet with her curds and whey, the Big Bad Wolf with his tablets (a mix of sweets and bouncy balls in a brown paper bag), etc.

There are a number of scenes which detail specific props, for example the figgy pudding baking, which are integral to the physical comedy.

### Staging

The action takes place in several locations: the kitchen inside the Book, outside the Book, the forest, outside the Giant's castle and inside the Giant's castle.

Projections of each setting could work well and is a quick and easy method; simple scenery can then be used in addition for each scene. A kitchen table, a 'tree' made from a stepladder or whirligig, a box or chair as a tuffet. The stage directions state a door, but an entrance/exit stage left, right and upstage centre will suffice. A fourth entrance through the audience can always be used too.

You might also use a fairy-tale-style wooden sign that is changed each scene which states: 'Outside the Fairytale House' or 'The Spooky Forest', etc. There are several opportunities to act in the audience, for example where the Wolves are plotting, which would add to the playful interactive pantomime nature of the piece.

The scenes at the Giant's castle involve a drawbridge and a moat, an underwater sequence and, inside, giant furniture and props. If you have staging platforms you can make a raised bridge that, in the absence of being drawn up and down, can simply be walked across once the password is said. If you cover the front of this, the Monster of the Moat can be hidden behind. More abstractly, a piece of long green material can be a slimy moat, and grey boxes/blocks stepping stones across. These changes would require slight adaption to the script of course.

Inside the Giant's house features oversized scenery which would need to be built. The chair will need to be a raised platform.

You will need a cage (cardboard bars held by stage hands work fine – this can be pivoted outwards to 'open'), while the rest of the action can take place on the floor, as it is the movement sequences with Mother Goose and Wolves which is the engaging action here, and the Wolves can be captured in the cage itself in the absence of an oven.

### Special props

The variously sized golden eggs can be a series of balloons, papier-mâché shapes, a beach ball, a gym ball; the oversized key and fork made from adapted brooms or cardboard tubing painted silver or gold.

**Music, sound effects and lighting**
The songs in this play are brilliant and will get the audience singing along too, which is an important feature of this 'family musical'. Bear this in mind when casting the roles.

Given the play is set at Christmas, and the first song is a carol, you could intersperse some festive songs throughout, making sure you have permissions, etc. Carols are usually licence-free.

Another idea is that you could use the original nursery rhymes spoken by the characters; the audience can play along with this too.

There are some specific special effects that add to the comedy, the Wolf's explosion in the cauldron for example, and these can be easily sourced online.


**Other considerations**
Audience interaction – there is lots of audience involvement here, by lots of different characters, which gives the play its lovely pantomime feel. There is no reason young actors cannot facilitate these moments, but they should be rehearsed with a live practice audience, and plans should be made for unexpected outcomes.

Choreographed movement sequences – as is effective in children's theatre there is a lot of visual comedy, including some slapstick routines. Most – including Act One, Scene Two with the Spider, Act One, Scene Three with Mother Goose and Tommy Tucker's baking, and others – are all explained in detail in the stage directions. Use the lesson plan for some further ideas but the key thing is to make sure they are well rehearsed, not too complicated and – above all – safe!

The underwater sequence can staged beautifully in slow motion and in a blue light, with some bubbly special effects if you like.

The ending sees Jack fighting the Giant, which is our exciting finale. The scene could end with Mother Goose trapping the Wolves bullfighter-style, though Little Jack would not get his 'big moment' – but he could be involved in the capture of the Wolves too.

Alternatively, the tussle between Jack and the Giant could be offstage, and we could only hear it. Real comedy could be created by the characters onstage reacting to sounds offstage of various punches, bops and an eventual splash in the moat. This would work for a shadow puppet fight too. If you use an actual onstage puppet for the Giant, then the fight can be more literal; you might wish to either run it in slow motion or, in the place of any contact between them, have Jack catapult something à la David and Goliath.

For the flying of the Goose and the hatching of Humpty Dumpty from the Golden Egg, a table top can represent the Goose's back, and the egg can be taken offstage, cracking sounds heard and the Humpty Dumpty character enter. I will leave you to decide whether you use real sheep or actors for the very end . . .!


**Lesson plan – Slapstick and physical comedy**
*Mother Goose's Golden Christmas* is full of lovely physical comedy; here are some activities to get that started.

*Starter activity*
In pairs ask students to create a sequence of mirrored movements using actions, facial expressions and movements – but no words. The focus is on good timing and imagination.

*Engaging*
Next set them the challenge of performing a sequence of slapstick comedy business. Teacher can demo: tapping on one shoulder and looking over the other, walking backwards and bumping into each other, miming a dropped banana skin and slipping over, ducking under an outstretched arm when someone points, running over and accidentally standing on someone's toe (stand slightly to the side, not on the actual toe!) etc. The focus is on reactions – there should be no or very little actual physical contact.

*Developing*
Using Jack's battle with the Giant at the end of the play as inspiration, students can devise a slapstick slow-motion fight sequence. Make sure all actions are planned and safe.

**Other activities**
It can be a fun task to take existing nursery rhymes and 'update' them to the modern day. So Red Riding Hood might be 'Red Riding Hoodie', Jack and the Beanstalk might be Sidney and the Skyscraper. These can be acted out in a series of still images, or can form a literacy task looking at narrative structure.

Puppetry basics activity from *The BFG* teacher notes might be useful here, as well as the character work from *The Gingerbread Man*.

# Mother Goose's Golden Christmas

**Book, music and lyrics by David Wood**

With sincere thanks to

John Hole

for whom this is my tenth

commissioned play, and without

whose confidence, help and

encouragement I might have

given up after the first.

*Mother Goose's Golden Christmas* was first presented at the Queen's Theatre, Hornchurch, on 19 December 1977, with the following cast:

| | |
|---|---|
| **Mother Goose** | Brian Hewlett |
| **Little Jack Horner** | David Brenchley |
| **Little Bo Peep** | Deirdre Dee |
| **Little Miss Muffet** | Nicolette Marvin |
| **Little Tommy Tucker** | Lennox Greaves |
| **Little Polly Flinders** | Patience Tomlinson |
| **Big Bad Wolf** | Jack Chissick |
| **Bigger Badder Wolf** | Mike Maynard |
| **Fairy Lethargia** | Penny Jones |
| **Goose** | Isobil Nisbet |
| **Giant** | Tim Pearce |
| **Spider** | Caroline Swift |
| **Monster of the Moat** | Caroline Swift |
| **Humpty Dumpty** | Caroline Swift |

*Directed by* Paul Tomlinson
*Settings by* David Knapman
*Musical direction by* David Carter

**Characters**

**Mother Goose**, *the purveyor of nursery rhymes, probably the 'dame' part, lovable old lady, looking after her nursery rhyme 'family'.*

**Little Bo Peep**, *weepy girl (because she is always losing her sheep!). Dressed in red (for reasons which will become apparent).*

**Little Tommy Tucker**, *fat, usually hungry boy – sings for his supper.*

**Little Miss Muffet**, *the most imaginative of the 'family' – her stories of meeting fearsome spiders are taken with a pinch of salt by the others.*

**Little Jack Horner**, *the nearest we get to a 'Simple Simon' or 'Idle Jack' part. Limited intelligence because his sole purpose in life is sitting in corners, putting his thumb in and pulling plums out.*

**Little Polly Flinders**, *grubby, skinny girl dressed in rags – the skivvy who cooks and cleans; but not looked down on or even discontented with her lot – this is her role in life and she enjoys it. Very shy – whispers a lot.*

**Goose**, *lovable, mute bird, must be capable of pathos, but humour as well; mimes to convey her thoughts, often interpreted by the audience.*

**Big Bad Wolf**, *a small, rather nervous villain.*

**Bigger Badder Wolf**, *a larger, rather confident villain.*

**Giant Bossyboots**, *the Wolves' employer. Ruthless, unsuccessful alchemist whose only aim is to make gold.*

**Spider**, *frightening frightener.*

**Fairy Lethargia**, *a lumpy, sleepy, reluctant fairy, who only emerges at Christmas time to sit on the Christmas tree. She can do magic spells, but only under pressure.*

**Monster of the Moat**, *a non-speaking monster, the guardian of the Giant's castle. Probably similar to the Loch Ness Monster and in segments, which divide.*

**Humpty Dumpty**, *a last-minute appearance – preferably played by a child.*

As the play is based upon the well-known collection of nursery rhymes called *Mother Goose's Nursery Rhymes*, the ideal period in which to set it is Victorian, with all the settings and costumes resembling a beautiful Victorian children's book.

Act One

| | |
|---|---|
| **Scene One** | The Book – home of the nursery rhyme characters |
| **Scene Two** | The Forest/Spider's Lair |
| **Scene Three** | The Book |
| **Scene Four** | The Forest, without the Spider's Lair |

Act Two

| | |
|---|---|
| **Scene One** | The Forest (optional scene) |
| **Scene Two** | Entrance to the Giant's Castle |
| **Scene Three** | In the Moat – under water |
| **Scene Four** | Entrance to the Giant's Castle |
| **Scene Five** | The Giant's Workshop |
| **Scene Six** | In the Sky |
| **Scene Seven** | The Book |

# Act One

## Scene One

*The Book. Home of the nursery rhyme characters. Dawn, Christmas Eve.*

*This is their equivalent of a house; indeed it has a door, and maybe windows. It is suggested that the Book is three-quarters open, the covers facing the audience. On the front cover is the title,* Mother Goose's Golden Christmas Annual, *with perhaps a picture representing Mother Goose flying on a goose, accompanied by several young people. As perhaps the ideal time in which to set the play is Victorian, the design of the cover could well be in the style of one of the famous children's book illustrations of the period – e.g. Arthur Rackham or Kate Greenaway. It may be considered a good idea to start with the tabs already out, so that the audience can see the Book and its title before the house lights go down. Alternatively, a painting of the book on a gauze front cloth would give the magical possibility of 'mixing through' to the real Book.*

*Music, as the lights come up on the Book.*

*The door of the Book opens and, surreptitiously,* **Little Miss Muffet** *creeps out, yawns and stretches, and looks both ways to see if anyone is coming. She beckons, and* **Little Jack Horner** *tiptoes out. They greet each other with excitement but no noise. Then* **Little Polly Flinders** *emerges, sweeping with a broom. The others shush her with a finger to their mouths and take away the broom, leaning it against the Book. As the three huddle together, as though discussing a secret plan,* **Little Tommy Tucker** *comes out, eating a large sausage or a piece of pie, and not looking where he is going. He bumps into the group, who turn on him and shush him. Finally,* **Little Bo Peep**, *with her shepherdess's crook, comes out, ignoring the others but looking into the early morning light – in the hope of seeing her lost sheep. She shrugs her disappointment as* **Little Jack Horner** *takes away her crook and leads her to the others. This section should not take long. The idea is not to set up the individual characters, but rather to convey the fact that these five people live in the Book, and, early this morning, having just woken up, are up to something secret.*

**Little Miss Muffet** *shuts the door, and in fairly soft voices they sing.*

SONG: **We Wish You a Merry Christmas**

*During the song the children bring forward a Christmas tree and, setting it to one side of the stage, start to decorate it with tinsel and baubles, etc., which they take from a largish box labelled 'Decorations', and which they wheel on for the purpose. Occasionally someone checks that no one is coming out of the door – the idea being, as we shall soon discover, that the children are doing this as a surprise for* **Mother Goose**.

**Little Miss Muffet, Little Jack Horner, Little Bo Peep, Little Tommy Tucker** and **Little Polly Flinders** (*singing*)
> We wish you a Merry Christmas
> We wish you a Merry Christmas
> We wish you a Merry Christmas
> And a Happy New Year.

> Good tidings we bring
> To you and your kin
> We wish you a Merry Christmas
> And a Happy New Year.

> Now bring us some figgy pudding
> Now bring us some figgy pudding
> Now bring us some figgy pudding
> And bring some out here.

> We wish you a Merry Christmas
> We wish you a Merry Christmas

*At this point the Christmas tree lights go on and the* **Children** *react happily.*

> We wish you a Merry Christmas

**Little Tommy Tucker** *is pushed forward. He gives a good tug on the bell-rope. The bell rings.*

> And a Happy New Year.

*Giggling with excitement, the* **Children** *hide to wait for the reaction.*

*After a short pause, we hear* **Mother Goose***'s voice as she comes to answer the door, hurriedly putting on a dressing-gown.*

**Mother Goose**    Who on earth can that be at this unearthly hour? (*She opens the door and steps out, and sees the lit-up tree. She gasps.*) Ah . . .! Look what's grown in the night. An electric light tree. Someone must have planted a bulb!

*The* **Children** *pop out from hiding, making* **Mother Goose** *jump. They gather round.*

**Children**    Tara! Surprise, surprise! Happy Christmas, Mother Goose, etc.

**Mother Goose**    Oh, little ones. All I can say is . . . (*Suddenly.*) Aaaaaah!

*All jump.*

**Little Tommy Tucker**    What's the matter, Mother Goose?

**Mother Goose**    You're standing on my foot, Tommy dear.

**Little Tommy Tucker**    Oh, sorry. (*He moves.*)

**Mother Goose**    Thank you, dear, and thank you, all of you, for such a lovely seasonal surprise. But haven't you forgotten something?

**Little Miss Muffet**   What?

**Mother Goose**   I'm not sure. But somehow it doesn't look complete . . .

*The* **Children** *all think hard.* **Mother Goose** *suddenly sees the audience.*

**Mother Goose**   Oh . . .! (*To the audience.*) Good morning. Hallo. Look, little ones, visitors. You're jolly early. I'm not even dressed yet. I don't usually open the door in my dressing-gown.

**Little Jack Horner**   I didn't know you *had* a door in your dressing-gown. Tara!

**Mother Goose**   Thank you, Jack. Anyway – (*To the audience.*) – now you're here, I'm Mother Goose and I look after all the nursery rhyme children and we all live in this big Book, and I know there's something missing off that Christmas tree. Can *you* spot it?

*The audience is encouraged to shout out that there is no fairy on the Christmas tree.*

Of course. That's it. They're right! The fairy. Where is she?

**Little Bo Peep**   She only works at Christmas. Sleeps the rest of the year.

**Mother Goose**   What a lazy fairy! Hibernating like a hedgehog. Anyone remember her name?

**Little Polly Flinders** *raises her hand.*

**Mother Goose**   Well, Polly?

**Little Polly Flinders** *whispers in* **Mother Goose**'*s ear, then smiles shyly.*

**Mother Goose**   That's right. Fairy Lethargia. We'd better give her an alarm call and wake her up. After three. One, two, three.

**All** (*calling*)   Fairy Lethargia.

*No reaction.*

**Mother Goose**   One, two, three.

**All** (*calling*)   Fairy Lethargia.

*No reaction.*

**Mother Goose**   We need a few more decibels, I reckon. (*To the audience.*) How about all joining in? Would you do that? Thank you. One, two, three.

**All** (*including the audience*)   Fairy Lethargia.

**Mother Goose**   And again. One, two, three.

**All**   Fairy Lethargia.

*Suddenly, a large yawn, accompanied perhaps by a drum roll, heralds the awakening of* **Fairy Lethargia**. *She crawls, unfairylike and anything but dainty, out of the* *decorations box. She holds a wand, complete with star on the end. She cannot stop yawning. This could possibly be accompanied by pretty, tinkling fairy music to point up the irony.*

**Fairy Lethargia**   Oh no, it's not Christmas time again already, is it? (*She gives a huge yawn.*)

**Mother Goose**   Yes. And you're late, Fairy Lethargia.

**Fairy Lethargia**   I'm sorry, I – ooh. (*Suddenly she sees the audience and makes an attempt to do a fairy balletic-type movement as she goes into rhyming couplets.*)

> Hallo, hallo, 'tis Christmas Eve and I am Fairy Lethargia,
> My wand and spells and magic powers are here to watch and guardjya
> Throughout the festive season my eyes on you I'll keep (*Yawning.*)
> Except when they start shutting, 'cos I need my beauty sleep. (*She falls asleep on
>    her feet.*)

**Mother Goose**   One, two, three.

**All** (*calling*)   Fairy Lethargia.

**Fairy Lethargia** *jumps awake.*

**Fairy Lethargia**   Oh no, it's not Christmas time again already, is it? (*She gives a huge yawn.*)

**Mother Goose**   Yes, it is.

**Little Miss Muffet**   And you're meant to be on the tree.

**Fairy Lethargia**   I'm not sitting on that tree. It's all prickly. And I might drop off.

**Little Jack Horner**   That's your trouble – you're *always* dropping off. Tara!

**Fairy Lethargia**   Cheek. Tell you what; we'll compromise. (*She waves her wand.*)
> My magic wand looks like a star, I'll stick it on the tree
> And like a beacon burning bright, it'll make you think of me.

*She arranges her wand on the tree.*

> Return I shall for turkey, for Christmas pud and booze
> Till then I think I'll say ta ta and have a little snooze.

*She nips back into the decorations box, yawns and vanishes from sight. NB: It may well be advisable for the box to extend a little into the wings, so that* **Fairy Lethargia** *can escape through one side to the wings between appearances.*

**Mother Goose**   Charming. Daintiness personified. She works too hard, that's her trouble. A twelve-hour year. She's the same every Christmas. Do you remember, little ones, when . . . (*She breaks off, then turns to the audience.*) Oh, I'm sorry. How rude. I haven't even introduced my family to you, have I? Tell you what, let's see if you can guess who they all are – because . . .

SONG: **Once Upon a Time**

**Little Bo Peep**
>It
>Really won't surprise us

**Little Jack Horner**
>If you recognise us

**All the Children**
>From a nursery rhyme

**Mother Goose**
>And I'm sure you've heard them
>Or even learnt them
>Once upon a time.

*The* **Children** *act out each other's story as appropriate. First,* **Little Bo Peep** *comes forward.*

**Mother Goose**
>Here's a girl all pale and wan
>And she's crying, so something's wrong

**Little Bo Peep**
>I can't help but weep
>I've lost all my sheep
>And don't know where they've gone.

*The music continues.*

**Mother Goose** (*speaking to the audience*)   Who is she?

*The audience may give her an answer. She ad libs her thanks.*

**All**
>She's
>Little Bo Peep
>Little Bo Peep
>From the nursery rhyme
>Little Bo Peep
>You must have learnt it
>Once upon a time.

**Little Jack Horner**
>I was eating Christmas pie
>In the corner, then – who knows why?

**Mother Goose**
>He put in his thumb
>And pulled out a plum –

**Little Jack Horner**
>What a good boy am I!

*Again* **Mother Goose** *asks the audience who he is.*

**All**

He's
Little Jack Horner
Little Jack Horner
From the nursery rhyme
Little Jack Horner
You must have learnt it
Once upon a time.

**Mother Goose**

Here's a girl you'll know, I s'pose
In the cinders she warmed her toes

**All** (*except* **Mother Goose** *and* **Little Polly Flinders**)

Her mother then caught her
And told off her daughter
For spoiling her new clothes.

*The audience shout out who it is.*

**All**

She's
Little Polly Flinders
Little Polly Flinders
From the nursery rhyme
Little Polly Flinders
You must have learnt it
Once upon a time.

**Little Tommy Tucker**

Now bring me some figgy pudding
Please bring me some figgy pudding –
I am singing for my supper

**Mother Goose**

What shall we give him?

**All** (*except* **Little Tommy Tucker**)

White bread and butter

**Little Tommy Tucker**

It's no wonder
I get fat

**Mother Goose**

Who can tell me . . .
Who is that?

*The audience shout out the answer.*

**All**

> He's
> Little Tommy Tucker
> Little Tommy Tucker
> From the nursery rhyme
> Little Tommy Tucker
> I'm sure you learnt it
> Once upon a time.

**Little Miss Muffet**

> In the forest yesterday
> I was eating my curds and whey

**Mother Goose**

> Along came a spider
> Who sat down beside her

**Little Miss Muffet**

> And frightened me away.

*The audience call out her name.*

**All**

> She's
> Little Miss Muffet
> Little Miss Muffet
> From the nursery rhyme
> Little Miss Muffet
> I'm sure you learnt it
> Once upon a . . .

> Little Miss Muffet
> Little Tommy Tucker
> Little Polly Flinders
> Little Jack Horner
> Little Bo Peep
> I'm sure you learnt them

**Girls**

> Once upon a time

**Boys**

> Once upon a time

**Girls**

> Once upon a time

**Boys**

> Once upon a time

**All**

> Once upon a time.

**Mother Goose**   There you are, I told you you knew them all already! Right, little ones, breakfast time. (*She calls loudly.*) Polly!

**Little Polly Flinders** *comes forward shyly.*

**Little Polly Flinders** (*whispering*)   Yes, Mother Goose.

**Mother Goose**   Put the kettle on.

*Music, as the* **Children** *revolve the Book, to reveal a room the other side. It is a kitchen with a large dining-table and a hearth complete with cinders, hob and traditional-style kettle. The Christmas tree and decorations box remain at the side of the stage. NB: The revolve of the Book could take place during the last chorus of the song.* **Little Polly Flinders** *puts the kettle on.* **Mother Goose** *and the others sit at the table.* **Mother Goose** *pours herself some cereal from a packet or jar, and passes it down the line. First* **Little Jack Horner,** *then* **Little Miss Muffet** *pour themselves some; then* **Little Tommy Tucker** *pours all the remaining cereal on to his plate. The music stops as* **Little Bo Peep** *– on the end – bursts into tears. NB: This section should be played at a fair speed.*

**Little Jack Horner**   Oh, stop being weedy, Bo Peep.

**Little Bo Peep**   I'm not being weedy. Tommy's taken all the cereal, the selfish pig.

**Little Tommy Tucker**   I'm a growing boy.

**Little Bo Peep**   Growing? Huh. If you grow any more you'll burst. Like a fat balloon.

**Mother Goose**   Stop arguing, you two. Bo Peep, there's more cereal in the cupboard. So stop crying. Tommy, go and fetch her some.

**Little Tommy Tucker** *does so.*

**Little Miss Muffet**   She's always crying.

**Little Bo Peep**   So would you if you kept losing your sheep. (*She starts sobbing again.*)

**Little Miss Muffet**   That's nothing compared with having to fight off great monster spiders every day.

**Little Jack Horner**   So you say.

**Little Miss Muffet**   What's that meant to mean?

**Little Jack Horner**   Well, *we* never see these giant spiders of yours. *No one* sees them except you.

**Little Miss Muffet**   Are you suggesting I invent them?

**Little Jack Horner**   No. I'm just saying I've never seen one.

**Little Bo Peep**   That's because he sits at home all day putting in his thumb and pulling out plums. What a waste of time.

**Little Tommy Tucker**   No, it's not. They're very nice plums.

**Little Bo Peep**    Well, we all know you're a greedy hog who never stops stuffing his face.

**Little Tommy Tucker**    I'd rather be a greedy hog who never stops stuffing his face than one of your miserable stupid sheep who keep wandering off . . .

**Little Bo Peep** *is about to retaliate.* **Mother Goose** *interrupts.*

**Mother Goose**    Ting-a-ling-a-ling-a-ling. End of round one. That's enough. It's Christmas, time of good cheer. Now, what's the matter, little ones?

*All the* **Children** *start to react angrily to the phrase 'little ones'. Then they think better of it. Silence.*

**Mother Goose**    Eh?

**Little Polly Flinders** *brings everyone a mug of tea.*

**Mother Goose**    Thank you, Little Polly.

*All the* **Children** *look at one another as if to say – 'there you are'.* **Little Polly Flinders** *sits.*

**Mother Goose**    What have I said now?

**Little Polly Flinders** (*whispering*)    Little.

**Mother Goose**    Little?

**Little Jack Horner**    Sorry, Mother Goose, but we're all getting a bit fed up with being 'Little'. *Little* Jack Horner.

**Little Miss Muffet**    *Little* Miss Muffet.

**Little Bo Peep**    We're all 'Little'.

**Little Tommy Tucker**    And we always have to do the same old 'little' things.

**Little Jack Horner**    Day after day after day.

**Little Polly Flinders** (*whispering*)    That's why we argue sometimes. It gives us something else to think about.

*The others nod.*

**Mother Goose**    I see. But, children, your nursery rhymes are so popular. Everyone knows them. You can't just stop doing what you do in them and start doing something else. People expect nursery rhymes to carry on for ever.

**Little Jack Horner**    But I'm fed up with sitting in corners pulling out plums. There must be something more to life than that.

**Little Bo Peep**    And I don't *enjoy* losing my sheep all the time. (*She starts to cry.*)

**Little Polly Flinders** (*whispering*)    I'd like to get away from my dirty old cinders sometimes. Not for always. Just sometimes.

**Little Tommy Tucker**   All I do is sing for my supper. That's child's play. I'd like a challenge. An adventure.

**Little Miss Muffet**   And I'm tired of being terrified by fierce spiders which nobody really believes I see anyway.

**Little Jack Horner**   In short, Mother Goose, we're bored. Bored with being 'Little' people of 'little' consequence.

*Pause.*

**Mother Goose** (*having an idea*)   I tell you what. I was wondering what I could give you all as a Christmas present. And now I know. I'll think up a brand new nursery rhyme story with all of you in it.

*The* **Children** *look interested.*

**Mother Goose**   An adventure story. Excitement. Danger. A story in which each one of you does great things, each one of you has his or her big moment. How about it?

**Children**   Yes, please; thank you, Mother Goose; how does it start? Let's hear it now; etc.

**Mother Goose** (*laughing*)   Hold on! Quiet! Give me a chance to cogitate. (*She has an idea.*) Magic. Every good story needs a bit of magic. Where can we find some magic?

*They all wait a moment – to allow the audience to come up with the solution if they want to.*

**Little Polly Flinders** (*whispering, pointing to the decorations box*)   Fairy Lethargia.

**Mother Goose**   Of course. Lethargia. We'd better wake her up. She can do something useful for once. One, two, three.

**All** (*calling*)   Fairy Lethargia.

**Fairy Lethargia** (*crawling from the box*)   What is it now? (*She yawns.*)

**Little Miss Muffet**   Will you come and be in our story?

**Fairy Lethargia**   No, I'm too tired for stories.

**Little Bo Peep**   Please. All we want is some of your magic.

**Fairy Lethargia** (*indignantly*)   What?

**Little Jack Horner**   Just a little.

**Little Tommy Tucker**   To make it a really special story.

**Fairy Lethargia** (*flattered*)   Oh, very well. If it's a special story, count me in. Let's see. (*She collects her wand from the tree and waves it.*)

To make your story special, to give it extra zip,
Three magic spells I'll let you have, and now I'll have a kip.

*She replaces the wand and, yawning, returns to the decorations box.*

**Mother Goose**    Thank you, Fairy Lethargia. Three spells. Mmm. We must only use them for emergencies and crises. Now, gather round, Little ones . . . I'm sorry, gather round, everybody, and I'll begin the story. Now, let's see.

*Music, as the* **Children** *listen to* **Mother Goose** *improvising the story. A lighting change here – narrowing to the 'family' group – would help the atmosphere.*

**Mother Goose**    Once upon a time, not very far away from here, at the other side of the forest, loomed a vast, mysterious, impenetrable stone castle. It was surrounded by a deep, inky-black moat in which lived a savage Monster who kept guard over the owner of the castle – the terrifying Giant Bossyboots. The Giant had only one interest in life – gold. Not that he had any, but he dreamed of possessing more gold than anyone else on earth. So he consulted all the old tomes about alchemy, trying to discover the secret of how to make gold. Then one day, as Mother Goose and her nursery rhyme children were sitting down to breakfast . . .

*From now on, the story takes over. The lighting changes and the music continues.*

*The* **Goose** *enters, perhaps in a follow spot. The* **Goose** *is tired and frightened. With wings flapping she breathes heavily to suggest she has been running or flying. She takes a short rest, looking off stage to check she is not being followed. Suddenly she sees the Book, rushes to it, searches till she finds the bell-rope and pulls it.*

*Inside, the* **Children** *and* **Mother Goose** *react to the bell This is really a two-level reaction – in one sense it's a natural reaction to hearing a doorbell, and in another sense it is excited anticipation, because the* **Children** *know this is part of* **Mother Goose**'s *story.*

**Little Bo Peep**    Maybe my sheep have come home!

*They jump up, dash to the door, open it and cluster round the* **Goose***, leading it, confused by all the fuss, downstage.* **Mother Goose** *watches, not getting too involved; she wants the* **Children** *to experience the excitement of this new story.*

**Little Miss Muffet**    Hallo, who are you?

**Little Jack Horner**    It's a duck! Hallo, ducky!

**Little Bo Peep**    No, it's not a duck. It's a goose. You're ignorant.

**Little Jack Horner**    Not as ignorant as your sheep. Baaaaah!

**Little Bo Peep** *bursts into tears again. The* **Goose** *reacts frightened, flapping its wings.*

**Little Tommy Tucker**    It's all right. Don't get in a flap. We're not going to hurt you.

**Little Miss Muffet**    Who are you? Where have you come from?

**Little Polly Flinders** *suddenly comes into her own, almost taking herself by surprise.*

**Little Polly Flinders**    Quiet! Sorry, but I think the Goose is frightened. (*To the* Goose.) It's all right; you can tell us.

*The* **Goose** *points to her beak and shakes her head.*

**Little Polly Flinders**    What's the matter?

*The audience will possibly shout out that the* **Goose** *cannot speak.*

**Little Polly Flinders**    You *can't* tell us? Oh, you can't speak?

*The* **Goose** *nods.*

**Little Polly Flinders**    Well, that doesn't matter. You can show us what you're trying to say and we'll all guess. (*Taking in the audience.*) Won't we? Now, are you lost?

*The* **Goose** *nods, then points off.*

**Little Jack Horner**    She's pointing to the forest.

*The* **Goose** *indicates 'beyond the forest'.*

**Little Polly Flinders**    What? Through the forest? The other side of the forest?

*The* **Goose** *nods.*

**Little Polly Flinders** (*asking the others*)    What's the other side of the forest?

*The audience may shout out 'The Giant's castle'. If not,* **Little Polly Flinders** *gets the answer herself – or from one of the others.*

**Little Polly Flinders**    The Giant's castle?

*The* **Goose** *nods nervously.*

**Little Tommy Tucker**    You want to go to the Giant's castle?

*The* **Goose** *immediately flaps her wings in panic, and shakes her head.*

**Little Polly Flinders**    No? What then?

*The audience may suggest that the* **Goose** *has come from the Giant's castle.*

**Little Polly Flinders**    Oh. You've *come* from the Giant's castle? Through the forest?

*The* **Goose** *nods.*

**Little Bo Peep**    You didn't see any lost sheep, did you?

*The* **Goose** *shakes her head.*

**The Others**    Shhh. Bo Peep, shut up, etc.

**Little Polly Flinders**    What were you doing in the castle?

*The* **Goose** *does a Marcel Marceau-type mime, using her hands/wings to suggest being locked in – showing imaginary walls.*

**Little Jack Horner**    Playing Blind Man's Buff?

**Little Miss Muffet**    Looking for a secret panel?

*The* **Goose** *shakes her head at each of these suggestions. The audience may help.*

**Little Polly Flinders**    You were locked in?

*The* **Goose** *nods.*

**Little Miss Muffet**    In a dungeon?

*The* **Goose** *shakes her head and mimes pacing up and down. Again, the audience should help.*

**Little Polly Flinders**    In a cage?

*The* **Goose** *nods.*

**Little Polly Flinders**    What were you doing in a cage?

*The* **Goose** *mimes laying eggs; sitting down then up. The audience are encouraged to help again.*

**Little Jack Horner**    Sitting in a hot bath.

**Little Polly Flinders**    No. Laying eggs?

*The* **Goose** *nods.*

**Little Polly Flinders**    And why should the Giant lock you in a cage laying eggs?

*The audience should be encouraged to reach the answer, using the following logical stages. If required,* **Little Polly Flinders** *can find the solution herself:*

*(1)  What does the* **Giant** *desire most? Gold.*

*(2)  What could eggs have to do with gold? They could be golden eggs.*

*(3)  Perhaps the* **Giant** *thought that this goose was the* **Goose** *that laid the Golden Egg?*

*(4)  Therefore he locked her in a cage, so that she couldn't escape, in the hope that she'd eventually lay a golden egg.*

**Little Polly Flinders**    But you never laid a Golden Egg?

*The* **Goose** *shakes her head.*

**Little Polly Flinders**    So you escaped. And now you're homeless?

*The* **Goose** *nods.*

**Little Miss Muffet**    You can live with us if you like, can't she, Mother Goose?

**Mother Goose** *'re-enters' the scene.*

**Mother Goose**    Well . . .

*All look at her, pleading . . .*

**Mother Goose**    With a name like mine, how can I refuse?

*The* **Goose** *reacts happily. All cheer.*

**Mother Goose**    What's your name, Goosey?

*The* **Goose** *shrugs her shoulders.*

**Mother Goose**    That's a funny name.

*The audience may shout out that she has not got a name.*

**Mother Goose**    You haven't got a name?

*The* **Goose** *shakes her head.*

**Mother Goose**    Well, that's terrible. We can't adopt you if we don't know what to call you. What are we to do?

**Little Tommy Tucker**    Let's think of a good goosey name for her.

**Mother Goose**    Good idea, Tommy. Any ideas?

*The* **Children** *cannot think of anything.*

**Mother Goose**    No? (*To the audience.*) Can *anyone* think of a good goosey name?

*The audience shout out ideas, some of which are put to the* **Goose***, who selects one – a different name for each performance. In the script let us call her Gertie.*

**Mother Goose**    Gertie? She likes Gertie? I know. Tommy. Sing a song for her.

**Little Tommy Tucker**    All right. It'll make a change from singing for my supper!

SONG: **The Song of the Goose** (*Part 1*)

**Little Tommy Tucker**
    Gertie!
    You needn't flap
    Gertie!
    Don't fly away
    Gertie!
    We'll take you under our wing
    So
    Gertie!
    Please stay.

Hey, I've got an idea. Why doesn't everyone (*Taking in the audience.*) join in whenever I sing the word Gertie? Would you do that? Then Gertie will see how many friends she's got to protect her from the Giant.

**Little Bo Peep**    Shall I give a signal with my crook? – Every time I lift it like this, we all shout 'GERTIE'. All right? Let's have a practice. (*She raises her crook.*)

**All** (*including the audience*)    Gertie!

**Little Bo Peep**    And again. (*She raises her crook.*)

**All** (*including the audience*)    Gertie!

**Little Bo Peep**    Lovely!

SONG: **The Song of the Goose** (*Part 2*)

**All** (*with audience*)
Gertie!

**Little Tommy Tucker**
You needn't flap

**All** (*with audience*)
Gertie!

**Little Tommy Tucker**
Don't fly away

**All** (*with audience*)
Gertie!

**Little Tommy Tucker**
We'll take you under our wing
So

**All** (*with audience*)
Gertie!

**Little Tommy Tucker**
Please stay.

**All**
Who escaped from the castle?

*All* (*with audience*)
Gertie!

**All**
Who escaped from the cage?

**All** (*with audience*)
Gertie!

**All**
Who escaped from the Giant?

**All** (*with audience*)
Gertie!

**All**
And left him in a rage?
Well it was

*Optional chorus*

**All** (*with audience*)
Gertie!

**All**
>You needn't flap

**All** (*with audience*)
>Gertie!

**All**
>Don't fly away

**All** (*with audience*)
>Gertie!

**All**
>We'll take you under our wing
>So

**All** (*with audience*)
>Gertie!

**All**
>Please stay,
>Yes, it was

*Final Chorus*

**All** (*with audience*)
>Gertie!

**All**
>You needn't flap

**All** (*with audience*)
>Gertie!

**All**
>Don't fly away

**All** (*with audience*)
>Gertie!

**All**
>We'll take you under our wing
>So

**All** (*with audience*)
>Gertie!

**All**
>Please stay.

**All** (*with audience*)
>Gertie!

*During the song the* **Goose** *gets happier and happier, dancing energetically.*

**Mother Goose**   Well done, everybody. Now, come on, all of you. Jobs. Jack – you can make the beds. Polly – washing-up. I need someone to help me make the figgy pudding.

**Little Tommy Tucker**   I will!

**Mother Goose**   All right. But fingers off my figgies. And someone to search for some holly to decorate the Book. Bo Peep?

**Little Bo Peep**   I'd rather stay here in case my sheep come home.

**Little Miss Muffet**   I'll go holly-hunting. Gertie can come too.

**Gertie** *nods.*

**Mother Goose**   Don't be long. (*She gives* **Little Miss Muffet** *a basket.*)

**Little Miss Muffet** (*as she and* **Gertie** *set off*)   No. It's not far to the forest. There's lots of holly there.

**Gertie** *stops abruptly at the mention of the word 'forest'. She trembles. Music echoes the danger.*

**Little Miss Muffet**   What's the matter, Gertie? The forest? Don't worry. (*Indicating the audience.*) We'll make sure you're safe, won't we?

**All**   Yes.

**Little Miss Muffet**   'Bye.

*Music.*

**Little Miss Muffet** *and* **Gertie** *set off, perhaps through the auditorium, towards the forest.*

*The others wave.*

**The Others**   'Bye.

**Mother Goose**   Come on, children, to work.

*They all revolve the Book back to its original position; then they enter the Book. Meanwhile, and after they are all in, the scene change takes place. If this needs a few extra seconds, it may be an idea to have a follow spot on* **Little Miss Muffet** *and* **Gertie** *as they progress through the auditorium, waving to the audience.*

## Scene Two

*The Forest/***Spider***'s Lair.*

*This set should not be too complex. It could consist of several cut-out trees and/or borders, if possible reminiscent of a potentially sinister Arthur Rackham-style forest. Intertwining branches, interesting shapes. Incorporated into this is a holly bush or two, plus a raised 'Tuffet' in front of the* **Spider***'s lair – this could be a gnarled old* *tree trunk: but it should not be designed in such a way that the audience will spot straight away that something nasty is going to pop out – the entrance of the* **Spider** *should be a surprise.*

*Sinister music as the lighting comes up on the rather spooky forest. Dramatic shadows made by the trees: perhaps some sinister noises – an owl hooting, a bat screeching.*

*The* **Big Bad Wolf** *enters, sniffing the ground ahead of him, searching for tracks. He moves stealthily, stopping every few steps and sniffing – using his nose like a metal detector. Suddenly he finds a scent.*

**Big Bad Wolf**    Aha . . . (*He scurries along, following it, head down, body bent over. After a few paces he bangs straight into a tree trunk.*) Ow! (*A sound like a wolf's howl. He rubs his head.*) I don't like this creepy forest. I'm going home. (*He stands upright, banging his head on an overhead branch.*) Ow! (*A bigger howl. He rubs his head.*) Oh, I can feel one of my turns coming on. Tranquilliser, quick. (*He fumbles for a very large bottle of pills.*) Oh, my nerves, my nerves they're in tags and ratters, raggers and tatty, tatties and rags, oh, they're in shreds, they really are. (*He pops a huge gob-stopper pill in his mouth. With his mouth full.*) That's bett . . . (*Suddenly he sees the audience. He reacts with violent surprise, spitting out the pill and half-retreating behind the tree. To the audience.*) Wh-wh-who are you? D-don't answer. I d-d-don't want to know. You didn't see that, do you understand, me t-taking that t-t-tranquilliser. I didn't take it. 'Cos I don't need t-t-tranquillisers. I'm f-f-fearless, n-nerveless, n-nothing frightens me. I'm the B-b-big B-b-bad W-w-wolf. No kid. And I'm strong, buff as old toots, I mean t-t-tough as old boots. So there. Ya boo! And that reminds me. Boo. I mean, that's what I'm here for. Looking, for a boo. Boo? Boo who? No, not boo-hoo, I mean, not looking for a boo, I mean looking for who you shouldn't say boo – to. Oh dear. (*He has an idea.*) Maybe you could help. You see, I jerk for the Wyant, I mean work for the Giant in the castle, and he has a sweet little pet, a snowy-white Goose we all love, and who loves us too. But today, horror of horrors, she's esca . . . she's disappeared, lost without trace, and the Giant is in tears, he's so worried about what awful fate may have befallen his little feathered friend. Now, all you kind animal lovers, hear my plea for a dumb creature in danger – and tell me, have you seen the Giant's Goose?

*The audience should shout out 'no' – they will realise the* **Big Bad Wolf** *is up to no good.*

Are you sure?

**Audience**    Yes.

**Big Bad Wolf**    Thank you. In that case I'd better go on searching. (*He puts his head down and starts sniffing again. Calling.*) Goosey, Goosey, Goosey. (*He starts to exit.*)

*The* **Bigger Badder Wolf** *enters suddenly.*

*The* **Big Bad Wolf** *bumps into him and jumps.*

**Big Bad Wolf**    Ooh! Oh, it's you. (*He takes out another tranquilliser, and pops it in his mouth – in fact 'palming' it.*)

**Bigger Badder Wolf**    Of course it's me. Pull yourself together. And stop taking those tranquillisers.

*He bangs the* **Big Bad Wolf** *on the back, but instead of making him spit it out, it in fact makes him swallow it. He reacts wide-eyed.*

**Bigger Badder Wolf**    Have you found the Goose?

**Big Bad Wolf**    N-n-no. I was just asking these kind people . . .

**Bigger Badder Wolf**    Yes, I heard. Huh. (*He turns on the audience.*) Now listen, you lot. I don't know who you are or why you're here, but something tells me you're all lying through your well-brushed teeth. You may think you can bamboozle the Big Bad Wolf with your devious tricks, but (*He cackles evilly.*) I'm the *Bigger Badder* Wolf and no one, but no one, fools me.

**Big Bad Wolf**    Hear, hear.

**Bigger Badder Wolf**    I am the greatest.

**Big Bad Wolf**    Hear, hear. And I am the second greatest.

**Bigger Badder Wolf**    Hear, hear.

**Big Bad Wolf** and **Bigger Badder Wolf**    And nobody stands in our way. Hear, hear.

*Both confidently turn inwards as though to move off, and bump into each other. Both jump and scream. The* **Big Bad Wolf** *reacts nervously, the* **Bigger Badder Wolf** *reacts angrily.*

SONG: **With a Huff and a Puff**

*The 'huh, huh' noise suggested is a combination of exhaled breath and a sinister laugh.*

**The Wolves**
> Huh huh huh huh huh huh huh
> With a huff and a puff
> We're rough and we're tough
> If you're climbing a tree, then
> We'll knock down your ladder.
> To make you feel sad
> Will make us feel glad

**Big Bad Wolf**
> 'Cos I'm big and bad

**Bigger Badder Wolf**
> He's big and bad
> And I

**Both**
> Huh huh huh huh huh

**Bigger Badder Wolf**
Am bigger and badder!

**Both**
Huh huh huh huh huh huh huh
With a huff and a puff
We're rough and we're tough
And we do dirty deeds for
A reas'nable figure,
And if people twig
We don't care a fig

**Big Bad Wolf**
'Cos I'm bad and big

**Bigger Badder Wolf**
He's bad and big
And I

**Both**
Huh huh huh huh huh

**Bigger Badder Wolf**
Am badder and bigger!

**Both**
If you're on your way home
On your own in the night
We'll be waiting in lurk
To give you a fright.
Huh huh huh huh huh huh huh
We'll creep up behind,
Then one leap in the dark
And you'll find
That our bite is far worse than our bark.

Huh huh huh huh huh huh huh
With a huff and a puff
We're rough and we're tough
We would rob our old granny
And not reimburse 'er;
It's not just a fad –
We've *always* been mad! –

**Big Bad Wolf**
'Cos I'm big and bad

**Bigger Badder Wolf**
He's big and bad
And I

**Both**

    Huh huh huh huh huh

**Bigger Badder Wolf**

    Am bigger and worser!

**Both**

    So watch out and don't cross our path
    It's years since we last had a bath
    Yes, we're dirty and vicious
    And highly suspicious
    With venom as vile as an adder –
    Two wolves at the door
    Means trouble in store
    One big and bad
    And one
    Huh huh huh huh huh
    Bigger and badder!

    Huh huh huh huh huh huh huh
    Huh!

*At the end of the song, the music continues.*

*The* **Big Bad Wolf** *and the* **Bigger Badder Wolf** *exit downstage, one each side, sniffing for the* **Goose**'s *tracks. The* **Big Bad Wolf** *exits left, the* **Bigger Badder Wolf** *exits right.*

*Simultaneously, from upstage right,* **Little Miss Muffet** *and* Gertie *enter, collecting holly in their basket.*

*The music continues. They are unaware of any danger, in spite of possible audience reaction. They advance downstage left to another holly bush.*

*The* **Big Bad Wolf,** *nose to the ground, enters upstage left and starts to cross the stage.*

*The audience shout a warning, whereupon* **Gertie** *turns and sees the* **Big Bad Wolf.** *She gets in a flap, and desperately tries to mime to* **Little Miss Muffet** *that they are in danger.*

*In the nick of time, sizing up the situation,* **Little Miss Muffet** *pulls* **Gertie** *off downstage left; in their panic they both drop their holly.*

*At the same time, the* **Big Bad Wolf** *picks up the* **Goose**'s *scent up right centre and triumphantly follows it downstage. The music stops.*

**Big Bad Wolf**  She's near. She's near. I can smack her trells – smell her tracks. Oh! Goosey, Goosey, Goosey! (*To the audience.*) I'm getting warm, aren't I?

**Audience**  No.

**Big Bad Wolf**  Oh, yes I am.

**Audience**   Oh, no you're not.

**Big Bad Wolf**   Oh, yes I am.

**Audience**   Oh, no you're not.

**Big Bad Wolf**   Oooooh – no I'm not. (*Sniffing.*) I've lost the scent again. Grrrr. Now listen, *please*, please help me or I'll get into trouble with the Bigger Badder Wolf. Which way did she go, eh? Did she go that way? (*He points offstage right.*)

**Audience** (*lying*)   Yes.

**Big Bad Wolf** (*pointing offstage left*)   This way?

**Audience**   No.

**Big Bad Wolf** (*pointing offstage right*)   That way?

**Audience**   Yes.

**Big Bad Wolf**   You're sure?

**Audience**   Yes.

**Big Bad Wolf**   You're not having me on?

**Audience**   No.

**Big Bad Wolf**   Thank you. (*He starts to exit downstage right.*)

*The* **Bigger Badder Wolf** *enters suddenly downstage right.*

*The* **Big Bad Wolf** *bumps into him, and jumps with fright.*

**Bigger Badder Wolf**   You useless, wittering, witless wolf. You're not the second greatest, not the third greatest, you're the three thousand, two hundred and forty-fourth greatest. Just. And (*To the audience.*) as for you lot – I was watching all the time. You're nothing but a mass of mamby-pamby flamboyantly fickle, feckless fibbers. The Goose went *that* way, and she had a girl with her and they were collecting holly.

**Big Bad Wolf**   Golly.

**Bigger Badder Wolf**   No, holly.

**Big Bad Wolf**   Ooh, you rotten lot. I trusted you.

**Bigger Badder Wolf**   Ha, ha, ha. Try fooling someone your own size next time. You can't fool the greatest.

**Big Bad Wolf**   And you can't fool the three thousand, two hundred and forty-fourth greatest. Just. Not a second time, anyway.

**Bigger Badder Wolf** (*to the audience*)   So, watch out.

**Big Bad Wolf** (*taking his pocket-watch out*)   Half-past eleven.

**Bigger Badder Wolf**   What?

**Big Bad Wolf**   Half-past eleven. You said 'watch out'.

**Bigger Badder Wolf** (*hitting him*)   Idiot. Come on.

*They start to exit.*

(*To the audience.*) Watch your step.

**Big Bad Wolf** (*watching his feet*)   If I watch my step, I can't see where I'm going. (*He bumps into the* **Bigger Badder Wolf.**)

**Bigger Badder Wolf**   Oh, for wickedness' sake . . . (*Hitting him.*) I'm telling *them* to watch *their* step.

*They start to move off.*

**Big Bad Wolf**   Ah. Yes. (*To the audience, as evilly as he can.*) Tread very, very carefully, or you'll put your foot in it.

*They growl – then both howl (OW!): they have each put their foot in the holly dropped by* **Gertie** *and* **Little Miss Muffet**. *If possible, we can see it sticking to their feet. Then they overbalance and sit in the holly.*

*Eventually the* **Big Bad Wolf** *and* **Bigger Badder Wolf** *run off screaming and shaking their paws in revenge at the audience.*

*Immediately, from upstage left,* **Little Miss Muffet** *and* **Gertie** *enter nervously: they edge downstage centre, then across right, looking warily about them.*

*The two* **Wolves** *enter upstage left on tiptoe.*

*The* **Wolves** *spot* **Little Miss Muffet** *and* **Gertie** *and, trying to 'shush' the audience, advance upon them. Hearing the audience's warning,* **Little Miss Muffet** *and* **Gertie** *see the* **Wolves** *and a short chase starts – possibly through the auditorium and back on to the stage. NB: This chase should not be too long or involved. Back on stage, all chase round a tree.*

*After one revolution of the tree* **Little Miss Muffet** *and* **Gertie** *escape offstage right.*

*The* **Wolves** *are left chasing each other round the tree. Eventually they bump into each other and fall over.*

*Furious, the* **Wolves** *look wildly about them, then exit downstage left. Immediately* **Little Miss Muffet** *and* **Gertie** *enter upstage right and dash downstage centre.*

**Little Miss Muffet**   Quick, Gertie, run home to the Book.

**Gertie** *wavers.*

**Little Miss Muffet**   Don't worry about me. I'll see you later.

**Gertie** *speeds off downstage right.*

**Little Miss Muffet,** *out of breath, sits down on the tuffet, and brings her curds and whey out of her basket. She begins to tuck in, hungrily and nervously.*

*Suddenly sinister music, as, from his lair, the large, furry, frightening* **Spider** *enters slowly. He sees* **Little Miss Muffet**, *exults, and advances towards her.*

*The audience scream a warning. The* **Spider** *arrives beside* **Little Miss Muffet**. *Sensing danger she slowly turns her head – in the wrong direction. Her head comes forward again; the* **Spider** *crosses behind her to the other side. She looks round again – in the other direction, thus missing the* **Spider** *again. Her head comes forward. She cannot understand the audience's concern. The* **Spider** *sits down beside her. Suddenly she 'feels' his presence and, with a slow burn, turns her head to face him. She sees him and screams. She leaps up and runs in a panic downstage right, then turns and runs across towards downstage left.*

*Meanwhile, the* **Spider** *retreats back into his lair, and the* **Wolves** *enter suddenly downstage left.*

**Little Miss Muffet** *runs straight into the arms of the* **Wolves**. *They hold on to her firmly.*

**Bigger Badder Wolf**   Got you. Ha, ha, ha. Now, little girl, where is she, eh?

**Big Bad Wolf**   Where's Goosey Goosey?

**Little Miss Muffet**   I don't know. Let me go, you're hurting.

**Bigger Badder Wolf**   Not until you help us find that scraggy bird.

*Suddenly there is a dramatic lighting change. Everything is black but for a small spotlight on* **Little Miss Muffet***'s face. The action freezes.*

SONG: **My Big Moment**

**Little Miss Muffet**
    This must be my big moment
    My moment of glory
    In the story
    This will be my closest shave
    This must be my big moment
    This is my time to be brave.

*At the end of the song the lights return to normal and the action starts again, the* **Wolves** *hanging on to the struggling* **Little Miss Muffet**.

**Little Miss Muffet**   All right, all right. I'll tell you. I'll tell you all I know.

**Bigger Badder Wolf**   Sensible. Right, where is she?

**Big Bad Wolf**   Where's Goosey Goosey?

**Little Miss Muffet**   But only if you stop hurting my arms.

**Bigger Badder Wolf**   All right.

*They release their grip.*

**Bigger Badder Wolf**   Now, where is she?

**Little Miss Muffet**   Come and sit down and I'll tell you.

*She sits to one side to the tuffet. The* **Big Bad Wolf** *moves towards her.*

**Bigger Badder Wolf**   Stop. (*To* **Little Miss Muffet**.) No trickery now.

**Little Miss Muffet**   Of course not. (*Sweetly.*) How could I ever trick two such clever wolves as you?

**Big Bad Wolf** (*flattered*)   Hey, she's right, B.B.W. We're the greatest.

**Bigger Badder Wolf**   Well, all right. But we've got our eyes on you.

*They sit down on the tuffet, the* **Big Bad Wolf** *next to* **Little Miss Muffet**, *and the* **Bigger Badder Wolf** *next to him.*

**Little Miss Muffet**   Are you hungry?

**Big Bad Wolf**   Starving. Didn't have any breakfast.

**Little Miss Muffet**   You can share my elevenses if you like. (*She offers her curds and whey.*)

**Big Bad Wolf**   Ooh, thanks. What is it?

**Little Miss Muffet**   Curds and whey.

**Big Bad Wolf**   Ughhh. Sounds horrible.

**Little Miss Muffet**   Try some.

**Bigger Badder Wolf**   Hold it. (*He sniffs the bowl.*) Could be poison.

**Little Miss Muffet**   Don't be silly. (*She takes some on her finger and eats it.*)

**Big Bad Wolf**   Yes. Don't be silly, B.B.W. (*He takes a spoonful.*) Mmm. Very tasty. Try some.

*The* **Bigger Badder Wolf,** *after a moment's hesitation, tries some.*

**Bigger Badder Wolf**   Mmmmm.

**Little Miss Muffet,** *in preparation for what is to happen, shuts her eyes tight.*

*Music, as the* **Spider** *emerges stealthily from his lair, and advances upon the* **Wolves**.

*The* **Bigger Badder Wolf** *is holding the bowl, tucking in greedily. The* **Spider**, *in pantomime fashion, taps the* **Bigger Badder Wolf** *on the shoulder. He thinks it is the* **Big Bad Wolf**.

**Bigger Badder Wolf**   Get off.

**Big Bad Wolf**   What?

**Bigger Badder Wolf**   You've had your turn. Don't be greedy.

*The* **Spider** *again taps the* **Bigger Badder Wolf** *on the shoulder.*

**Bigger Badder Wolf**   I said get off.

**Big Bad Wolf**   I don't know what you're talking about.

*The* **Spider** *sits down beside the* **Big Bad Wolf***.*

**Bigger Badder Wolf**   Stop bashing me.

**Big Bad Wolf**   I didn't bash you. (*Turning to the* **Spider***.*) Did I?

*The* **Spider** *shakes his head. The* **Big Bad Wolf***'s head returns front.*

**Big Bad Wolf**   No. Cheek. I never touched you.

*The* **Big Bad Wolf** *does an enormous double take, sees the* **Spider** *again, and, terrified, exits.*

*The* **Bigger Badder Wolf***, who is still tucking in, does not see the* **Big Bad Wolf** *go. The* **Spider** *moves along the tuffet, bringing himself next to the* **Bigger Badder Wolf***. He digs him in the ribs.*

**Bigger Badder Wolf**   I've told you, don't do that. You've had your share.

*The* **Spider** *taps his knee.*

**Bigger Badder Wolf**   And don't tickle my leg either.

*The* **Spider** *does it again.*

**Bigger Badder Wolf**   I'm warning you . . .

*The* **Bigger Badder Wolf** *taps the* **Spider***'s 'knee'. The* **Spider** *shakes with laughter. The* **Bigger Badder Wolf** *suddenly does a double 'thinks' look, and gingerly reaches out and touches the* **Spider***'s knee – it clearly does not feel like the* **Big Bad Wolf***'s knee. He runs his hand up and down the* **Spider***'s leg/legs, gradually getting panic-stricken.*

*Finally, the* **Bigger Badder Wolf** *looks round, sees the* **Spider***, screams and dashes off, throwing down the bowl and spoon.*

*Hearing the scream,* **Little Miss Muffet** *opens her eyes and, summoning up all her courage, turns to see the* **Spider***. The* **Spider** *cheekily and endearingly waves a leg or two.* **Little Miss Muffet** *tentatively waves back, then stretches across and shakes hands with the* **Spider***. They share a moment of triumph over the* **Wolves***. She gives him a kiss and waves goodbye. He waves back with all his legs.*

**Little Miss Muffet** *exits towards home, i.e. downstage right.*

*The* **Spider** *picks up the bowl of curds and whey and starts to gobble it up. The lights fade.*


**Scene Three**

*Back at the Book*

*Music.* **Mother Goose***,* **Little Jack Horner***,* **Little Tommy Tucker***,* **Little Bo Peep** *and* **Little Polly Flinders** *enter.*

*During the song they could well be effecting the scene change back to the Book,
revolving it to display the inside, then decorating it, etc., and preparing the table and
props for the cookery scene that follows.*

**SONG: Getting Ready for Christmas**

**Mother Goose, Little Jack Horner, Little Bo Peep, Little Tommy Tucker** *and*
**Little Polly Flinders** (*singing*)
We're getting ready for Christmas
We're getting ready for Christmas Day
Building a snowman
From cotton-wool snow
Hanging up the holly
And the mistletoe
We're getting ready
Getting ready for Christmas
Ready,
Steady –

We're getting ready for Christmas
We're getting ready for Christmas Day
Filling the stockings
As full as can be
Wrapping up the presents
For the Christmas tree
We're getting ready
Getting ready for Christmas
Ready,
Steady –

It's nearly time for the celebrations
Fun and festivity lie in store
It's time to put up the decorations
With a welcoming Christmas wreath upon the door

We're getting ready for Christmas
We're getting ready for Christmas Day
Roasting the chestnuts
And chopping the wood
Blowing up balloons and
Helping stir the pud
We're getting ready
Getting ready for Christmas
Ready,
Steady –
Go!

*Suggested instrumental verse for dance.*

> We're getting ready for Christmas
> We're getting ready for Christmas Day
> Shining a candle
> From each window pane
> Making paper hats and
> Miles of paper chain
> We're getting ready
> Getting ready for Christmas
> Ready,
> Steady –

> It's nearly time for the celebrations
> Fun and festivity lie in store
> It's time to put up the decorations
> With a welcoming Christmas wreath upon the door.

> We're getting ready for Christmas
> We're getting ready for Christmas Day
> Stuffing the turkey
> And scrubbing the floors
> Sweeping out the chimney
> For old Santa Claus
> We're getting ready
> Getting ready for Christmas
> Ready,
> Steady –
> Go, go, go –
> Christmas
> Hallo.

**Little Jack Horner, Little Bo Peep** *and* **Little Polly Flinders** *exit to do more decorating on the 'outside' of the Book.*

**Mother Goose** *and* **Little Tommy Tucker** *remain behind to prepare the figgy pudding. The following slapstick-style scene could be embellished further into a 'speciality' if it is felt that not enough scope is given here: but it should not last too long, as, however funny it may be, it does hold up the plot.*

**Mother Goose** (*putting on an overall and chef's hat*)   Now, Tommy, time to make the figgy pudding.

**Little Tommy Tucker** (*singing*) Now bring me some figgy pudding, Now bring me . . .

**Mother Goose**   Yes, all right, dear. Be a good boy and fetch me the dough.

**Little Tommy Tucker**   Dough?

**Mother Goose**   Dough. D.O. Dough.

**Little Tommy Tucker**   Oh. Dough. Right ho. (*He goes to the back of the set, singing as he works.*) Do, ray, me, fah, so, la, te (*Coming forward with the tray of dough.*) DO!

**Mother Goose** (*busy doing something else, e.g. weighing out currants, so not looking.*)   Hurry up, dear.

**Little Tommy Tucker** *staggers under the weight of the dough, and puts it down, on the floor in front of the table. He has to crouch to do this, so is temporarily out of* **Mother Goose***'s vision.*

**Mother Goose**   (*Looking up and not seeing him.*) Tommy!

**Little Tommy Tucker** *stands up. She sees him.*

**Mother Goose**   Stop playing, dear (*Coming round to the front of the table.*) and (*One step per word.*) go-fetch-the-dough. (*On the word 'dough' she steps in the dough.*) Ohhhh!

*Together they pull it off her boot.*

**Little Tommy Tucker**   Oh. You've put your foot in it!

**Mother Goose**   Now concentrate, Tommy. (*Returning behind the table.*) Place the dough *here*. (*Patting the end of the table, then returning to counting her currants.*)

**Little Tommy Tucker** *struggles with the dough, which should be rather pliable and elastic.*

**Mother Goose**   *Here.* (*She gives another pat.*)

**Little Tommy Tucker** *manages to put the dough down where* **Mother Goose** *wants it.*

**Mother Goose**   *Here.* (*This time her hand crashes into the dough.*) Ughhhh!

**Little Tommy Tucker**   You've put your hand in it now.

**Mother Goose**   Tommy, a little con-cen-tra-tion if you please.

**Little Tommy Tucker**   Con-cen-tra-tion.

**Mother Goose** *kneads the dough into a large ball. A rolling-pin is visible on the table.*

**Mother Goose**   Take the dough (*She hands it to him.*) and roll it.

**Little Tommy Tucker**   Eh?

**Mother Goose** (*back with her currants*)   Roll it. Hurry up.

**Little Tommy Tucker** *shrugs his shoulders and rolls the ball of dough along the floor.*

**Little Tommy Tucker**   Wheeee!

**Mother Goose** (*seeing this*)   No, no, no, Tommy. Use the rolling-pin. (*She hands him the rolling-pin.*) This. (*She returns to her currants.*)

**Little Tommy Tucker** *takes the rolling-pin, and after a moment's hesitation, uses it as a bat to roll the dough further along the floor.*

**Mother Goose** (*seeing this*)   No, no, no, Tommy. (*Deliberately.*) Roll it with the rolling-pin, thus. (*She mimes the movement.*)

**Little Tommy Tucker** (*echoing the movement*)   Thus.

**Mother Goose**   Thus.

**Little Tommy Tucker**   Thus.

*It now becomes a rhythmic movement, complete with knees bend, etc. Both enjoy it.*

**Mother Goose**   Thus.

**Little Tommy Tucker**   Thus.

*As they continue,* **Mother Goose** *gets carried away.*

**Mother Goose** (*suddenly*)   Stop it! Now get on with it, Tommy, and con-cen-trate.

**Little Tommy Tucker** *mouths the word 'con-cen-trate' with her. He starts rolling the dough correctly, except that he is still doing it on the floor.*

**Mother Goose** (*seeing this.*)   No, no, no, Tommy. Not on the floor. On the table. On the table.

**Little Tommy Tucker** *immediately jumps on the table, giving* **Mother Goose** *a fright.*

**Mother Goose**   Aaaaah! Not you, the dough.

**Little Tommy Tucker**   Oh. (*He collects the dough, puts it on the table and starts rolling it with the rolling-pin. If possible, as the dough gets flatter and bigger, it spreads on to* **Mother Goose***'s outstretched hand and arm, so that they get rolled too. In rolling rhythm.*) Thus. Thus. Thus.

*He eventually notices the bump, investigates, and, looking for where the bump leads, traces it up the arm to find* **Mother Goose***'s long-suffering face staring at him. She slowly lifts her hand, letting the dough hang.*

**Mother Goose/Little Tommy Tucker**   Con-cen-trate.

**Mother Goose**   Now, fetch the baking tin.

**Little Tommy Tucker** *goes to the back of the set.* **Mother Goose** *scatters the currants over the dough and wraps it over, 'folding in the ends'.* **Little Tommy Tucker** *brings forward a tin, then suddenly screams, and drops the tin like a hot brick, with a clatter.*

**Mother Goose** (*with a jump*)   What was that?

**Little Tommy Tucker**   The baking tin. It's baking! Tara!

**Mother Goose** (*dividing the dough in two*)   Don't be silly. Now, we'll make one family-size figgy pudding (*She places half the dough in the tin, and scatters dusting powder on it.*) and a dozen small ones. (*She starts dividing the other half into smaller tennis-ball-size sections.*)

*Suddenly* **Little Tommy Tucker***'s attention is drawn to the baking tin, where the pudding is 'rising' rapidly. In fact this is done with a balloon blowing up beneath the dough. NB: This may have to be in a different tin, switched for the original one. This could have a thin layer of dough over the balloon, which pushes it up when blown up. As the pudding gets bigger and bigger,* **Little Tommy Tucker** *grabs* **Mother Goose***'s attention. They both look at it, then* **Mother Goose** *prods it with a wooden spoon* (*with a pin attached*). *It bursts, spraying dough or dusting powder over their faces.*

**Mother Goose**   Self-raising flour! (*Returning to the small ones.*) Right, Tommy. Into the oven.

*The oven could be 'under the table' or in another part of the set.* **Tommy** *starts to get in it.*

**Mother Goose**   Not you. The figgy puddings.

**Tommy** *gets out of the oven. To music,* **Mother Goose** *starts throwing the balls of dough to* **Little Tommy Tucker***, the idea being that he should transfer them to the oven. If the actor playing* **Little Tommy Tucker** *can juggle, he could go into a short routine here. Eventually, he has too many to hold and* **Mother Goose** *is throwing more, without looking at him.*

*At this point,* **Little Jack Horner, Little Bo Peep** *and* **Little Polly Flinders** *enter.*

**Little Tommy Tucker** *throws the 'balls' to them; they spread out and catch the 'balls' in a circular chain. The last one returns the 'balls' to the table for* **Mother Goose** *to pick up and throw at* **Little Tommy Tucker** *again. She is unaware that this is going on, of course. The catching game, to music, continues for a short while. Then* **Mother Goose** *notices what is going on. Her immediate reaction is one of annoyance, but this changes to amusement and enjoyment. She suddenly picks up a frying pan or similar object and, as the 'balls' come back to her, whacks them, cricket or tennis-style. The first few she hits stay on the stage. Then* **Little Tommy Tucker** *starts throwing into the 'chain' 'balls' from another source. These are cotton-wool balls, and are clouted fair and square by* **Mother Goose** *into the audience. NB: This fairly traditional panto routine could be omitted; the cookery scene could end on the line 'Self-raising flour', at which point the others enter.*

*Suddenly, as the fun with the audience is in full flood,* **Gertie** *enters from the forest and runs to the door and pulls the bell-rope.*

*The 'game' freezes at the sound of the bell.*

**Little Bo Peep**   Is that my sheep?

**Mother Goose**   No, it's Little Miss Muffet and Gertie back from holly hunting, I expect.

**Little Jack Horner** *opens the door; in rushes* **Gertie** *in a flurry, flapping her wings. They all cluster round her.*

**Little Jack Horner**, **Little Tommy Tucker** and **Little Bo Peep**.
   What is it?
   What's the matter? etc.
   What's happened, Gertie? etc.

**Gertie** *is confused.*

**Mother Goose**   Quiet. You can see she's in a state. Polly. Come and do your stuff.

**Little Polly Flinders** *comes forward.*

**Little Polly Flinders**   What is it, Gertie? Did you meet somebody?

**Gertie** *nods, and does a wolf impersonation. The audience will probably help interpret.*

**Little Polly Flinders**   What? A monster? The Giant? A wolf?

**Gertie** *nods, and mimes 'two'.*

**Little Polly Flinders**   Two wolves?

**Little Bo Peep** (*freezing with terror*)   Wolves?

**Little Polly Flinders**   Did they chase you?

**Gertie** *nods.*

**Mother Goose**   Where's Little Miss Muffet?

**Gertie** *mimes a boxing match.*

**Little Polly Flinders**   She's fighting them?

**Gertie** *nods.*

**Mother Goose**   Ooh. (*She swallows hard.*) I hope she's careful. (*Trying not to appear too worried.*) She had a clean apron on this morning. (*She blinks away a tear.*)

**Little Tommy Tucker**   She'll be all right, Mother.

**Little Bo Peep**   Wolves! (*She bursts into tears.*)

**Little Jack Horner**   Don't cry, Bo Peep; Little Miss Muffet will be back soon.

**Little Bo Peep**   I'm not worried about her, I'm worried about my poor little sheep. Alone in the forest. Surrounded by wolves. Wolves like nothing better than sheep – to eat! I'll never see them again.

*The others look at one another and shrug their shoulders, as she dashes out of the door, to 'outside' the Book, which then revolves to reveal the outside cover again.*
**Little Bo Peep** *looks out in all directions, hoping for a glimpse of her sheep.*

SONG: **Sheep, Sheep**

**Little Bo Peep**
    Sheep, sheep
    This is Bo Peep
    Oh can you hear
    What I say?
    Or have you strayed
    Too far?

    Sheep, sheep
    I'm losing sleep
    Oh don't you know
    How I care
    Please tell me where
    You are.

*One by one, the others –* **Little Jack Horner, Little Tommy Tucker** *and* **Little Polly Flinders** *– put their heads over or round the Book.*

**Little Jack Horner** (*speaking*)   Baaaaaaaa!

**Little Tommy Tucker** (*speaking*)   Baaaaaaaa!

**Little Polly Flinders** (*speaking*)   Baaaaaaaa!

**All three** (*speaking*)   Baaaaaaaa!

**Little Bo Peep** *swings round, thinking her sheep have been found. When she sees it is the others sending her up, she is cross, but tries to preserve her dignity.*

**Little Bo Peep** (*speaking*)   Oh, it's you.

*The other three sing with a sheep-like wobble in their voices.*

**Little Polly Flinders, Little Tommy Tucker** *and* **Little Jack Horner** (*singing together*)
    Baaaaaa! Baaaaaa!
    We've not strayed far
    And we'll return
    Very soon
    This afternoon
    You'll see.

    Baaaaaa! Baaaaaa!
    Daft things we are!
    But if you leave
    Us alone
    We'll hurry home
    For tea.

**Little Bo Peep** *tries to take no notice.*

**Little Bo Peep**
>   Sheep, sheep
>   This is Bo Peep
>   Oh tell me why
>   Must you go?
>   Why are you so
>   Unkind?

**Little Polly Flinders, Little Tommy Tucker** *and* **Little Jack Horner** (*singing together*)
>   Baaaaaa! Baaaaaa!
>   Stupid we are
>   But we'll come back
>   Without fail
>   Bringing our tails
>   Behind.

**Little Bo Peep**
>   Sheep, sheep

**Little Polly Flinders, Little Tommy Tucker** *and* **Little Jack Horner**    Baaaaaa! Baaaaaa!

*Dabbing her eyes,* **Little Bo Peep** *has a final look, shakes her head and goes back in the Book.*

**Little Polly Flinders, Little Tommy Tucker** *and* **Little Jack Horner**    Baaaaaa! Baaaaaa!

**Little Bo Peep**
>   Sheep, sheep.

*Their heads disappear from view.*

*Sinister chord as the* **Bigger Badder Wolf** *enters, rubbing his hands in glee; he has seen* **Little Bo Peep** *go in. He is followed by the* **Big Bad Wolf**, *head down sniffing the tracks. The* **Bigger Badder Wolf** *stops. The* **Big Bad Wolf** *bumps into him. The* **Bigger Badder Wolf** *hits him.*

**Big Bad Wolf**    Sorry, B.B.W. (*Nervously he takes out a tranquilliser.*)

**Bigger Badder Wolf** (*imitating*)    Sorry, B.B.W. (*Crossly.*) And stop taking tranquillisers.

*He knocks it out of the* **Big Bad Wolf**'s *hand, making it bounce high in the air. The* **Bigger Badder Wolf** *catches it under his hat Alternatively it is allowed to bounce out into the auditorium.*

**Big Bad Wolf**    Sorry, B.B.W.

**Bigger Badder Wolf**    And stop saying 'Sorry, B.B.W.' It gets on my nerves.

**Big Bad Wolf**   Sorry, B.B.W. (*He realises too late, and clamps his hand over his mouth.*)

**Bigger Badder Wolf**   Now, listen. Tracks end here, right?

**Big Bad Wolf**   Right here, right.

**Bigger Badder Wolf** (*pointing to the Book*)   Goose in there, therefore, right?

**Big Bad Wolf**   Right there, therefore, right.

**Bigger Badder Wolf**   Problem: to get inside, right? And not to be left outside, right?

**Big Bad Wolf**   Ah! Right. Not left outside, but right inside, right! Not outside left but inside right to centre forward and shoot and it's a goal! Hooray! (*He jumps up and down.*)

*The* **Bigger Badder Wolf** *clamps his hand over the* **Big Bad Wolf**'s *mouth.*

**Bigger Badder Wolf**   Shhh. Solution: take off your coat.

**Big Bad Wolf**   What?

**Bigger Badder Wolf**   Take off your coat.

**Big Bad Wolf**   I'll catch cold.

**Bigger Badder Wolf**   You'll catch more than a cold if you don't. Now (*Helping him out of his coat.*) take it off and turn it inside out, right?

**Big Bad Wolf**   Inside out, right. Not outside in, left. Inside out . . .

**Bigger Badder Wolf**   And don't start all that again.

**Big Bad Wolf**   I didn't start it. You started it.

*By this time, the* **Big Bad Wolf**'s *coat is back on – inside out, revealing the thick sheepskin lining,.*

**Bigger Badder Wolf**   Now. Baaaa.

**Big Bad Wolf**   I beg your pardon?

**Bigger Badder Wolf**   Baaaa. Baaaaa! (*He encourages the* **Big Bad Wolf** *to copy the noise.*)

*The* **Big Bad Wolf** *has not a clue what he is on about.*

**Big Bad Wolf**   Baaaa?

**Bigger Badder Wolf** (*nodding*)   Baaaaa! (*Louder and more manic.*) Baaaaaa!

**Big Bad Wolf**   Do you want a tranquilliser?

**Bigger Badder Wolf**   Oh, give me strength!

**Big Bad Wolf**   No, but it'll calm you down.

**Bigger Badder Wolf**   You baaaa.

**Big Bad Wolf**   Me baaaa?

**Bigger Badder Wolf**   Yes, you baaaa. Look, didn't you hear that girl bleating on about her lost sheep?

*The* **Big Bad Wolf** *nods.*

**Bigger Badder Wolf** (*slowly and clearly*)   Well, *you* are now a wolf in sheep's clothing, right? And that means . . .

*He is stopped by a shout off.*

**Little Miss Muffet**   Mother Goose! Mother Goose!

**Bigger Badder Wolf**   Look out!

*The* **Bigger Badder Wolf** *drags the* **Big Bad Wolf** *off to hide. They exit the side opposite the one they entered – i.e. not the side established as leading to the forest.* **Little Miss Muffet** *rushes on from the forest: she rings frantically on the bell.*

**Little Miss Muffet**   Mother Goose! Quick.

*The door opens and* **Mother Goose**, **Gertie** *and the four other* **Children** *emerge, and cluster round her.* **Little Polly Flinders** *carries the kettle with her.*

**All**   She's back. Thank goodness you're safe. Are you all right? etc.

**Little Miss Muffet** (*breathless*)   Wolves. After Gertie. From the Giant's castle. They're coming.

**Little Bo Peep**   What are we going to do?

**Little Jack Horner**   Shut ourselves in the Book.

*All turn to go in the door.*

**Little Miss Muffet**   No.

*They stop.*

They're strong. They'll smash the door down if they know Gertie's inside. (*She grabs* **Gertie**.) I'll hide with her in the forest.

**Little Polly Flinders**   Can I come?

**Little Jack Horner**   And me.

**Little Tommy Tucker**   Me too! I'll bring the figgy pud. All right, Mother Goose?

**Mother Goose**   I suppose so, dear. But do take care, all of you.

**Little Tommy Tucker** *rushes in and collects some figgy pudding.*

**Little Bo Peep**   I'd better stay here, in case my sheep turn up. (*She starts sniffing.*)

**Mother Goose**   Very well, dear.

**Little Miss Muffet**   Come on.

*Little Miss Muffet leads a nervous Gertie off. The others follow – they exit towards the forest, Mother Goose waving.*

**Mother Goose**   I'll see you off.

*She exits. Little Bo Peep goes back in the Book and shuts the door. Immediately, music is heard as the Wolves enter from the other side.*

*The Bigger Badder Wolf pushes the disguised Big Bad Wolf to the door. The Big Bad Wolf rings the bell, then bends over to look more like a sheep.*

**Big Bad Wolf**   Baaaaa! Baaaaaa!

*The door opens.*

*The Bigger Badder Wolf backs away to avoid being seen, and in fact exits on the forest side, looking eagerly towards the Book. This is to prevent the audience thinking he is chasing after the others.*

**Little Bo Peep** *emerges.*

**Big Bad Wolf**   Baaaaaa!

**Little Bo Peep** (*yelling with delight*)   Little sheep! You've come home!

*She falls upon the 'sheep', stroking and hugging him. By this time the audience may well be screaming a warning.*

You're safe from the Wolves, now. Come in.

*She takes him in and shuts the door behind them. Pause. Suddenly, a bloodcurdling scream is heard. The door opens again and Little Bo Peep, screaming, tries to get out, but each time is seen to be pulled roughly back inside. Growling noises from the Big Bad Wolf. But Little Bo Peep has her crook with her and manages to stave off the Wolf with it. NB: It may be possible to work out a short routine using the crook as a catching device. Little Bo Peep could emerge from the door a couple of times, but be suddenly caught round the neck with the crook and hauled in again. Then the situations could be reversed, with Little Bo Peep catching the Big Bad Wolf by the neck trying to drag him inside so she can get out. Finally the door is shut, and we imagine the Big Bad Wolf is a little stunned inside. Little Bo Peep, screaming still, rushes downstage right, nearly exits, then, remembering that the others went in the other direction, turns round and starts to run offstage left.*

**Mother Goose** *enters downstage left.*

**Little Bo Peep** *is stopped in her tracks.*

**Little Bo Peep**   Oh, Mother Goose, Mother Goose. (*She flings herself into Mother Goose's arms, pointing indoors to where the Big Bad Wolf is. Hysterically.*) A wolf, a wolf. Rang the bell and I thought it was one of my sheep and let him in and . . . ohhh! (*She sobs.*)

**Mother Goose**   There, there, dear. You're safe now. Stop crying.

*The sobbing lessens with the reassuring pats on the back.*

**Little Bo Peep**    I'm sorry. I can't help it. He was so horrible – and he's still in the Book!

**Mother Goose**    There, there.

*For the first time,* **Little Bo Peep** *looks up, through tear-stained eyes, at* **Mother Goose**.

**Little Bo Peep**    Oh, Mother Goose, how strong your arms are.

**Mother Goose**    All the better to comfort you, my dear.

*Music chord.*

**Little Bo Peep**    Oh, Mother Goose. (*A little uncomfortable.*) How big your eyes look today.

**Mother Goose**    All the better to watch over you, my dear.

*Music chord.*

**Little Bo Peep** (*nervously*)    Oh, Mother Goose, how long and sharp your teeth look.

**Mother Goose**    All the better to *bite* you with, my dear.

*Music. Dramatic struggle, but not too long, in which 'Mother Goose' is revealed to be the* **Bigger Badder Wolf** *in disguise – in fact, wearing* **Mother Goose***'s dress. NB: This revelation should, if possible, come as a real surprise to the audience. The tussle ends with the* **Big Bad Wolf** *entering from the Book, rubbing his head; he is finishing off writing a note, which he speedily attaches to the door. Then he helps subdue the struggling, screaming* **Little Bo Peep**. *They lift her up and tuck her under their arms. Suddenly the lighting changes dramatically, to solely a follow spot on* **Little Bo Peep**. *Simultaneously the action freezes.*

SONG: **My Big Moment** (*reprise*)

**Little Bo Peep** (*singing*)
>This must be my big moment
>My moment of glory
>In the story
>This will be my closest shave
>This must be my big moment
>This is my time to be brave.

*At the end of the song, the lighting reverts and the action starts again, and the growling* **Wolves** *carry off the struggling* **Little Bo Peep**. *They exit downstage left towards the forest. Simultaneously,* **Mother Goose** *enters upstage left, in her undies, still spinning from the shock of being attacked by the* **Bigger Badder Wolf**.

*The audience may well shout out that* **Little Bo Peep** *has been caught, or that the* **Wolves** *have left a note. In any case, she staggers to the door, goes to open it, notices the note, rips it off the door and studies it.*

**Mother Goose** (*reading*)   'We, the Wolves of the Giant's castle, wish to inform Mother Goose that Little Bo Peep is in our clutches. If you ever want to set eyes on her again you must bring the Giant's Goose into the forest within the hour and we will do a swap. The Goose for Little Bo Peep. Yours threateningly, The Big Bad Wolf and the Bigger Badder Wolf.' Oh, no. What's to be done? (*Calling.*) Children! (*Remembering.*) They've all gone. Poor Little Bo Peep. Poor Gertie. Now calm down, Mother Goose, calm down, don't panic, don't panic, don't panic. (*Pause. She takes a deep breath to calm down. Suddenly she shouts.*) HE – LP! Emergency, emergency. He – lp! (*She has an idea.*) Fairy Lethargia, of course. (*To the audience.*) Quick, let's wake her up. One, two, three.

**Audience** *and* **Mother Goose** (*calling together*)   Fairy Lethargia.

**Mother Goose**   Once more. One, two, three.

**Audience** *and* **Mother Goose** (*calling together*)   Fairy Lethargia

*A yawning, stretching* **Fairy Lethargia** *eases her way out of the decorations box.*

**Fairy Lethargia**   Cor dear, I'm up and down like a blinking yoyo . . . oh. (*She sees the audience as she climbs out, puts on her act again.*)

Hallo, hallo, it's Christmas Eve, and I'm your Christmas Fairy
My spells will get you out of spots and situations hairy . . .

(*Suddenly she sees* **Mother Goose.**) Ha, ha, ha, ha.

**Mother Goose**   What's the matter?

**Fairy Lethargia**   You look funny with your undies on.

**Mother Goose**   I look funnier with them off.

**Fairy Lethargia**   Ha, ha, ha, ha.

**Mother Goose**   Stop laughing. This looks serious.

**Fairy Lethargia**   It doesn't from where I'm standing. Ha, ha.

**Mother Goose**   I've been hijacked by a wolf. And Little Bo Peep's been kidnapped. Wolfnapped. I need the first of our three spells, please.

**Fairy Lethargia**   Oh.

**Mother Goose**   Oh what?

**Fairy Lethargia**   OK. (*Taking the wand off the tree.*) What's it to be?

**Mother Goose**   Er. (*She thinks.*) Miss Muffet and Polly and Tommy and Jack – oh, and Gertie – I need them here, so we can decide what to do.

**Fairy Lethargia**   Where are they now?

**Mother Goose**   If I knew that, I wouldn't ask for a spell to get them back, would I?

**Fairy Lethargia**   All right, all right, don't get your knickers in a twist. (*She looks at* **Mother Goose**'*s undies and giggles again.*)

**Mother Goose**   I'll go and find my dressing-gown.

*She goes in the door.*

**Fairy Lethargia** *takes up a pose, holds up the wand, and starts the spell, accompanied by not-very-graceful movements.*

SONG: **Fairy Lethargia's Magic Spell**

**Fairy Lethargia**
    Gertie and Little Miss Muffet
    And Tommy and Polly and Jack
    Abracadabra, hocus pocus
    Magic the lot of them back.

*At the end of the spell, the four* **Children** *and* **Gertie** *return 'by magic'. This could be achieved by use of trap doors, flash boxes, a swift blackout, etc. At any event, all five return, and are surprised to find themselves transported back to the Book.* **Little Tommy Tucker** *carries a substantially reduced figgy pudding;* **Little Polly Flinders** *carries her kettle.*

**Fairy Lethargia** *curtsies to acknowledge possible audience applause – depending on how well the magical appearances were done!*

**Little Jack Horner** (*waking up*)   What's happened?

**Fairy Lethargia**   Spell number one's happened, that's what. Pretty spectacular, eh? (*She blows her fingernails, or does some other self-congratulatory movement.*)

**Little Tommy Tucker**   We're back.

**Little Miss Muffet**   But why?

**Mother Goose** *enters from the Book; she wears her dressing-gown.*

**Mother Goose**   Oh, thank goodness. Well done, Lethargia. Have a rest, dear. Children, listen.

*The* **Children** *and* **Gertie***, still 'waking up', gather round* **Mother Goose***.*

**Mother Goose**   Little Bo Peep has been wolfnapped. By the kids . . . I mean, kidnapped by the Wolves.

*This jerks them into life.*

**Children**   What? How? Where have they taken her? etc.

**Mother Goose**   Shhh. Listen. They left a note saying that if we ever want to see her again, we must meet them in the forest.

**Gertie** *involuntarily flaps her wings.*

**Mother Goose**   Then they will give us back Little Bo Peep on condition that we – that we – well, children, that we – in exchange as it were – give them back – (*She can hardly bring herself to say it.*) – Gertie.

*Music.* **Gertie** *slowly turns away from the group, and, head down, sadly waddles downstage. She is obviously crying. NB: This must not be overdone – it is a very tender moment. The others watch her.*

**Mother Goose**    Gertie, dear. I wouldn't have had this happen for all the world, you know that, don't you?

**Gertie** *nods.*

**Mother Goose**    But what can I do? Eh? I must save Little Bo Peep. I'm sorry.

**Gertie** *nods and, resigned, starts moving off towards the forest. The music builds as the others all set off too. A sad procession, which* **Fairy Lethargia** *joins.* **Little Polly Flinders** *still has her kettle. The lights fade.*


**Scene Four**

*The Forest – without the* **Spider***'s Lair.*

*The music continues as the scene changes. The following sequence is all done in mime to music. If desirable, a forest front cloth could fly in to cover the scene change. The two snarling* **Wolves** *enter, carrying a distressed* **Little Bo Peep***. They pause for a few moments to shake their fists at the audience, who should be booing them. The* **Bigger Badder Wolf** *removes* **Mother Goose's** *dress, while the* **Big Bad Wolf** *retains a grip on* **Little Bo Peep***. The dress is thrown roughly on the ground, and maybe stamped on. Then they exit, or, if a front cloth is not being used – it may be possible, for example, for them to enter through the auditorium and reach the stage just as the scene change has been effected, taking the dress off on the way – they hide behind a tree.*

*The music continues, playing a sad version of the* **Goose's** *song, as* **Gertie***, with the* **Children***,* **Mother Goose** *and* **Fairy Lethargia***, enter the forest. They, too, could come through the auditorium, or go across the front cloth, or simply arrive in the forest. They find* **Mother Goose's** *dress on the ground, and know they are on the right route.* **Mother Goose** *takes the dress with her. The* **Children** *surround* **Gertie** *protectively.*

*Suddenly, the* **Wolves** *and* **Bo Peep** *emerge. The two sides confront each other.* **Little Bo Peep** *outstretches her arms for help.* **Mother Goose***, firmly but sympathetically, forces the* **Children** *to let* **Gertie** *go. Each one kisses her goodbye.* **Mother Goose** *takes her by the wing and advances to 'no-man's land' in the centre.*

*The* **Wolves** *bring* **Little Bo Peep** *forward. The exchange is made.* **Little Bo Peep** *embraces* **Mother Goose***, who leads her back to the 'family'.*

*Meanwhile, the* **Wolves** *grab* **Gertie** *and perhaps put a rope round her neck, before roughly forcing her to go with them towards the Giant's castle. The others watch them disappear, with obviously conflicting emotions – relief for* **Little Bo Peep's** *safety and sadness at* **Gertie's** *disappearance.*

*The music stops.*

**Little Bo Peep**   Where's Gertie going?

**Mother Goose**   Back to the Giant's castle. It was either her or you, dear.

**Little Bo Peep**   But we can't just let her be locked up in a cage again. (*To the others*.) Can we?

**Little Miss Muffet**   She's right.

**Little Tommy Tucker**   But what else can we do? Mother Goose?

**Mother Goose**   It's up to you, children. Remember, this is *your* story, *your* adventure . . .

*Pause.* **Fairy Lethargia** *falls asleep on her feet.*

**Little Jack Horner**   We'll rescue Gertie.

**All**   Hear, hear; hooray, etc.

**Little Polly Flinders** (*plucking up courage*)   And – and – and teach that stinking old Giant Bossyboots a lesson he'll never forget.

**All**   Hear, hear; hooray, etc.

**Mother Goose**   But don't forget it'll be dangerous – we'll have to face the forest and the castle and the Wolves and the Giant, not to mention the Monster of the Moat.

**Little Tommy Tucker**   They'll help make it a real adventure.

**Little Miss Muffet**   And we've still got two of Fairy Lethargia's spells left. Haven't we?

**Fairy Lethargia** *is still asleep on her feet. All turn to see her. She snores.*

**Little Bo Peep**   She's nodded off again.

**Mother Goose**   Come on, then, everybody. One, two, three.

**All**   Fairy Lethargia.

**Fairy Lethargia** (*suddenly waking with a start*)   Oooh! (*Lifting her wand, and putting on her act.*)

Hallo, hallo, 'tis Christmas Eve, and I'm . . .

**All** (*shouting her down*)   No! Quiet! Shh! etc.

**Fairy Lethargia**   What's going on?

SONG: **Off to the Rescue**

*They all sing except* **Fairy Lethargia**, *who joins in at an appropriate moment.*

Off through the forest
Off to the castle

Off to the rescue we race;
Summon up courage
Tackle the Monster
Challenge the Giant and put those two Wolves in their place;
We must find her
We can't be that far behind her
We'll follow the track
And bring our Goose back
Leave no stone unturned
Till we have returned
With her found
Safe and sound.

Off through the forest
Off to the castle
Off to the rescue we race;
Nothing can stop us
We won't be beaten
We'll do our best for our quest must be no wild goose chase;
When we see her
Somehow we'll force them to free her
We know that it's right
We'll stand up and fight
Then back to the Book
By hook or by crook
We'll vamoose
With our Goose!
Off to the rescue
Off to the rescue . . .

*Suddenly* **Little Jack Horner** *trips over something and falls over. He shouts out. The music stops, all except a tremolo rumble of excitement.*

**Little Miss Muffet**    Enjoy your trip?

**Little Jack Horner** (*getting up*)    There's something there – in that patch of grass.

*They look. Suddenly* **Little Polly Flinders** *finds something.*

**Little Polly Flinders**    Look.

**Little Miss Muffet**    An egg.

**Mother Goose**    A *golden* egg. It's beautiful.

**Little Tommy Tucker**    Gertie must have laid it . . .

**Little Bo Peep**    So she *is* the Goose that laid the Golden Egg.

**Fairy Lethargia** (*taking control*)    That's right. She was so grateful to you all for showing her kindness that she laid it for you.

*Into couplets – but not sent up.*

> Throughout your quest, this egg will be your lucky charm
> As long as you don't lose it, you can come to no harm.

**Little Bo Peep**   Thank you, Gertie.

**Little Tommy Tucker**   We'll pay you back.

**Little Polly Flinders/Little Miss Muffet/Little Jack Horner**   We're on our way!

SONG: **Off to the Rescue** (*continued*)

**All**

> Off to the rescue
> Off to the rescue
> This Golden Egg will protect us from danger we know
> So
> Off to the rescue
> We go.

*As the song ends, the 'Quest' exits.*

**Fairy Lethargia** *waves farewell. Then she replaces her wand on the Christmas tree, yawns and stretches and gets back into the decorations box. The music swells as the lighting narrows down to the star on the wand. Then it fades to a blackout.*

*The Christmas tree, with the wand on it as a star, remains in view throughout the interval.*

## Act Two

### Scene One

*NB: This scene is optional. Its function is to re-establish the plot, but this may be felt to be unnecessary.*

*The Edge of the Forest (front cloth), with the Giant's castle visible in the distance.*

*The entr'acte music becomes sinister as the house lights go down.*

*The* **Wolves** *enter, dragging* **Gertie** *behind them. She still has the sack over her head. The* **Wolves** *savagely push and pull her, playing up to the audience reaction against them. Finally they exit the other side. The music changes, and from offstage we hear singing. The 'Quest' then enters continuing the song.* **Little Polly Flinders** *still carries her kettle.* **Mother Goose** *has put on her dress and carries her dressing-gown.*

SONG: **Off to the Rescue** (*reprise*)

**Mother Goose, Little Miss Muffet, Little Jack Horner, Little Bo Peep, Little Tommy Tucker** *and* **Little Polly Flinders** (*singing together*)
> Off through the forest
> Off to the castle
> Off to the rescue we race
> Summon up courage
> Tackle the Monster
> Challenge the Giant and put those two Wolves in their place;
> We must find her
> We can't be that far behind her . . .

*The music continues under the following dialogue.*

**Little Miss Muffet** (*excited*)   There's the castle. It's not far.

**Little Bo Peep**   Looks really spooky. (*Wanting reassurance.*) Where's the Golden Egg?

**Little Jack Horner**   Tommy's eaten it.

**Little Tommy Tucker**   I haven't.

**Mother Goose**   Here it is. (*She takes it from her pocket.*)

**Little Polly Flinders** (*whispering in amazement*)   It's bigger.

**Mother Goose**   What, dear?

**Little Polly Flinders**   The egg's grown. It's bigger.

**Mother Goose**   So it is.

**Little Jack Horner**   How eggstraordinary! Tara!

*All groan at the pun.*

SONG: **Off to the Rescue** (*reprise, continued*)

**All**

> Off to the rescue
> Off to the rescue
> Our Golden Egg will protect us from danger we know
> So
> Off to the rescue
> We go.

*As the song ends, they all exit towards the castle.*

*The lights fade to a blackout.*


## Scene Two

*The Entrance to the* **Giant**'*s Castle.*

*Huge studded double doors dominate the scene upstage – giving an idea of the gigantic scale of the castle. In front of the doors is a raised drawbridge. A sign says 'BEWARE OF THE MONSTER OF THE MOAT', and downstage is a bank, to suggest the moat between it and the doors. Perhaps a lighting effect could suggest water reflections from the moat. On the bank is a bell-push or bell-rope; if it is the latter, it could extend up into the flies, as though going up to a bell tower. Another sign says 'RING THE BELL AND UTTER THE PASSWORD'.*

*The* **Wolves** *enter dragging* **Gertie**.

**Bigger Badder Wolf**    Ring the bell.

**Big Bad Wolf**    What?

**Bigger Badder Wolf**    Ring the bell.

**Big Bad Wolf** (*nervously*)    I'd rather not.

**Bigger Badder Wolf**    What do you mean (*Imitating.*) 'I'd rather not'? We can't get inside unless we ring the bell.

**Big Bad Wolf**    You ring it, then.

**Bigger Badder Wolf**    Why me?

**Big Bad Wolf**    You're more musical than I am.

**Bigger Badder Wolf**    Don't be so stupid. What's the matter with you? Why won't you ring the bell?

**Big Bad Wolf**    It m-m-means m-m-moving towards the m-m-moat and the M-m-m-monster.

**Bigger Badder Wolf**    The Monster isn't worried about you.

**Big Bad Wolf**    No, but I'm a little worried about *him*.

**Bigger Badder Wolf**    Oh, for wickedness' sake – hold this horrible bird.

*The* **Big Bad Wolf** *does so. The* **Bigger Badder Wolf** *strides confidently up to the bell-rope and pulls it. He returns.*

**Bigger Badder Wolf**    There you are. Nothing to it.

*The very loud boom of the deep, ominous, clanging bell makes them both jump. From high up in the flies we hear the sound of a sash window being raised. The* **Wolves** *look up.*

**Giant's Voice** (*booming down from the flies*)    Password.

**Bigger Badder Wolf**    Password.

**Bigger Badder Wolf** *and* **Big Bad Wolf** (*chanting together*)
    Copper and silver leave us cold
    What we want is lots of gold.

**Giant's Voice**    Again.

**Bigger Badder Wolf**    Why? Don't you believe us?

**Giant's Voice**    Yes. But I enjoy hearing it.

**Bigger Badder Wolf** *and* **Big Bad Wolf** (*chanting together*)
    Copper and silver leave us cold
    What we want is lots of gold.

**Giant's Voice**    You may enter.

**Bigger Badder Wolf**    Thanks, boss. We've got the Goose.

**Giant's Voice**    Splendid. (*He laughs – a hollow, evil, booming laugh.*)

*With a sinister creaking sound, the drawbridge lowers, and clanks on to the bank. Music, as the* **Wolves** *and* **Gertie** *start to go across. The* **Big Bad Wolf** *is nervous, and surreptitiously takes out a tranquilliser and pops it in his mouth. The* **Bigger Badder Wolf** *catches him at it, and slaps him on the back. The gob-stopper-size tranquilliser pops out – into the moat. The* **Wolves** *react worried, and even more so when they hear the sound of the* **Monster**, *underwater, being woken up, hit by the flying gob-stopper – a sort of 'ow' sound, followed by a roar of anger. The* **Wolves** *cling on to each other as well as* **Gertie**, *as, suddenly, an enormous head – rather like the head of the Loch Ness Monster – rears us from the moat, and advances towards them, snapping its jaws and uttering frightening sounds.*

*The* **Wolves** *manage to edge their way along the drawbridge, pushing* **Gertie** *ahead of them. They reach the doors, enter the castle – more sinister creaking sounds – and close the doors.*

*The drawbridge raises itself, perhaps hitting the* **Monster** *on the 'chin' as it does so. The* **Monster**, *disappointed, returns under the water with a dissatisfied moan. The music continues.*

**Little Miss Muffet** *enters downstage, and beckons on* **Mother Goose** *and the other* **Children**. *They enter on tiptoe.* **Mother Goose** *still carries her dressing-gown – she puts it down in a suitable place during the following scene.*

**Little Jack Horner** (*loudly*)   Cor, it's gigantic!

**All**   Shhhh!

*They all huddle downstage, organised by* **Mother Goose**, *and start to whisper tactics. They are stopped by the booming sound of the* **Giant**'s *voice.*

**Giant's Voice** (*from the flies above*)   Hallo, Goosey. Welcome home. Ha, ha, ha. Into your cage, there's a good bird.

*There is the clank of a cage door closing and a key turning.*

Now, back on the job. I want a Golden Egg, do you hear? A Golden Egg. And if you don't lay it soon, you'll be shut in a dungeon without food or water till you rot. So lay, blast you, lay.

*Giant footsteps are heard retreating.* **Mother Goose** *and the* **Children** *react to the speech, shaking their fists up towards the flies.*

**Little Jack Horner** (*loudly, incensed*)   Mother Goose . . .

**All**   Shhh.

**Little Jack Horner** (*whispering*)   Mother Goose, let me rescue Gertie from that big bully Bossyboots. Let Little Jack Horner be Jack the Giant-killer.

**Mother Goose**   It's your story, dear; so good luck.

**All**   Good luck, Jack. Take care, etc.

**Mother Goose**   Don't forget the Golden Egg. (*She hands it to him.*)

*             *             *             *             *

*The following three speeches should be inserted if Act Two, Scene One has been omitted.*

**Little Polly Flinders**   The egg's grown. It's bigger.

**Mother Goose**   So it is.

**Little Jack Horner**   How eggstraordinary. Tara!

*             *             *             *             *

**Little Bo Peep**   How are you going to get in the castle?

**Little Jack Horner**   I'll swim across the moat.

**Little Tommy Tucker**   But look (*He points to the sign – 'BEWARE OF THE MONSTER OF THE MOAT'.*) 'Beware of the Monster of the Moat.'

**Little Jack Horner**   I'm not frightened of a Monster – I've got the Golden Egg.

*Dramatic rumble music as* **Little Jack Horner** *approaches the moat. The others huddle together, watching.* **Little Jack Horner** *stands on the edge of the bank and flexes his legs and arms as if to dive into the moat. As an afterthought, he turns back and waves to the 'family'. As he does so, the* **Monster**'s *head rears up, unseen by him, but visible to the others and to the audience. All try to warn him. He smiles disbelievingly, and turns back to find himself virtually nose to nose with the* **Monster**. *He screams and jumps impulsively, and in his panic to escape, throws his arms in the air, allowing the Golden Egg to fly from his hand and fall into the watery depths of the moat. A splash sound effect could enhance this. The* **Monster** *disappears again, the 'threat' having gone.*

**Little Miss Muffet**    Now look what you've done.

**Little Jack Horner** (*hardly able to believe it*    I'm sorry. I jumped.

**Little Tommy Tucker**    So did the Golden Egg. Right into the moat.

**Little Bo Peep** (*on the verge of tears*)    We'll never rescue Gertie now.

**Little Miss Muffet**    What can we do? Mother Goose?

**Mother Goose**    Is it an emergency?

**Little Bo Peep** (*emotionally*)    Of course it is. We must get the Golden Egg back.

**Mother Goose**    If it's an emergency, there's only one thing to do –

*Pause, during which the audience may call out, 'Get Fairy Lethargia' –*

**Little Polly Flinders** (*eventually, whispering*)    Call Lethargia.

**Mother Goose**    What, dear?

**Little Polly Flinders** (*louder*)    Call Fairy Lethargia.

**Mother Goose**    Bullseye! Come on, everyone! (*Looking at the castle.*) But not too loudly. One, two, three.

**All** (*including* **audience**; *calling together*)    Fairy Lethargia.

*They look towards the decorations box – still in position at the side of the stage.*

*A loud yawn heralds* **Fairy Lethargia**'s *arrival from the box.*

**Fairy Lethargia**    Up, down, up, down, up, down. I'm not a flipping Jack-in-the-Box, you know.

**Mother Goose**    It's an emergency.

**Fairy Lethargia**    It always is. (*Suddenly noticing the castle.*) Oo-er. Where are we? I'll say this much. Your story's very moving.

**Little Tommy Tucker**    Moving?

**Fairy Lethargia**    Yes – it's never in the same place twice. Just as well I don't get travel-sick. Whose is this humble abode, eh?

**Little Miss Muffet**    The Giant's.

**Fairy Lethargia**    Ooh, I don't like giants.

**Little Miss Muffet**    Why not?

**Fairy Lethargia**    They always look down on people! Right, come on. (*She yawns.*) I can't hang around all afternoon. I thought this was an emergency.

**Little Bo Peep** (*crossly*)    It is. But you won't let us get a word in edgeways.

**Fairy Lethargia**    Ooooh! Hark at her. Fairies have feelings, you know. I know when I'm not wanted. (*She yawns.*) Night, night. (*She starts to climb back into the box.*)

**Mother Goose**    You've offended her now. Fairy Lethargia, please, you must help.

**Fairy Lethargia**    Why? You're all right. You've got the Golden Egg. Night.

**Little Jack Horner**    But that's the whole point. We haven't.

**Fairy Lethargia**    Eh? (*She stops.*)

**Little Jack Horner** (*sheepishly, pointing to the moat*)    I dropped the egg in the water.

**Fairy Lethargia** (*after a pause to take in the news*)    You dropped the egg in the water? Knowing you, I'm surprised you didn't add a pinch of salt, turn the gas on and boil it for three minutes. All right, I'll help. You'll have to dredge the bed of the moat. Like looking for buried treasure.

**Little Miss Muffet**    We *are* looking for buried treasure.

**Mother Goose**    What can we use to try and scoop it up?

*The audience may shout solutions.*

**Little Polly Flinders** (*eventually*)    We could try my kettle! (*She holds it up.*) And I've got some string . . . (*She produces the string and starts to tie it on the handle.*)

**Little Tommy Tucker**    No, Polly, that'll never work. Anyway, I've made my mind up. *I'm* going to find it – like a pearl diver.

**Mother Goose**    You're most certainly not, Tommy dear. Not with Daughter of Dracula in there gnashing her mashers.

**Little Tommy Tucker**    If Jack can grapple with the Giant, I can mix it with a Monster.

**Fairy Lethargia**    Fighting words, Little Tommy T. But why not use Polly's kettle too?

**Little Tommy Tucker**    How?

**Fairy Lethargia**    Stand there and I'll show you! (*She positions him.*) Right. A bit of a hush, please. A bit of atmosphere.

SONG: **Fairy Lethargia's Magic Spell** (*reprise*)

**Fairy Lethargia**
Spell number two is on Tommy
Him with the little fat tum . . .

**Little Tommy Tucker** (*speaking*)    Here! No need to be personal.

**The Others**    Shhh.

**Fairy Lethargia**    Don't be so touchy. The magic has to know who to work on . . .

**Little Tommy Tucker**    It's all very well . . .

**Fairy Lethargia**
Oh, all right. I'll start again. (*She sings.*)
Spell number two is on Tommy
Another young Tom he'll become;
Abracadabra, hocus pocus
Magic him into Tom Thumb

*As the spell ends, there is a flash and a bang, and magically* **Little Tommy Tucker** *disappears. Perhaps a trap could be used for this, in conjunction with a flash box, or a very short blackout would effect it. In his place there is a similarly dressed doll about nine inches high. The music continues.*

**Mother Goose**    Oo-er! Tommy! He's gone.

**Fairy Lethargia**    No, he hasn't. Look.

**Mother Goose** *sees the doll.*

**Mother Goose**    Oh, Tommy, I know I kept saying you ought to diet, but I didn't mean it, dear, I didn't mean it!

**Fairy Lethargia**    Shh. Polly, put Tom Thumb in your kettle.

*Very gently,* **Polly** *does so.*

**Fairy Lethargia**    Now, lower the kettle into the moat . . .

**Mother Goose**    Take care, dear, Tommy's in your hands.

*Gingerly,* **Little Polly Flinders** *picks up the kettle, holding it by the string. Suddenly the lighting snaps to blackout, all except for a follow spot on* **Little Polly Flinders**. *The action freezes as she sings.*

SONG: **My Big Moment** (*reprise*)

**Little Polly Flinders**
This must be my big moment
My moment of glory
In the story
This will be my closest shave
This must be my big moment
This is my time to be brave.

**Little Polly Flinders** *turns and makes her way towards the moat. The lights fade to a blackout, and the scene changes very rapidly. NB: It may be possible to start the scene change during the song – perhaps by bringing in black tabs behind* **Little Polly Flinders**.

**Scene Three**

*In the Moat.*

*The following sequence, which takes place underwater, is all mimed and moved to music. It could possibly be done in ultraviolet lighting, or using 'black art', or it could be done using projection or lighting effects, depending on the scale of the production and the facilities available. It should take place downstage of the 'entrance to the Giant's castle' set, because the change back, as well as the change into the underwater sequence, should be very quick. The sequence is 'magnified', so that 'Tom Thumb' can be played by the normal-sized* **Little Tommy Tucker**. *Therefore, in due course, the kettle, the* **Monster** *and the Golden Egg should all be 'blown-up' versions. NB: The* **Monster** *cannot realistically be expected to be to scale. The overall effect of the sequence, apart from the exciting nature of* **Little Tommy Tucker***'s venture underwater, could be one of pure magic – using all the best 'tricks' the theatre can offer.*

*The scene underwater could be enhanced by rocks and waving weeds. To start with there could be a 'ballet' of fishes of different shapes and sizes. With a large cast, these could be actors, but the effect could be gained in ultraviolet lighting with cut-outs on rods operated by puppeteers dressed in black; or, perhaps projection or large 'mobiles' operated from the flies could achieve this. Then the huge kettle arrives, as though let down by* **Little Polly Flinders** *on the string. Ideally it floats in gently from the flies and comes to rest on the bed of the moat, scattering the fishes. If this is impractical, the scene could start with the kettle already in position. The kettle will most probably be a cut-out – an enlargement of the normal-sized one.*

*'***Tom Thumb***' clambers out of the kettle. The actor can enter between the tabs after the kettle has flown in, and climb over the cut-out. He looks warily about, then starts searching for the Golden Egg – behind rocks, weeds, etc. When he is out of sight, the* **Monster** *of the moat enters; played by four or more actors, each one a 'segment'. It is long like a centipede, all the legs moving in unison. It is not unlike the Loch Ness Monster, perhaps, but the head looks frightening, its jaws snapping as it stomps along. Clearly from the audience point of view, it should look amusing as well as frightening. Suddenly, after a 'dance' around, it sees the kettle and reacts startled – a jolt going from segment to segment, accompanied by the relevant feet jumping back in surprise.*

*The* **Monster** *goes to examine the kettle more carefully. Perhaps the head peeps behind it, or perhaps the whole body investigates the back of it. At the same time '***Tom Thumb***' struggles back with the 'blown-up' Golden Egg – about his own height. A cut-out is more practical than a shaped object. He starts struggling to put* *the Golden Egg inside the kettle. With a great effort he manages it, but, just before it disappears from view, the* **Monster** *re-emerges and sees it – and* '**Tom Thumb**'. *Stamping its feet in fury, it backs away ready to 'charge'.* '**Tom Thumb**', *still at ground level, sees the* **Monster**, *reacts with fear; then the action freezes, the lighting dramatically changes to a follow spot on* '**Tom Thumb**' *and the music goes into 'My Big Moment', which* '**Tom Thumb**' *mimes. It could be amusing to have a garbled underwater singing voice offstage. Then the lighting and the action revert to their former states.*

*Now follows an exciting moved/choreographed section during which the Monster 'charges'* '**Tom Thumb**', *who has to nip sharply out of the way. Perhaps he could acrobatically 'leapfrog', in stages from segment to segment. At least twice he manages to escape the 'charge'. Then the* **Monster** *adopts a subtler approach and attempts to 'surround'* '**Tom Thumb**' *with itself – the head and the tail meeting. He escapes between the feet. Then, surrounding him again, the* **Monster** *does its 'coup' – it divides into individual segments, as many as the actors inside, each of which has its own face, and, ideally, snapping jaws. This can be incorporated effectively into a visually exciting pattern, as* '**Tom Thumb**' *weaves his way in and out of the little Monsters.*

*Finally he tricks them, perhaps by encouraging them to advance on him like a rugby scrum, then escaping, leaving them heads together in a circle, revolving. He climbs back up into the kettle, not forgetting to give two big tugs on the string. He disappears inside.*

*The kettle rises up, as if pulled by* **Little Polly Flinders**. *The* **Monster** *or Monsters, frustrated, watch it go. The lights fade to a blackout.*

## Scene Four

*The Entrance to the* **Giant**'s *Castle.*

*The scene changes back, as speedily as possible, to the position at the end of Scene Two.* **Little Polly Flinders** *is pulling the kettle up from the bed of the moat, watched by the other* **Children** *and* **Mother Goose**, *with* **Fairy Lethargia**, *who has nodded off again.* **Little Polly Flinders** *carefully brings the kettle downstage. The others cluster round.*

**Little Bo Peep**    Well?

**Little Polly Flinders** (*producing the egg*)    He's done it! Look.

**Little Miss Muffet** (*gasping*)    It's grown again. It's twice the size!

*Indeed it has grown.*

**Little Jack Horner**    How eggsciting! Tara!

*All groan.*

**Mother Goose**    Children, less levity, more gravity. Where's our Little Tommy?

**Little Polly Flinders** (*taking out the doll*)    Here he is.

**Mother Goose** (*taking it*)    I do believe he's even smaller. He's shrunk in the wash! Lethargia!

**Fairy Lethargia** (*waking quickly*)    Hallo, hallo, 'tis Christmas time . . . (*Realising.*) Oh. Beg pardon. Did it work?

**Mother Goose**    Yes, thank you. But we'd like our Tommy back to scale, please.

**Fairy Lethargia**    Spell three. Right.

**Mother Goose**    Spell three? Wrong. Spell two, part two. You can't leave him like that. We might tread on him.

**Fairy Lethargia**    Oh, all right. I'll do Spell two in reverse. That ought to work. Put him over there.

**Mother Goose** *positions the doll on the ground, holding it with one hand, standing it on her other hand.* **Fairy Lethargia** *concentrates, using her fingers to 'count' through the tricky reversed spell.*

SONG: **Fairy Lethargia's Magic Spell** (*reprise*)

**Fairy Lethargia**
Thumb Tom into him magic
Pocus hocus, Arbadacarba
Become he'll Tom young another
Tommy on is two number spell.

*There is a sudden flash and/or blackout.*

*Magically,* **Little Tommy Tucker** *returns, taking the place of the doll.* **Mother Goose** *is still crouched on the ground holding an ankle now.*

**All**    Hooray; well done, Lethargia; hallo, Tommy, etc.

**Little Tommy Tucker** (*blinking, getting his bearings*)    Hallo. Thanks.

**Fairy Lethargia**    Everyone all right?

**Mother Goose**    Aaaaaaah!

**Little Tommy Tucker** (*looking down*)    Hallo, Mother Goose. What are you doing down there?

**Mother Goose**    You're standing on my hand, Tommy dear.

**Little Tommy Tucker**    Oh, sorry. (*He steps off.*)

**Mother Goose** *gets up, rubbing her hand.*

**Fairy Lethargia** *goes back to the decorations box and climbs inside, yawning.*

**Little Tommy Tucker**    Thanks for holding the string, Polly.

**Little Polly Flinders**    Did you see the Monster?

**Little Tommy Tucker**    Yes, he was vast, and he divided . . .

*He is interrupted by the booming roar of the* **Giant**'s *voice and footsteps from above. All react, and draw back, listening.*

**Giant's Voice**    Goosey, Goosey. I'm coming. Is my Golden Egg ready? (*Pause.*) Grrrrh. Nothing. (*A roar of anger, with fists beating on a table.*) Lay, blast you, lay, or you'll be my Christmas dinner. Roasted alive.

*Giant footsteps are heard receding.*

**Mother Goose**    Save your memoirs for another day, Tommy. This one could be Gertie's last.

**Little Jack Horner**    Right. My turn. Give me the Golden Egg.

**Little Bo Peep**    How are you going to get in the castle?

**Little Miss Muffet**    You can't swim the moat.

**Little Jack Horner** (*heroically*)    I'm going to ring the bell and order them to lower the drawbridge.

**Mother Goose**    But look, dear, the sign says 'Utter the password'. We don't know the password.

*The audience should shout out that they know it, because they heard the* **Wolves** *use it.*

(*To the audience.*) *You* know it? Can you tell us what it was, please? (*She pieces it together and then repeats it.*)
    Copper and silver leave us cold
    What we want is lots of gold.

Got it, Jack? Off you go, dear, and good luck.

*The others whisper good luck, as they draw back to watch. Music, as* **Little Jack Horner** *strides to the bell and rings it. The very loud, deep clang sends a shudder through everyone. From above, the* **Giant**'s *footsteps approach the window.*

**Giant's Voice**    Password.

**Little Jack Horner**
    Copper and silver leave us cold
    What we want is lots of gold.

**Giant's Voice**    You may enter.

*With a sinister creaking sound, the drawbridge lowers, and clanks on to the bank.*

*Summoning up his courage,* **Little Jack Horner** *strides into the castle. The drawbridge stays down.*

*The four* **Children** *gather round* **Mother Goose**. *They look worried.*

**Mother Goose** (*sensing the reason for their long faces*)    He'll be all right, children. And there's nothing we can do to help by worrying. We just have – to try and concentrate on something else. Listen . . .

SONG: **When You're Feeling Worried**

*It is suggested that during the song, tabs come in behind* **Mother Goose** *and the* **Children**, *to accommodate the scene change. Ideally, the drawbridge would still be visible but this may well be impractical.*

*This is a cumulative song, in the style of 'One Man Went to Mow'. The activities mentioned in each verse should each have a big action or gesture to accompany them every time they are sung. The recurring whistle should give some of them trouble.*

**Mother Goose**
>     When you're feeling worried
>     And your skies are looking grey
>     Just whistle a tune
>     (*Whistle.*)
>     And very soon
>     Your worry will hurry away.

(*Speaking.*) Of course, you don't *have* to whistle a tune. Any ideas?

**Little Miss Muffet**
>     When you're feeling worried
>     And your skies are looking grey
>     Try physical jerks
>     It always works.

**Little Miss Muffet** *and* **Mother Goose**
>     Just whistle a tune
>     (*Whistle.*)
>     And very soon
>     Your worry will hurry away.

**Little Tommy Tucker**
>     When you're feeling worried
>     And your skies are looking grey
>     Eat treacly pud
>     And you'll feel good.

**Little Tommy Tucker, Little Miss Muffet** *and* **Mother Goose**
>     Try physical jerks
>     It always works
>     Just whistle a tune
>     (*Whistle.*)
>     And very soon
>     Your worry will hurry away.

**Little Bo Peep**
> When you're feeling worried
> And your skies are looking grey
> Try bouncing a ball
> Against a wall.

**Little Bo Peep, Little Tommy Tucker, Little Miss Muffet** *and* **Mother Goose**
> Eat treacly pud
> And you'll feel good
> Try physical jerks
> It always works
> Just whistle a tune
> (*Whistle.*)
> And very soon
> Your worry will hurry away.

**Little Polly Flinders**
> When you're feeling worried
> And your skies are looking grey
> Go pick up a broom
> And sweep the room.

**Little Polly Flinders, Little Bo Peep, Little Tommy Tucker, Little Miss Muffet**
*and* **Mother Goose**
> Try bouncing a ball
> Against a wall
> Eat treacly pud
> And you'll feel good
> Try physical jerks
> It always works
> Just whistle a tune
> (*Whistle.*)
> And very soon
> Your worry will hurry away.

*During the last chorus,* **Fairy Lethargia** *is woken up by the noise, and pops out of the decorations box to see what is going on. She decides to join in.*

**Fairy Lethargia**
> When you're feeling worried
> And your skies are looking grey
> Just have a good yawn
> And sleep till dawn

**Fairy Lethargia, Little Polly Flinders, Little Bo Peep, Little Tommy Tucker,**
**Little Miss Muffet** *and* **Mother Goose**
> Go pick up a broom
> And sweep the room

    Try bouncing a ball
    Against a wall
    Eat treacly pud
    And you'll feel good
    Try physical jerks
    It always works
    Just whistle a tune
    (*Whistle.*)
    And very soon
    Your worry will hurry away.

**All**

    When you're feeling worried
    And your skies are looking grey
    Start marching along
    And sing this song
    Just have a good yawn
    And sleep till dawn
    Go pick up a broom
    And sweep the room
    Try bouncing a ball
    Against a wall
    Eat treacly pud
    And you'll feel good
    Try physical jerks
    It always works
    Just whistle a tune
    (*Whistle.*)
    And very soon
    Your worry will hurry
    Your worry will hurry
    Your worry will hurry away

(*Shouting.*) Don't worry!

*At the end of the song, all the* **Children** *have cheered up.*

**Mother Goose**    There you are. Are you still worried about Jack?

**Children**    No.

**Mother Goose**    Good. Mother Goose was right, wasn't she?

**Children**    Yes.

**Mother Goose** *suddenly frowns and bites her nails and taps her foot nervously and scratches her neck, etc., then she starts whistling.*

**Little Polly Flinders**    What's the matter, Mother Goose?

**Mother Goose**   Oooh. I'm so worried I can't stand it. (*She calls.*) Jack. Jack. I'm coming to help you, dear.

*She grabs her dressing-gown and runs off.*

(*As she goes.*) Go home, children. And don't worry!

*Ideally,* **Mother Goose** *would dash along the drawbridge into the castle, just before it closes: but perhaps she runs off and as the lights fade to a blackout we hear the clanking sound of the drawbridge rising, thus giving the impression that she has just made it in time.*

**Scene Five**

*The* **Giant**'*s Workshop.*

*In this set, everything is magnified. There is a high window, open, and an overgrown chair and table, which stretches off, thus making the table-top accessible from the wings one side. The chair should be constructed in such a way that normal-sized people can use it as a stepping-stone to the table-top. On the table is a cage with a barred door;* **Gertie** *is inside. Throughout the whole set there should be not a trace of the colour gold. On stage level are several steaming cauldrons, foaming beakers, test tubes, etc., and tomes piled high. To one side is a giant oven, with a dial marked 'OFF', 'ON', 'HOT', 'HOTTER' and 'OUCH'. On a shelf or side table are visible several large tins or jars, marked 'CUSTARD POWDER', 'MUSTARD POWDER', 'GUN POWDER', 'CHOWDER POWDER', 'ITCHING POWDER', 'TALCUM POWDER'. A vase of daffodils and a lighted candle are also visible. The large tomes are open, covers facing the audience: 'TEACH YOURSELF ALCHEMY' and 'GOLD-MAKING FOR BEGINNERS'.*

*As the scene starts, the heads of the two* **Wolves** *menacingly creep up over the books. They laugh nastily. The heads return to their reading. Suddenly* **Bigger Badder Wolf** *speaks.*

**Bigger Badder Wolf**   Aha! Here's an experiment we haven't tried.

**Big Bad Wolf**   Aha! (*He tries to imitate the* **Bigger Badder Wolf**, *but it turns into a cough.*) Read it out, B.B.W.

**Bigger Badder Wolf** (*reading slowly and deliberately*)   How to make a bar of gold. (*He rubs his hands in anticipation.*)

**Big Bad Wolf**   A bar of gold!

**Bigger Badder Wolf**   Take one heavy brick.

**Big Bad Wolf**   One heavy brick. (*He finds one, and staggers with the weight.*)

**Bigger Badder Wolf**   Drop it . . .

**Big Bad Wolf**   Drop it. (*He drops it on the* **Bigger Badder Wolf**'*s foot.*)

**Bigger Badder Wolf**    Aaaaah! What did you do that for?

**Big Bad Wolf**    You said 'drop it'.

**Bigger Badder Wolf**    I hadn't finished. Drop it in a cauldron.

**Big Bad Wolf**    Ah. Drop it in a cauldron. (*He does so.*)

**Bigger Badder Wolf**    Add one yellow daffodil.

**Big Bad Wolf**    One yellow daffodil. (*He finds one, sniffs it, sneezes and throws it in the cauldron.*)

**Bigger Badder Wolf** (*lyrically*)    Add the golden tones of the song of the yellow-hammer.

**Big Bad Wolf**    Eh?

**Bigger Badder Wolf**    The yellow-hammer.

**Big Bad Wolf**    Oh. (*He produces a large yellow hammer – the sort for banging in nails.*) Got one.

**Bigger Badder Wolf** (*not seeing, too busy reading the experiment*)    Good. Make it sing.

*The* **Big Bad Wolf** *looks mystified, then looks at the hammer and encouragingly 'la las' a few notes. No reaction from the hammer.*

**Big Bad Wolf**    B.B.W.

**Bigger Badder Wolf**    Mm?

**Big Bad Wolf**    The yellow hammer doesn't want to sing.

**Bigger Badder Wolf**    Well, bash it on the head.

**Big Bad Wolf**    Eh?

**Bigger Badder Wolf** (*impatiently*)    Bash it on the head.

*After a doubting pause, the* **Big Bad Wolf** *smashes the hammer down on the* **Bigger Badder Wolf**'*s head.*

**Bigger Badder Wolf**    Ow! What are you doing? What's this?

**Big Bad Wolf**    A yellow hammer.

**Bigger Badder Wolf**    For wickedness' sake! I meant a bird, a yellow-hammer bird. Oh, never mind. Stir in a spoonful of custard powder.

*The* **Big Bad Wolf** *runs his hand along the jars or tins, calling them out as he goes.*

**Big Bad Wolf**    Talcum powder, itching powder, chowder powder, gun powder, mustard powder, custard powder.

*He takes down the jar and pours some in. He replaces the jar.*

**Bigger Badder Wolf** (*before the* **Big Bad Wolf** *has finished, making him hurry*)    And a pinch of mustard powder.

*The* **Big Bad Wolf** *dashes back, and, by mistake, takes down the gun powder. He pours some in. The audience must realise his mistake.*

**Big Bad Wolf**    Mustard powder. One pinch of. (*He replaces the jar.*)

**Bigger Badder Wolf**    Expose to the golden rays of the sun.

**Big Bad Wolf**    We can't. There's no sun today. (*Pointing out of the window.*) It's cloudy.

**Bigger Badder Wolf**    We'll have to find a substitute. (*He looks around.*) Ah. Try the golden rays of that candle instead.

**Big Bad Wolf**    Oh, right.

*He takes the lighted candle and throws it in the cauldron. Immediately there is a loud explosion and smoke from the cauldron. The impact knocks the* **Wolves** *over. As they recover, the* **Bigger Badder Wolf** *starts hitting the* **Big Bad Wolf.** *Suddenly the* **Giant***'s voice is heard.*

**Giant's Voice** (*off*)    Wolves! Wolves!

*They spring to attention.*

**Bigger Badder Wolf**    Yes, boss?

**Big Bad Wolf**    Y-y-yes, b-b-boss?

**Giant's Voice**    Any Golden Eggs from that Goose yet?

**Bigger Badder Wolf**    Just checking, boss. (*He deliberately takes the large key to the cage from inside his coat and hands it to the* **Big Bad Wolf.**) Cage. (*He glances to the cage on the table above.*)

**Big Bad Wolf** (*realising the implication*)    Oh n-no, n-no, n-not m-me, p-please.

**Bigger Badder Wolf**    Why not you?

**Big Bad Wolf**    You know I can't stand heights. I'll get giddy. I'll have one of my turns. (*He reaches for a tranquilliser.*)

**Bigger Badder Wolf**    Oh, come on then.

*Music, as he pushes the* **Big Bad Wolf** *to the chair.*

*A brief comic interlude as they climb up – the* **Big Bad Wolf** *falling on or stepping on the* **Bigger Badder Wolf,** *who pushes him on ahead.*

*Eventually they reach the cage, unlock the door and, pushing* **Gertie** *aside, look inside. They shake their heads and close and lock the door. The music stops.*

**Bigger Badder Wolf**    Nothing. We'd better go and tell him.

**Big Bad Wolf** (*nervously*)    Ooh.

*The music starts again as the* **Wolves** *exit along the table into the wings – towards where the* **Giant** *is presumably sitting at the other end.*

*After a pause,* **Little Jack Horner** *enters from the opposite side. He takes in the huge furniture and creeps about checking nobody is around. He puts his finger to his mouth to make sure the audience remain quiet and don't give the game away.*

**Little Jack Horner** *spots* **Gertie** *in the cage; or it may be better for him to whisper 'Where's Gertie?' to the audience, and incorporate their help – not vocally, but pointing to the cage. He climbs up the chair and arrives on the table. He tiptoes to the cage.*

**Little Jack Horner** (*whispering*)   Gertie! Psst. It's me. Jack.

**Gertie** *rushes excitedly to the bars, flapping her wings.*

**Little Jack Horner**   Shhh. I've come to rescue you. (*He tries the cage door.*) Where's the key?

**Gertie** *indicates the* **Wolves** *offstage, and the audience, not forgetting to whisper, interpret.*

**Little Jack Horner**   The Wolves. Oh. (*He ponders what to do.*)

**Mother Goose**, *still carrying her dressing-gown, enters stealthily.*

**Mother Goose** (*whispering*)   Jack, Jack.

**Little Jack Horner** *jumps in surprise, then recovers and looks down from the table top, just as* **Mother Goose** *is passing below, so her back is now turned away from him.*

**Little Jack Horner** (*in a loud whisper*)   Mother Goose!

**Mother Goose** *nearly has a heart attack and ducks under the chair seat.* **Little Jack Horner** *slips from the table on to the chair seat. He kneels, then slowly slides his head over the edge; simultaneously* **Mother Goose** *slowly slides her head out from underneath. The heads meet, making* **Mother Goose** *and* **Little Jack Horner** *nearly jump out of their skins.*

**Mother Goose** (*recovering*)   Oh, it's you, dear. What a relief. I'm all of a quiver. Like a nervous jelly.

**Little Jack Horner** (*whispering*)   Shhh!

*The sudden roar of the* **Giant**'s *voice is heard, offstage.*

**Giant's Voice** (*off*)   What? Still no Golden Egg? Right, Goosey Goosey; you've had your last chance. Ha, ha, ha, ha.

*The laughter approaches.*

**Little Jack Horner** (*whispering*)   Quick, he's coming. Gertie's locked in the cage up here but the Wolves have the key.

**Mother Goose** (*after a pause, whispering*)   I know, dear. Put the Golden Egg in the cage. The Giant will want it, the Wolves will have to open the cage to take it out, and . . . (*She is too late.*)

**Giant** (*calling*)    Goosey Goosey! Ha, ha, ha, ha.

**Mother Goose** *retreats under the chair.* **Jack** *leaps back on to the table and carefully puts the Golden Egg through the bars of the cage. Then he spots a dining fork – large scale – on the table top, and arms himself with it. Finally he hides at the side of the cage.*

*Suddenly the* **Wolves** *enter, on the table, leading in the* **Giant**, *who should naturally be as large as possible. It may be an idea to use another actor's voice from a microphone off, so that a huge headmask could be employed.*

SONG: **Fee Fi Fo Fum**

*During the song, the* **Wolves** *climb down from the table via the chair.* **Mother Goose**, *hiding, looks terrified as the* **Wolves** *pass so near her.*

**Giant**
Fee fi fo fum
I am the Giant, here I come
Fee fi fo fum
Goosey for dinner, yum yum yum.

Fee

**Wolves**
Fee

**Giant**
Fi

**Wolves**
Fi

**Giant**
Fo

**Wolves**
Fo

**Giant**
Fum

**Wolves**
Fum

**Giant**
I am the Giant, here I come.
Fee

**Wolves**
Fee

**Giant**
Fi

**Wolves**
Fi

**Giant**
Fo

**Wolves**
Fo

**Giant**
Fum

**Wolves**
Fum

**Giant**
Goosey, prepare to meet my tum.

**Giant** (*speaking*)    Wolves!

**Wolves**    Yes, boss?

**Giant**    Light the oven.

**Wolves**    Yes, boss.

*The **Wolves** go to the oven and turn the dial, which makes an unpleasant ratchet noise, gleefully through 'HOT', and 'HOTTER' to 'OUCH'. **Gertie** is reacting.*

**Giant**    We'll see if Goosey Goosey tastes better than she works. Ha, ha, ha, ha.

*The **Bigger Badder Wolf** opens the oven door a little – a red glow tells us the oven is on.*

**Giant**    Stubborn bird. All I wanted was one Golden Egg.

*The audience may well shout out, 'Look in the cage'.*

(*Eventually.*) But you wouldn't lay. So now you'll pay. Wolves!

**Wolves**    Yes, boss?

**Giant**    Open the cage.

**Wolves**    Yes, boss.

*The **Bigger Badder Wolf** deliberately hands the key to the **Big Bad Wolf**.*

**Big Bad Wolf**    Oh, no, please, not again . . .

**Bigger Badder Wolf**    Go on. Hurry up.

**Giant** (*roaring*)    What are you muttering about?

**Bigger Badder Wolf**    Nothing, boss.

**Big Bad Wolf**    N-n-nothing, b-b-boss.

*Reluctantly the* **Big Bad Wolf** *climbs up on to the table. A dramatic drum roll as he approaches the cage. He puts the key in the lock, turns it and opens the door.*

Come on, Goosey, Goosey.

*Leaving the key in the lock, he grabs* **Gertie**, *who tries to point out the Golden Egg. This proves difficult, and she is pulled out of the cage and a few steps away from it before the* **Big Bad Wolf** *realises.*

It's no use struggling, I'm too strong . . . (*If the audience are shouting.*) What? (*He suddenly spots the Golden Egg.*) Hey! She's done it! She's done it! B-b-boss, l-look – a Golden Egg. (*He takes it reverently from the cage – it is quite large now, say eighteen inches high – and holds it out.*)

**Giant** (*roaring*)   What? Aaaaaaah! At last, at last! Gold. Real gold! Ah ha ha ha.

*The* **Giant** *takes the Golden Egg and, roaring with laughter, does the nearest a* **Giant** *can to hopping about with joy, stroking and kissing the Golden Egg.*

*The* **Big Bad Wolf** *stands smiling on the table top. The* **Bigger Badder Wolf** *is still by the oven.*

*Music.* **Little Jack Horner** *creeps round from his hiding place by the cage and prods the* **Big Bad Wolf** *with the outsize fork. The* **Big Bad Wolf** *nearly has heart failure – he could have fallen over the edge! He turns, sees* **Little Jack Horner** *and reacts terrified.* **Little Jack Horner** *stalks him round with the fork. Meanwhile* **Gertie** *hangs back by the cage door and the* **Bigger Badder Wolf** *is too busy watching the ecstatic* **Giant** *to notice. Suddenly the* **Big Bad Wolf** *has an idea. He brings out his tranquillisers and starts throwing them at* **Little Jack Horner**, *who has to use the fork as a shield: but the tranquillisers run out, and the* **Big Bad Wolf** *puts up his hands in submission.* **Little Jack Horner** *forces him at fork point back, round and into the cage, the door of which* **Gertie** *holds open for him. They slam the door shut, turn the key and remove it from the lock. They raise their arms/wings in triumph.*

**Mother Goose** *manages to peep out occasionally from under the chair, and glean some idea of* **Little Jack Horner**'s *progress. Now, she watches him bring the key of the cage to the edge of the table top. He indicates he is going to throw it down and she stands by to catch it.*

*He throws, but she misses, and it hits the floor. The sound is heard by the* **Bigger Badder Wolf**, *who turns and sees* **Mother Goose**. *In a rage, he advances on her. She picks up the key and tries to fend him off with it. He grabs the other end and they have a heave-ho tug-of-war with it, ending with the* **Bigger Badder Wolf** *tripping over a tome and falling. But* **Mother Goose** *has let go of the end of the key, and soon the* **Bigger Badder Wolf** *is up again, advancing on her and using the key as a weapon.*

**Mother Goose** *looks wildly around and spots her dressing-gown, which is a red one. There follows a short, amusing bullfighting sequence to appropriate music, with* **Mother Goose** *using her dressing-gown as a cape, and the* **Bigger Badder Wolf** *charging her. On one of his charges, he overruns, bumping into the still drooling*

**Giant**, *who notices, and turns – just in time to see the* **Bigger Badder Wolf** *charge in the other direction, towards* **Mother Goose**, *who has manoeuvred herself to the oven. At the last minute she opens the door and the* **Bigger Badder Wolf** *charges straight into the red glowing oven.* **Mother Goose** *shuts the door, and raises her arms in a bullfighter's triumph.* **Little Jack Horner** *and* **Gertie** *have watched from above. But now the* **Giant** *is ranting and roaring and advancing towards the table, arms flailing with rage, that his henchmen have been disposed of. In his excitement he drops the Golden Egg, which is caught by* **Mother Goose** *below. Just as the* **Giant** *appears to aim a blow towards* **Little Jack Horner** *and* **Gertie**, *the action freezes and the lighting changes to just a follow spot on* **Little Jack Horner**.

SONG: **My Big Moment** (*reprise*)

**Little Jack Horner**
　　This must be my big moment
　　My moment of glory
　　In the story
　　This will be my closest shave
　　This must be my big moment
　　This is my time to be brave.

*The lighting returns to its former state and the action resumes.* **Little Jack Horner** *and the* **Giant** *fight their duel – the action climax of the drama! The actual mechanical details of the combat will have to be left to the ingenuity of the individual directors, having regard for the capabilities and limitations of their* **Giant**. *Clearly, a lavish production might have a* **Giant** *capable of more mobility and tricks – like picking up* **Little Jack Horner** *with one hand – than a more modest production: or some directors may feel it better to see the* **Giant** *only in silhouette, thus using back-projection on to a screen. Another idea is that the* **Giant** *could be a huge puppet, even operated from inside. It might be possible for* **Little Jack Horner** *to leap on the* **Giant**'s *shoulders, or to have a sort of sword fight with him; the* **Giant** *could use his dagger and* **Little Jack Horner** *the fork. If the actor playing* **Little Jack Horner** *were athletic or acrobatic, further exciting ideas could develop, using ropes on which to swing to the ground, etc. Certainly* **Gertie** *should help the cause with the odd peck – her comeuppance against her cruel master adds an important element of poetic justice: and* **Mother Goose** *can shout encouragement; but she should not be actively involved in the battle, because this is* **Little Jack Horner**'s *moment of glory. Naturally the contest ends in triumph for* **Little Jack Horner**, *as the* **Giant** *topples from the high window and falls to the moat below. A huge splash is followed by the snapping of jaws and the contented munching of the* **Monster of the Moat**. *Victory yells of triumph from all, as* **Little Jack Horner** *climbs down the chair to floor-level, where* **Mother Goose** *hugs him.*

**Little Jack Horner**　　Back to the Book.

**Mother Goose**　　Take the Golden Egg, dear. It's grown again.

**Little Jack Horner**　　What we've come to eggspect! Tara!

**Mother Goose** *groans. They set off for the exit. Meanwhile,* **Gertie***, on the table top, tries gingerly to put one foot down towards the chair in an attempt to get down. Now she flaps her wings. The audience may call out to* **Mother Goose** *and* **Little Jack Horner***.*

**Little Jack Horner**   (*Eventually, suddenly remembering*) Gertie!

*They turn back.*

(*Seeing* **Gertie***.*) Come on.

**Gertie** *shakes her head and mimes flight.*

**Little Jack Horner**   She can't get down, Mother Goose.

**Mother Goose**   Cooped up in that cage for so long she can't fly any more.

**Little Jack Horner**   But we can't leave without her. She's the reason we came.

**Mother Goose**   Crisis time. (*To the audience, indicating the decorations box*) One, two, three.

**All** (*including audience*)   Fairy Lethargia.

*Pause*

**Fairy Lethargia** (*in the box*)   Co–ming!

**Fairy Lethargia** *struggles, yawning, out of the decorations box and goes to collect her wand.*

Right. Spell three. And you'd better look sharp. I'm so drained, my wings are beginning to droop and my wand's wilting. (*Turning and seeing the* **Giant***'s workshop.*) Oo-er, I'm shrinking too!

**Mother Goose**   No, you're not. We're in the Giant's workshop.

**Fairy Lethargia**   Oh. Well, I don't like it. I want to go home.

**Mother Goose**   So do we. But Gertie's stuck.

**Gertie** *flaps her wings.*

**Fairy Lethargia**   Right. No problem. You two – up on the table.

**Little Jack Horner** *and* **Mother Goose** *climb up.*

**Fairy Lethargia**   Huddle together and hang on tight. Fasten your seat belts for spell three. (*She comes forward.*)

SONG: **Fairy Lethargia's Magic Spell** (*reprise*)

*It may be practical to bring in tabs behind* **Fairy Lethargia** *as she sings the spell, to facilitate the scene change, or the tabs could fly in behind the table, but in front of the rest of the* **Giant***'s workshop. This would mean that* **Gertie***,* **Mother Goose** *and* **Little Jack Horner** *could be visible during the spell.*

**Fairy Lethargia**
Gertie and Jack and his Mother
All want to go home – so do I
Abracadabra, hocus pocus
Make us all able to fly.

*At the end of the song, there is a flash, leading, as quickly as possible, into the following scene.*

**Scene Six**

*In the Sky.*

*We see* **Gertie** *in flight, complete with* **Mother Goose** *and* **Little Jack Horner** *'on board' her. They are joined by* **Fairy Lethargia** *flying under her own steam. This sequence should take only a minute or two, and can be done in several different ways:*

*(1) The table could become a platform on which they all stand, and lighting makes it look as though they are suspended in mid-air, flying.*

*(2) Projection of moving clouds against the sky could give an impression of movement, plus, perhaps, some sort of wind machine offstage.*

*(3) The whole thing could be done in ultraviolet lighting in front of black tabs. The sequence could start with small cut-out figures in rods, 'walked across' by stage-hands clad in black, changing over to medium-sized ones, then ending up with the real characters, being pulled across on a black truck, invisible against the black tabs.* **Fairy Lethargia** *could be on a separate one.*

*(4) Kirby's Flying Ballet.*

*The scene could be very effective because it represents the traditional picture of* **Mother Goose** *of nursery rhyme fame – flying on a goose. Also, if it can be made to look magical, it will be a very exciting visual moment.*

**Mother Goose**    You're flying, Gertie. This is your big moment.

SONG: **Her Big Moment**

**Mother Goose, Little Jack Horner** *and* **Fairy Lethargia**
This must be her big moment
Her moment of glory
In the story
This must be her closest shave
This must be her big moment
This is her time to be brave
This must be her big moment
This is her time to be brave.

*As the song ends, the lights fade to a blackout.*

**Scene Seven**

*Back at the Book.*

*As quickly as possible, the lights go up on the 'cover' side of the Book. It is dusk:* **Little Miss Muffet, Little Polly Flinders, Little Bo Peep** *and* **Little Tommy Tucker** *are putting the final touches to the Christmas decorations: but they are not happy – because they are worried about* **Mother Goose, Little Jack Horner** *and* **Gertie.** *A table of food lies untouched. During the song even* **Little Tommy Tucker** *refuses to eat anything.*

SONG: **Getting Ready for Christmas** (*reprise*)

*A slow, sad version.*

**Little Miss Muffet, Little Bo Peep, Little Tommy Tucker** *and* **Little Polly Flinders**
We're getting ready for Christmas
We're getting ready for Christmas Day
Building a snowman
From cotton-wool snow
Hanging up the holly
And the mistletoe . . .

*Suddenly they hear the loud beating of wings overhead. Dramatic musical rumble. They look up into the flies and follow* **Gertie's** *'progress' across the stage above their heads.*

**Little Miss Muffet**    It's them! Look!

*The others cheer, and 'watch'* **Gertie** *land, offstage.*

SONG: (*continued*)

*The song speeds up.*

**Little Miss Muffet, Little Bo Peep, Little Tommy Tucker** *and* **Little Polly Flinders**
We're getting ready
Getting ready for Christmas
Ready
Steady –
Go, go, go –

**Mother Goose** *enters, with* **Little Jack Horner** *and* **Gertie.** *The others warmly greet them.*

**All,** *with* **Mother Goose** *and* **Little Jack Horner**
Christmas
Hallo.

*At the end of the song, all chatter animatedly – 'What happened?', 'Did you see the Giant?', 'Thank goodness you're safe', etc., etc.*

**Fairy Lethargia** *enters, almost on her knees with tiredness. She stands, looking at the excited 'family group', none of whom see her.*

*She coughs to get their attention: no reaction; and again; no reaction. So she puts her fingers in her mouth and does a vibrant, shrill whistle. All shut up and turn to her.*

**Fairy Lethargia**   Is that it, then? Till next year? (*She yawns.*) I can't twinkle much longer.

**Mother Goose**   But Christmas Day hasn't begun yet!

**Fairy Lethargia**   No, but the story's finished, isn't it? Must be; you've had your three spells.

**Mother Goose**   Yes, almost. The children wanted adventure, something out of the ordinary, and we've certainly had that; and they've all been so brave that I for one will never think of them as 'Little' again. But, Fairy Lethargia, you must keep your eyes open a little longer. It's time for our Christmas party. (*She calls.*) Polly!

**Little Polly Flinders** (*confidently*)   Yes, Mother Goose?

**Mother Goose**   Put the kettle on!

*Laughter.*

**Little Polly Flinders** *goes inside.*

*Music, as* **Gertie** *comes forward and gently pecks* **Mother Goose,** *who turns.* **Gertie** *embraces her.*

**Little Jack Horner**   She's saying thank you!

**Gertie** *bows to all the* **Children**.

**Mother Goose**   Well, Gertie, the best way you can thank us is to stay with us as long as you like. Right, everyone?

*All nod and agree.*

**Gertie** *suddenly runs offstage, nudging* **Little Jack Horner** *and* **Little Tommy Tucker** *offstage too.*

**Mother Goose**   What's she up to now?

**Gertie** *returns with the two boys carrying the Golden Egg – even larger, say thirty inches high – wrapped with ribbon and with a label.* **Gertie** *presents it to* **Mother Goose**.

**Mother Goose**   For me? Oh, thank you, Gertie. It won't grow any more, will it?

**Little Jack Horner**   It's getting a little eggcessive! Tara!

*All groan.*

**Mother Goose**   Oh, look, a label. (*Reading.*)
Happy Christmas to you,
Happy Christmas to you,

Happy Christmas, dear Mother Goose,
Happy Christmas to you.

Thank you.

**Gertie** *mimes singing.*

**Little Jack Horner**   She says, let's sing it. Come on, then. Everybody.

SONG: **Happy Christmas to You**

*The audience is encouraged to join in this, the equivalent of a songsheet.*

**All**, *including audience, except* **Mother Goose**
   Happy Christmas to you
   Happy Christmas to you
   Happy Christmas, dear Mother Goose,
   Happy Christmas to you.

**Little Jack Horner** (*speaking*)   Once more. With eggstra voice!

**All**, *including audience except* **Mother Goose**
   Happy Christmas to you
   Happy Christmas to you
   Happy Christmas, dear Mother Goose,
   Happy Christmas to you.

*At the end of the song, the music continues as the Golden Egg, to everyone's surprise, starts moving. Then it 'grows' arms and legs and a head. It in fact 'hatches'.*

**Mother Goose**   Hallo, dear. Who are you?

**Humpty Dumpty**   Humpty Dumpty.

**Mother Goose**   Humpty Dumpty?

SONG: **Humpty Dumpty Sat on a Wall**

**Humpty Dumpty** *acts out his nursery rhyme.*

**Humpty Dumpty**
   Humpty Dumpty sat on a wall
   Humpty Dumpty had a great fall
   All the king's horses and all the king's men
   Couldn't put Humpty Dumpty together again.

*At the end of the song, all clap.*

**Mother Goose**   Thank you, Humpty Dumpty. You're a very welcome addition to my nursery rhyme family. And we'll all take care to see you don't fall off that wall too often.

**Little Polly Flinders** *enters with the kettle.*

**Little Polly Flinders**   Kettle's boiled!

**Mother Goose**   Then it's time for the party.

*Music, as* **Fairy Lethargia** *comes forward in her best rhyming couplet fashion.*

**Fairy Lethargia**
Now Mother Goose's story has been well and truly told'n
For her and for her family, this Christmas will be golden.

*If possible,* **Fairy Lethargia** *waves her wand two or three times causing magical lighting changes to occur in stages, each accompanied by a musical chord.*

SONG: **Mother Goose's Golden Christmas**

*During the song, if possible, the whole set, and perhaps some of the costumes, become enriched with gold – streamers, glitter, lights, etc. There is no reason why, as a gesture of goodwill, the 'baddies' should not arrive during the song, to be made welcome by Mother Goose and her family. Thus the number could be a curtain call in itself – also, being the final number, the more singing voices on stage the merrier.*

**All**
It's Mother Goose's Golden Christmas
So come and join us ev'ryone.

So
Come and join us
Come and join us
Come on in
The party has begun
It's Mother Goose's Golden Christmas
Come and join us ev'ryone
It's Mother Goose's Golden Christmas
Come and join us ev'ryone.

It's a day we shall remember
Throughout the coming year
That golden day in December
When our troubles seem to disappear

So
Come and join us
Come and join us
Come on in
The party has begun
It's Mother Goose's Golden Christmas
Come and join us ev'ryone
It's Mother Goose's Golden Christmas
Come and join us ev'ryone.

Never mind the wintry weather
Forget the rain and snow

With all the fam'ly together
Celebrating in the fireside glow

So
Come and join us
Come and join us
Come on in
The party has begun
It's Mother Goose's Golden Christmas
Come and join us ev'ryone
It's Mother Goose's Golden Christmas
Come and join us ev'ryone.

So
Come and join us
Come and join us
Come on in
The party has begun
It's Mother Goose's Golden Christmas
Come and join us ev'ryone
It's Mother Goose's Golden Christmas
Come and join us ev'ryone.

**Girls**
So
Come and join us

**Boys**
Come and join us

**Girls**
So
Come and join us

**Boys**
So
Come and join with Mother

**Girls**
It's Mother

**All**
Goose's Golden Christmas
Come and join us ev'ryone.


**Optional Extra Scene**

*At the end of the song, the cast bow, and the audience should think it is the end; but suddenly* **Little Bo Peep** *bursts into tears.*

**Mother Goose**   Oh no, Bo Peep. What's the matter? We're all meant to be happy. It's the end of the story.

**Little Bo Peep**   How can I be happy? I still haven't found my sheep. (*She sobs.*)

**Mother Goose**   Oh dear. We can't finish like this. Fairy Lethargia, can't you help?

**Fairy Lethargia**   Well, I'm so tired, my magic's almost run out, but (*Taking in the audience.*) if everyone could chip in and give me a hand, I dare say . . .

**Mother Goose**   Oh, we will. (*To the audience.*) Won't we?

**All**   Yes.

**Fairy Lethargia**   Right, then. After me. Abracadabra, help Bo Peep.

**All**   Abracadabra, help Bo Peep.

**Fairy Lethargia**   Hocus pocus, find her sheep.

**All**   Hocus pocus, find her sheep.

**Fairy Lethargia**   Smashing. Now, let's put it together and say it as loud as we can. After three. One, two, three.

**All** (*as* **Fairy Lethargia** *waves her magic wand*)
   Abracadabra, help Bo Peep
   Hocus pocus, find her sheep.

*A flash; and then by magic,* **Little Bo Peep**'*s sheep – real – are revealed. Perhaps they could 'enter' from the decorations box or simply be led on stage. All cheer.* **Little Bo Peep** *is happy again.*

SONG: (*continued*)
   So
   Come and join us
   Come and join us
   Come on in
   The party has begun
   It's Mother Goose's Golden Christmas
   Come and join us ev'ryone
   It's Mother Goose's Golden Christmas
   Come and join us ev'ryone.

**Girls**
   So
   Come and join us

**Boys**
   Come and join us

**Girls**
   So
   Come and join us

**Boys**

So
Come and join with Mother

**Girls**

It's Mother

**All**

Goose's Golden Christmas
Come and join us ev'ryone.

*Curtain.*

www.ingramcontent.com/pod-product-compliance
Ingram Content Group UK Ltd.
Pitfield, Milton Keynes, MK11 3LW, UK
UKHW020655280225
455688UK00004B/126

9 781350 174924